Anonymous

Letters and messages of Rutherford B. Hayes

Anonymous

Letters and messages of Rutherford B. Hayes

ISBN/EAN: 9783337810351

Printed in Europe, USA, Canada, Australia, Japan

Cover: Foto ©ninafisch / pixelio.de

More available books at **www.hansebooks.com**

LETTERS AND MESSAGES

OF

RUTHERFORD B. HAYES,

PRESIDENT OF THE UNITED STATES,

TOGETHER WITH

LETTER OF ACCEPTANCE

AND

INAUGURAL ADDRESS.

WASHINGTON:
1881.

LETTER OF ACCEPTANCE

OF THE

REPUBLICAN NOMINATION FOR PRESIDENT OF THE UNITED STATES.

JULY 8, 1876.

LETTER OF ACCEPTANCE.

COLUMBUS, OHIO, *July* 8, 1876.

GENTLEMEN: In reply to your official communication of June 17, by which I am informed of my nomination for the office of President of the United States by the Republican National Convention at Cincinnati, I accept the nomination with gratitude, hoping that, under Providence, I shall be able, if elected, to execute the duties of the high office as a trust for the benefit of all the people. I do not deem it necessary to enter upon any extended examination of the declaration of principles made by the Convention. The resolutions are in accord with my views, and I heartily concur in the principles they announce. In several of the resolutions, however, questions are considered which are of such importance that I deem it proper to briefly express my convictions in regard to them. The fifth resolution adopted by the Convention is of paramount interest. More than forty years ago a system of making appointments to office grew up, based upon the maxim " to the victors belong the spoils." The old rule, the true rule, that honesty, capacity, and fidelity constitute the only real qualification for office, and that there is no other claim, gave place to the idea that party services were to be chiefly considered. All parties in practice have adopted this system. It has been essentially modified since its first introduction. It has not, however, been improved. At first the President, either directly or through the heads of department, made all the appointments, but gradually the appointing power, in many cases, passed into the control of members of Congress. The offices in these cases have become not merely rewards for party services, but rewards for services to party leaders. This system destroys the independence of the separate departments of the Government. " It tends directly to extravagance and official incapacity." It is a temptation to dishonesty; it hinders and impairs that careful supervision and strict accountability by which alone faithful and efficient public service can be secured; it obstructs the prompt removal and sure punishment of the unworthy; in every way it degrades the civil service and the character of the Government. It is felt, I am confident, by a large majority of the members of Congress, to be an intolerable burden and an unwarrantable hindrance to the proper discharge of their legitimate duties. It ought to be abolished. The reform should be thorough, radical, and complete. We should return to the principles and practice of the founders of the Government—supplying by legislation, when needed, that which was formerly the established custom. They neither expected nor desired from the public officers any partisan service. They meant that public officers should give their whole service to the Government and to the people. They meant that the officer should be secure in his tenure as long as his personal character remained untarnished and the performance of his duties satisfactory. If elected, I shall conduct the administration of the Government upon these principles, and all constitutional powers vested in the Executive will be employed to establish this reform. The declaration of principles by the Cincinnati Convention makes no announcement in favor of a single Presidential term. I do not assume to add to that declaration; but believing that the restoration of the civil service to the system established by Washington and followed by the early Presidents can be best accomplished by an Executive who is under no temptation to use the patronage of his office to promote his own re-election, I desire to perform what I regard as a duty in now stating my inflexible purpose, if elected, not to be a candidate for election to a second term.

On the currency question I have frequently expressed my views in public, and I stand by my record on this subject. I regard all the laws of the United States relating to the payment of the public indebtedness, the legal-tender notes included, as constituting a pledge and moral obligation of the Government, which must in good faith be kept. It is my conviction that the feeling of uncertainty inseparable from an irredeemable paper currency, with its fluctuations of value, is one of the great obstacles to a revival of confidence and business, and to a return of prosperity. That uncertainty can be ended in but one way— the resumption of specie payments. But the longer the instability of our money system is permitted to continue, the greater will be the injury inflicted upon our economical interests and all classes of society. If elected, I shall approve every appropriate measure to accomplish the desired end; and shall oppose any step backward.

The resolution with respect to the public-school system is one which should receive the hearty support of the American people. Agitation upon this subject is to be apprehended, until, by constitutional amendment, the schools are placed beyond all danger of sectarian control or interference. The Republican party is pledged to secure such an amendment.

The resolution of the Convention on the subject of the permanent pacification of the country, and the complete protection of all its citizens in the free enjoyment of all their constitutional rights, is timely and of great importance. The condition of the Southern States attracts the attention and commands the sympathy of the people of the whole Union. In their progressive recovery from the effects of the war, their first necessity is an intelligent and honest administration of government which will protect all classes of citizens in their political and private rights. What the South most needs is "peace," and peace depends upon the supremacy of the law. There can be no enduring peace if the constitutional rights of any portion of the people are habitually disregarded. A division of political parties resting merely upon sectional lines is always unfortunate and may be disastrous. The welfare of the South, alike with that of every other part of this country, depends upon the attractions it can offer to labor and immigration, and to capital. But laborers will not go, and capital will not be ventured where the Constitution and the laws are set at defiance, and distraction, apprehension, and alarm take the place of peace-loving and law-abiding social life. All parts of the Constitution are sacred and must be sacredly observed—the parts that are new no less than the parts that are old. The moral and national prosperity of the Southern States can be most effectually advanced by a hearty and generous recognition of the rights of all, by all—a recognition without reserve or exception. With such a recognition fully accorded it will be practicable to promote, by the influence of all legitimate agencies of the General Government, the efforts of the people of those States to obtain for themselves the blessings of honest and capable local government. If elected, I shall consider it not only my duty, but it will be my ardent desire to labor for the attainment of this end.

Let me assure my countrymen of the Southern States that if I shall be charged with the duty of organizing an administration, it will be one which will regard and cherish their truest interests—the interests of the white and of the colored people both, and equally; and which will put forth its best efforts in behalf of a civil policy which will wipe out forever the distinction between North and South in our common country. With a civil service organized upon a system which will secure purity, experience, efficiency, and economy, a strict regard for the public welfare solely in appointments, and the speedy, thorough, and unsparing prosecution and punishment of all public officers who betray official trusts; with a sound currency; with education unsectarian and free to all; with simplicity and frugality in public and private affairs, and with a fraternal spirit of harmony pervading the people of all sections and classes, we may reasonably hope that the second century of our existence as a Nation will, by the blessing of God, be pre-eminent as an era of good feeling and a period of progress, prosperity, and happiness.

Very respectfully, your fellow-citizen,

R. B. HAYES.

To the Hons. EDWARD MCPHERSON, WM. A. HOWARD, JOS. H. RAINEY, AND OTHERS. *Committee of the National Republican Convention.*

INAUGURAL ADDRESS

OF THE

PRESIDENT OF THE UNITED STATES.

MARCH 5, 1877.

INAUGURAL ADDRESS.

FELLOW-CITIZENS: We have assembled to repeat the public ceremonial, begun by Washington, observed by all my predecessors, and now a time-honored custom, which marks the commencement of a new term of the Presidential office. Called to the duties of this great trust, I proceed, in compliance with usage, to announce some of the leading principles on the subjects that now chiefly engage the public attention, by which it is my desire to be guided in the discharge of those duties. I shall not undertake to lay down irrevocably principles or measures of administration, but rather to speak of the motives which should animate us, and to suggest certain important ends to be attained in accordance with our institutions and essential to the welfare of our country.

At the outset of the discussions which preceded the recent Presidential election, it seemed to me fitting that I should fully make known my sentiments in regard to several of the important questions which then appeared to demand the consideration of the country. Following the example, and in part adopting the language, of one of my predecessors, I wish now, when every motive for misrepresentation has passed away, to repeat what was said before the election, trusting that my countrymen will candidly weigh and understand it, and that they will feel assured that the sentiments declared in accepting the nomination for the Presidency will be the standard of my conduct in the path before me, charged, as I now am, with the grave and difficult task of carrying them out in the practical administration of the Government so far as depends, under the Constitution and laws, on the Chief Executive of the Nation.

The permanent pacification of the country upon such principles and by such measures as will secure the complete protection of all its citizens in the free enjoyment of all their constitutional rights is now the one subject, in our public affairs, which all thoughtful and patriotic citizens regard as of supreme importance.

Many of the calamitous effects of the tremendous revolution which has passed over the Southern States still remain. The immeasurable benefits which will surely follow, sooner or later, the hearty and generous acceptance of the legitimate results of that revolution, have not yet been realized. Difficult and embarrassing questions meet us at the threshold of this subject. The people of those States are still impoverished, and the inestimable blessing of wise, honest, and peaceful self-government is not fully enjoyed. Whatever difference of opinion may exist as to the cause of this condition of things, the fact is clear, that, in the progress of events, the time has come when such government is the imperative necessity required by all the varied interests, public and private, of those States. But it must not be forgotten that only a local government which recognizes and maintains inviolate the rights of all is a true self-government.

With respect to the two distinct races whose peculiar relations to each other have brought upon us the deplorable complications and perplexities which exist in those States, it must be a government which guards the interests of both races carefully and equally. It must be a government which submits loyally and heartily to the Constitution and the laws—the laws of the Nation and the laws of the States themselves—accepting and obeying faithfully the whole Constitution as it is.

Resting upon this sure and substantial foundation, the superstructure of beneficent local governments can be built up, and not otherwise. In furtherance of such obedience to the letter and the spirit of the Constitution, and in behalf of all that its attainment implies, all so-called party interests lose their apparent importance, and party lines may well be permitted to fade into insignificance. The question we have to consider for the immediate welfare of those States of the Union is the question of government or no government, of social order and all the peaceful industries and the happiness that belong to it, or a return to barbarism. It is a question in which every citizen of the Nation is deeply interested, and with respect to which we ought not to be, in a partisan sense, either Republicans or Democrats, but fellow-citizens and fellow-men, to whom the interests of a common country and a common humanity are dear.

The sweeping revolution of the entire labor system of a large portion of our country, and the advance of four millions of people from a condition of servitude to that of citizenship, upon an equal footing with their former masters, could not occur without presenting problems of the gravest moment, to be dealt with by the emancipated race, by their former masters, and by the General Government, the author of the act of emancipation. That it was a wise, just, and Providential act, fraught with good for all concerned, is now generally conceded throughout the country. That a moral obligation rests upon the National Government to employ its constitutional power and influence to establish the rights of the people it has emancipated, and to protect them in the enjoyment of those rights when they are infringed or assailed, is also generally admitted.

The evils which afflict the Southern States can only be removed or remedied by the united and harmonious efforts of both races, actuated by motives of mutual sympathy and regard. And while in duty bound and fully determined to protect the rights of all by every constitutional means at the disposal of my administration, I am sincerely anxious to use every legitimate influence in favor of honest and efficient local self-government as the true resource of those States for the promotion of the contentment and prosperity of their citizens. In the effort I shall make to accomplish this purpose I ask the cordial co-operation of all who cherish an interest in the welfare of the country, trusting that party ties and the prejudice of race will be freely surrendered in behalf of the great purpose to be accomplished. In the important work of restoring the South it is not the political situation alone that merits attention. The material development of that section of the country has been arrested by the social and political revolution through which it has passed, and now needs and deserves the considerate care of the National Government, within the just limits prescribed by the Constitution and wise public economy.

But, at the basis of all prosperity, for that as well as for every other part of the country, lies the improvement of the intellectual and moral condition of the people. Universal suffrage should rest upon universal education. To this end, liberal and permanent provision should be made for the support of free schools by the State governments, and, if need be, supplemented by legitimate aid from national authority.

Let me assure my countrymen of the Southern States that it is my earnest desire to regard and promote their truest interests, the interests of the white and of the colored people both, and equally, and to put forth my best efforts in behalf of a civil policy which will forever wipe out in our political affairs the color line, and the distinction between North and South, to the end that we may have not merely a united North or a united South, but a united country.

I ask the attention of the public to the paramount necessity of reform in our civil service, a reform not merely as to certain abuses and practices of so-called official patronage, which have come to have the sanction of usage in the several departments of our Government, but a change in the system of appointment itself, a reform that shall be thorough, radical, and complete: a return to the principles and practices of the founders of the Government. They neither expected nor desired from public officers any partisan service. They meant that public officers should owe their whole service to the Government and to the people. They meant that the officer should be secure in his tenure as long as his personal character remained untarnished, and the performance of his duties satisfactory. They held that appointments to office were not to be made nor expected merely as rewards for partisan services, nor merely on the nomination of members of Congress, as being entitled in any respect to the control of such appointments.

The fact that both the great political parties of the country, in declaring their principles prior to the election, gave a prominent place to the subject of reform of our civil service, recognizing and strongly urging its necessity, in terms almost identical in their specific import with those I have here employed, must be accepted as a conclusive argument in behalf of these measures. It must be regarded as the expression of the united voice and will of the whole country upon this subject, and both political parties are virtually pledged to give it their unreserved support.

The President of the United States of necessity owes his election to office to the suffrage and zealous labors of a political party, the members of which cherish with ardor, and regard as of essential importance, the principles of their party organization. But he should strive to be always mindful of the fact that he serves his party best who serves his country best.

In furtherance of the reform we seek, and in other important respects a change of great importance, I recommend an amendment to the Constitution prescribing a term of six years for the Presidential office, and forbidding a re-election.

With respect to the financial condition of the country, I shall not attempt an extended history of the embarrassment and prostration which we have suffered during the past three years. The depression in all our varied commercial and manufacturing interests throughout the country, which began in September, 1873, still continues. It is very gratifying, however, to be able to say that there are indications all around us of a coming change to prosperous times.

Upon the currency question, intimately connected as it is with this topic, I may be permitted to repeat here the statement made in my letter of acceptance, that, in my judgment, the feeling of uncertainty inseparable from an irredeemable paper currency, with its fluctuation of values, is one of the greatest obstacles to a return to prosperous times. The only safe paper currency is one which rests upon a coin basis, and is at all times and promptly convertible into coin.

I adhere to the views heretofore expressed by me in favor of congressional legislation in behalf of an early resumption of specie payment, and I am satisfied not only that this is wise, but that the interests as well as the public sentiment of the country imperatively demand it.

Passing from these remarks upon the condition of our own country to consider our relations with other lands, we are reminded by the international complications abroad, threatening the peace of Europe, that our traditional rule of non-interference in the affairs of foreign nations has proved of great value in past times, and ought to be strictly observed.

The policy inaugurated by my honored predecessor, President Grant, of submitting to arbitration grave questions in dispute between ourselves and foreign Powers, points to a new and incomparably the best instrumentality for the preservation of peace, and will, as I believe, become a beneficent example of the course to be pursued in similar emergencies by other nations.

If, unhappily, questions of difference should at any time during the period of my administration arise between the United States and any foreign Government, it will certainly be my disposition and my hope to aid in their settlement in the same peaceful and honorable way, thus securing to our country the great blessings of peace and mutual good offices with all the nations of the world.

Fellow-citizens, we have reached the close of a political contest marked by the excitement which usually attends the contests between great political parties, whose members espouse and advocate with earnest faith their respective creeds. The circumstances were, perhaps, in no respect extraordinary, save in the closeness and the consequent uncertainty of the result.

For the first time in the history of the country, it has been deemed best, in view of the peculiar circumstances of the case, that the objections and questions in dispute with reference to the counting of the electoral votes should be referred to the decision of a tribunal appointed for this purpose.

That tribunal—established by law for this sole purpose; its members, all of them, men of long-established reputation for integrity and intelligence, and, with the exception of those who are also members of the Supreme Judiciary, chosen equally from both political parties; its deliberations—enlightened by the research and the arguments of able counsel—was entitled to the fullest confidence of the American people. Its decisions have been patiently waited for, and accepted as legally conclusive by the general judgment of the public. For the present, opinion will widely vary as to the wisdom of the several conclusions announced by that tribunal. This is to be anticipated in every instance where matters of dispute are made the subject of arbitration under the forms of law. Human judgment is never unerring, and is rarely regarded as otherwise than wrong by the unsuccessful party in the contest.

The fact that two great political parties have in this way settled a dispute, in regard to which good men differ as to the facts and the law, no less than as to the proper course to be pursued, in solving the question in controversy, is an occasion for general rejoicing.

Upon one point there is entire unanimity in public sentiment, that conflicting claims to the Presidency must be amicably and peaceably adjusted, and that when so adjusted the general acquiescence of the Nation ought surely to follow.

It has been reserved for a Government of the people, where the right of suffrage is universal, to give to the world the first example in history of a great Nation, in the midst of a struggle of opposing parties for power, hushing its party tumults, to yield the issue of the contest to adjustment according to the forms of law.

Looking for the guidance of that Divine Hand by which the destinies of nations and individuals are shaped, I call upon you, Senators, Representatives, Judges, fellow-citizens, here and everywhere, to unite with me in an earnest effort to secure to our country the blessings, not only of material prosperity, but of justice, peace, and union—a Union depending not upon the constraint of force, but upon the loving devotion of a free people; "and that all things may be so ordered and settled upon the best and surest foundations, that peace and happiness, truth and justice, religion and piety, may be established among us for all generations."

LETTER OF INSTRUCTION

TO THE

LOUISIANA COMMISSION.

APRIL 2, 1877.

LETTER OF INSTRUCTION.

WASHINGTON, *April* 2, 1877.

GENTLEMEN: I am instructed by the President to lay before you some observations upon the occasion and objects which have led him to invite you, as members of the commission about to visit the State of Louisiana, to undertake this public service.

Upon assuming his office the President finds the situation of affairs in Louisiana such as to justly demand his prompt and solicitous attention; for this situation presents as one of its features the apparent intervention of the military power of the United States in the domestic controversies which, unhappily, divide the opinions and disturb the harmony of the people of that State. This intervention, arising during the term and by the authority of his predecessor, throws no present duty upon the President, except to examine and determine the real extent and form and effect to which such intervention actually exists, and to decide as to the time, manner, and conditions which should be observed in putting an end to it. It is in aid of his intelligent and prompt discharge of this duty that the President has sought the service of this commission to supply by means of its examination, conducted in the State of Louisiana, some information that may be pertinent to the circumspection and security of any measure he may resolve upon.

It will be readily understood that the service desired of and intrusted to this commission does not include any examination into or report upon the facts of the recent State election, or of the canvass of the votes cast at such election. So far as attention to these subjects may be necessary the President cannot but feel that the reports of the committees of the two Houses of Congress, and other public information at hand, will dispense with and should preclude any original exploration by the commission of that field of inquiry.

But it is most pertinent and important, in coming to a decision upon the precise question of executive duty before him, that the President should know what are the real impediments to regular, legal, and peaceful procedures under the laws and constitution of the State of Louisiana by which the anomalies in government there presented may be put in course of settlement without involving the element of military power as either an agent or a make-weight in such solution. The successful ascertainment of these impediments, the President would confidently expect, would indicate to the people of that State the wisdom and the mode of their removal. The unusual circumstances which attended and followed the State election and canvass, from its relation to the excited feelings and interests of the Presidential election, may have retarded, within the State of Louisiana, the persuasive influences by which the great social and material interests common to the whole people of a State, and the pride of the American character as a law-abiding nation, ameliorate the disappointments and dissolve the resentments of close and zealous political contests. But the President both hopes and believes that the great body of the people of Louisiana are now prepared to treat the unsettled results of their State election with a calm and conciliatory spirit. If it be too much to expect a complete concurrence in a single government for that State, at least the President may anticipate a submission to the peaceful resources of the laws and the constitution of the State of all their discussions, at once relieving themselves from the reproach, and their fellow-citizens of the United States from the anxieties, which must ever attend a prolonged dispute as to the title and the administration of the government of one of the States of the Union.

The President, therefore, desires that you should devote your first and principal attention to a removal of the obstacles to an acknowledgment of one government for the purpose of an exercise of authority within the State, and a representation of the State in its relations to the General Government, under section four of article four of the Constitution of the United States, leaving, if necessary, to judicial or other constitutional arbitrament within the State the question of ultimate right. If these obstacles should prove insuperable from whatever reason, and the hope of a single government in all its departments be disappointed, it should be your next endeavor to accomplish the recognition of a single Legislature as the depositary of the representative will of the people of Louisiana. This great department of government rescued from dispute, the rest of the problem could gradually be worked out by the prevalent authority which the legislative power, when undisputed, is quite competent to exert in composing conflict in the co-ordinate branches of the Government.

An attentive consideration of the conditions under which the Federal Constitution and the acts of Congress provide or permit military intervention by the President in protection of a State against domestic violence, has satisfied the President that the use of this authority in determining or influencing disputed elections in a State is most carefully to be avoided. Undoubtedly, as was held by the Supreme Court in the case of Luther *vs.* Borden, the appeal from a State may involve such an inquiry as to the lawfulness of the authority which invokes the interference of the President in supposed pursuance of the Constitution. But it is equally true that neither the constitutional provision nor the acts of Congress were framed with any such design. Both obviously treated the case of domestic violence within a State as of outbreak against law and the authority of established government which the State was unable to suppress by its own strength. A case wherein every department of the State government has a disputed representation, and the State, therefore, furnishes to the Federal Government no internal political recognition of authority upon which the Federal Executive can rely, will present a case of so much difficulty that it is of pressing importance to all interests in Louisiana that it should be avoided. A single Legislature would greatly relieve this difficulty, for that department of the State government is named by the Constitution as the necessary applicant, when it can be convened, for military intervention by the United States.

If, therefore, the disputing interests can concur in or be reduced to a single Legislature for the State of Louisiana, it would be a great step in composing this unhappy strife.

The President leaves entirely to the commission the conciliatory influences which, in their judgment formed on the spot, may seem to conduce to the proposed end. His own determination that only public considerations should inspire and attend this effort to give the ascendency in Louisiana to the things that belong to peace, is evinced by his selection of commissioners who offer to the country, in their own character, every guarantee of the public motives and methods of the transactions which they have undertaken. Your report of the result of this endeavor will satisfy the President, he does not doubt, of the wisdom of his selection of and of his plenary trust in the commission.

A second and less important subject of attention during your visit to New Orleans will be the collection of accurate and trustworthy information from the public officers and prominent citizens of all political connections as to the State of public feeling and opinion in the community at large upon the general questions which affect the peaceful and safe exercise, within the State of Louisiana, of all legal and political rights, and the protection of all legal and political privileges conferred by the Constitution of the United States upon all citizens. The maintenance and protection of these rights and privileges, by all constitutional means, and by every just, moral, and social influence, are the settled purpose of the President in his administration of the Government. He will hope to learn from your investigations that this purpose will be aided and not resisted by the substantial and effective public opinion of the great body of the people of Louisiana.

The President does not wish to impose any limit upon your stay in Louisiana that would tend to defeat the full objects of your visit. He is, however, extremely desirous to find it in his power, at the earliest day compatible with a safe exercise of that authority, to put an end to even the appearance of military intervention in the domestic affairs of Louisiana, and he awaits your return with a confident hope that your report will enable him promptly to execute a purpose he has so much at heart.

The President desires me to add, that the publication of the results of your visit he shall hope to make immediately after their communication to him.

I have the honor to be, with great respect, your obedient servant,

WM. M. EVARTS.

To the Honorables CHARLES B. LAWRENCE, JOSEPH R. HAWLEY, JOHN M. HARLAN, JOHN C. BROWN, and WAYNE MACVEAGH, *Commissioners.*

EXECUTIVE ORDER

IN RELATION TO

MILITARY INTERVENTION OF THE GENERAL GOVERNMENT IN THE AFFAIRS OF THE STATE OF LOUISIANA.

APRIL 20, 1877.

EXECUTIVE ORDER.

EXECUTIVE MANSION, *Washington, April 20, 1877.*

SIR: Prior to my entering upon the duties of the Presidency there had been stationed by order of my predecessor in the immediate vicinity of the building used as a State-house in New Orleans, La., and known as Mechanics' Institute, a detachment of United States infantry. Finding them in that place, I have thought proper to delay a decision of the question of their removal until I could determine whether the condition of affairs is now such as to either require or justify continued military intervention of the National Government in the affairs of the State.

In my opinion there does not now exist in Louisiana such domestic violence as is contemplated by the Constitution as the ground upon which the military power of the National Government may be invoked for the defence of the State. The disputes which exist as to the right of certain claimants to the chief executive office of that State are to be settled and determined, not by the Executive of the United States, but by such orderly and peaceable methods as may be provided by the constitution and the laws of the State. Having the assurance that no resort to violence is contemplated, but, on the contrary, the disputes in question, are to be settled by peaceful methods, under and in accordance with law, I deem it proper to take action in accordance with the principles announced when I entered upon the duties of the Presidency.

You are therefore directed to see that the proper orders are issued for the removal of said troops at an early date from their present position to such regular barracks in the vicinity as may be selected for their occupation.

R. B. HAYES.

To the Hon. GEO. W. McCRARY,
Secretary of War.

REPORT

OF THE

LOUISIANA COMMISSION.

APRIL 24, 1877.

REPORT OF THE LOUISIANA COMMISSION.

NEW ORLEANS, *April* 24, 1877.

To the PRESIDENT OF THE UNITED STATES:

SIR: In accordance with your request the undersigned have visited this city and passed the last sixteen days in ascertaining the political situation of Louisiana, and endeavoring to bring about a peaceful solution of its difficulties. In view of the declaration in the letter of the Secretary of State, that we should direct our efforts to the end of securing the recognition of a single Legislature as the depositary of the representative will of the people of Louisiana, leaving, if necessary, to the judicial or other constitutional arbitrament within the State the question of the ultimate right, and in view of your determination to withdraw the troops of the United States to their barracks as soon as it could be done without endangering the peace, we addressed ourselves to the task of securing a common Legislature and undisputed authority competent to compose the existing political contentions and preserve peace without any aid from the National Government. To this end we endeavored to assuage the bitterness and animosity we found existing on both sides, so as to secure public opinion less unfavorable to such concessions as were indispensable to our success in obtaining such Legislature, and such general acquiescence in its authority as would insure social order. We have had full conferences with two gentlemen who claim the gubernatorial office, and with many members of their respective governments in their executive, judicial, and legislative departments. We have also conversed very freely with large delegations of men of business, with many of the district judges, and with hundreds of prominent citizens of all parties and races, representing not only this city but almost every parish in the State. We have also received many printed and written statements of fact and legal argument, and every person with whom we came in contact has shown an earnest desire to give us all possible information bearing on the unfortunate political divisions in the State.

The actual condition of affairs on our arrival in this city may be briefly stated as follows: Governor Packard (we shall speak of both gentlemen by the title they claim) was at the State-house with his

Legislature and friends and armed police force. As there was no quorum in the Senate, even upon his own theory of law, his Legislature was necessarily inactive. The supreme court, which recognized his authority, had not attempted to transact any business since it was dispossessed of its court-room and the custody of its records on the 9th day of January, 1877. He had no organization of the militia, alleging that his deficiency in that respect was owing to the obedience to the orders of President Grant to take no steps to change the relative position of himself and Governor Nicholls. His main chance was upon the alleged legal title, claiming that it was the constitutional duty of the President to recognize it, and to afford him such military assistance as might be necessary to enable him to assert his authority as Governor. Governor Nicholls was occupying Odd Fellows' Hall as a State-house. His Legislature met there, and was actively engaged in business of legislation. All the departments of the city government of New Orleans recognized his authority. The supreme court, nominated by him, and confirmed by the Senate, was holding daily sessions, and had heard about two hundred cases. The time for the collection of taxes had not arrived, but considerable sums of money, in the form of taxes, had been voluntarily paid into his treasury, out of which he was defraying the ordinary expenses of the State government. The Nicholls Legislature had a quorum in the Senate upon either the Nicholls or Packard theory of law, and a quorum in the House on the Nicholls, but not on the Packard theory. The Packard Legislature had a quorum in the House on its own theory of law, but, as already stated, not in the Senate, and was thus disabled from any legislation that would be valid even in the judgment of its own party. The commission found it to be very difficult to ascertain the precise extent to which the respective governments were acknowledged in the various parishes outside of New Orleans; but it is safe to say that the changes which had taken place in parishes after the organization of the two governments, January 9, 1877, were in favor of the Nicholls government. The claim to the legality of the supreme court, composed of Chief Justice Manning and his associates, who were nominated by Governor Nicholls, and confirmed by his Senate, rests upon the same basis as the title of Governor Nicholls and his Senate. The claim to the legality of the supreme court, composed of Chief Justice Ludeling and his associates, rests either upon their right to hold over in case the Nicholls court is illegal, or upon the legality of the Kellogg-Packard Senate, which confirmed the judges upon the nomination of Governor Kellogg, and while it had a returning-board quorum. We have briefly sketched the actual position as we found it.

THE LEGAL STATUS.

We will now state the legal question upon which the right of these respective governments depends. The constitution of the State of Louisiana requires that the "returns of all elections for members of the General Assembly shall be made to the Secretary of State." It also provides that "qualified electors shall vote for Governor and Lieutenant-Governor at the time and place of voting for Representatives. The returns of every election shall be sealed up and transmitted by the proper returning officers to the Secretary of State, who shall deliver them to the Speaker of the House of Representatives on the second day of the General Assembly then to be holden. Members of the General Assembly shall meet in the House of Representatives and examine and count the votes." It will be observed that this provision of the Constitution requires the returns of votes for Governor and Lieutenant-Governor to be sealed up and transmitted by the proper returning officers to the Secretary of State, and the same provision is made, in substance, as to members of the General Assembly; but, in 1870, the Legislature passed an act, amended in 1872, which created a body called the returning board, consisting of five members, to be appointed by the Senate, and to be returning officers for all elections in the State. The act provides that "the commissioners of election, at each poll or voting-place, shall count the votes, making the list of names of all persons voted for and the officers for which the votes were given, number of votes received by each, number of ballots contained in the box, and the number rejected, and reasons therefor, and to make duplicates of such lists, and send one to the supervisor of registration of the parish of Orleans and one to the Secretary of State." The law further requires the supervisors of registration to consolidate the returns received from the different polling-places and forward them, with the originals, to the returning board. The act further provides "that if there shall be any riot, tumult, acts of violence, intimidation, and disturbance, bribery or corrupt influences at any places within said parish, at or near any poll or voting-place, or places of registration or revision of registration, which riot, tumult, acts of violence, intimidation, and disturbance, bribery or corrupt influences, shall prevent or tend to prevent a fair, free, peaceable, and full vote of all qualified electors, it shall be the duty of the commissioners to make a statement of such facts and forward the same to the supervisor of registration with his returns of election, and the supervisors of registration shall forward the same to the returning board." The returning board is required to investigate statements of intimidation, and to exclude from the returns, which it makes to the Secretary of State, the returns received by it from those polls or voting-places where a fair election has been prevented by the causes above named. The same law further declares—

"It shall be the duty of the Secretary of State to transmit to the clerk of the House of Representatives, and to the secretary of the Senate of the last General Assembly, a list of the names of such persons as, according to the returns, shall have been elected to either branch of the General Assembly; and it shall be the duty of the clerk and secretary to place the names of Representatives and Senators elect upon the roll of the House and Senate respectively, and those Representatives and Senators whose names are so placed by the clerk and secretary respectively, in accordance with the foregoing provisions, and none other, shall be competent to organize the House of Representatives or Senate."

It is claimed by the counsel for the Nicholls government that this act, so far as it interposes the returning board exercising those powers of exclusion between the parish supervisor of registration, with his consolidated report, and the Secretary of State, is, when applied to the election of members of the General Assembly, of Governor, and Lieutenant-Governor, a plain violation of those provisions of the constitution of Louisiana which say the returns of all elections for members of the General Assembly shall be made to the Secretary of State; and, in reference to Governor and Lieutenant-Governor, the returns of every election "shall be sealed up and transmitted by the proper returning officers to the Secretary of State," who shall deliver them to the Speaker of the House of Representatives. On the other hand, it is insisted by the counsel for the Packard government that the Legislature has power to create this returning board and give it the authority with which the act clothes it. It is also claimed by them that the constitutionality of the act has been settled by the supreme court of the State, but the Nicholls party denied that the question was decided by the supreme court in a manner that could be considered authoritative. It should be further stated that it was not claimed by the counsel for Governor Nicholls that the Legislature could not create a returning board and clothe it with these powers in regard to the appointment of the Presidential electors, since the provisions of the State constitution on which they rely relate only to the election of members of the Legislature, of Governor, and Lieutenant-Governor. We quote the following sentence from one of their printed arguments:

"Indeed, as to Presidential electors, the mode of their appointment is, by the Constitution of the United States, left to the discretion of the Legislature of the State, therefore the General Assembly of Louisiana might create any tribunal whatever and confide the appointment of electors for President and Vice-President to it; consequently it may properly authorize such a tribunal in the case of the election of Presidential electors by the people to count the votes and decide and declare who were entitled to seats in the electoral college."

As matters stood on our arrival here the legal title of the respective claimants to the office of Governor depended upon the question we have stated. There was no judicial tribunal acknowledged to be authoritative by both parties by which it could be solved for reasons already given. The only hope of a practical solution was by the union of so many members of the rival Legislatures as would make a Legislature with a constitutional quorum, in both Senate and House, of members whose title to seats is valid under either view of the law. With a Legislature of undisputed authority the settlement of other questions could, as stated in the letter of instruction to our commission from the Secretary of State, be gradually worked out by the prevalent authority which legislative power, when undisputed, is quite competent to exert in composing conflicts in co-ordinate branches of the Government. Within the last three days this first great step in restoring peace to the State has been accomplished. In consequence of a withdrawal of members from the Packard to the Nicholls Legislature the latter body has now eighty-seven returning-board members in the House and thirty-two in the Senate. Sixty-one members constitute a constitutional quorum in the House and nineteen in the Senate.

CONCLUSIONS OF THE COMMISSION.

It is proper that we should say in conclusion, that it was in view of the foregoing facts, especially the consolidation of the Legislatures and our knowledge of the condition of Louisiana, derived from personal contact with the people, that we were induced to suggest, in our telegram of the 20th instant, that the immediate announcement of the time when the troops would be withdrawn to their barracks would be better for the peace of Louisiana than to postpone such announcement to some distant day. The commissioners, holding various shades of political belief, cannot well concur in any sketch of the past or probable future of Louisiana. We have foreborne in this report to express any opinion on the legal questions arising upon the foregoing statement of facts, because our letter of instructions seemed to call for a statement of facts rather than an expression of opinion by the commissioners. We all, however, indulge in confident hopes of better days for all races in Louisiana. Among the reasons for these hopes are the resolutions of the Nicholls Legislature and the letter of Governor Nicholls, herewith submitted, and which has already been given to the public.

With an earnest hope that the adjustment which has been made of the political controversies of Louisiana will be of lasting benefit to that State, and be approved by the patriotic people of all sections, we have the honor to be, your obedient servants,

CHARLES B. LAWRENCE.
JOSEPH R. HAWLEY.
JOHN M. HARLAN.
JOHN C. BROWN.
WAYNE MacVEAGH.

PROCLAMATION

CONVENING

THE TWO HOUSES OF CONGRESS.

MAY 5, 1877.

PROCLAMATION.

BY THE PRESIDENT OF THE UNITED STATES OF AMERICA.

A PROCLAMATION.

Whereas the final adjournment of the Forty-fourth Congress without making the usual appropriations for the support of the Army for the fiscal year ending June 30, 1878, presents an extraordinary occasion requiring the President to exercise the power vested in him by the Constitution to convene the Houses of Congress in anticipation of the day fixed by law for their next meeting:

Now, therefore, I, RUTHERFORD B. HAYES, President of the United States, do, by virtue of the power to this end in me vested by the Constitution, convene both Houses of Congress to assemble at their respective chambers at 12 o'clock noon on Monday, the fifteenth day of October next, then and there to consider and determine such measures as, in their wisdom, their duty and the welfare of the people may seem to demand.

In witness whereof I have hereunto set my hand, and caused the seal of the United States to be affixed.

Done at the city of Washington this fifth day of May, in the year of our Lord one thousand eight hundred and seventy-seven, and [SEAL.] of the Independence of the United States of America the one hundred and first.

R. B. HAYES.

By the President:
  WM. M. EVARTS,
    Secretary of State.

LETTER

ON

THE CONDUCT TO BE OBSERVED BY OFFICERS OF THE GENERAL GOVERNMENT IN RELATION TO ELECTIONS.

MAY 26, 1877.

LETTER.

EXECUTIVE MANSION,
Washington, May 26, 1877.

MY DEAR SIR: I have read the partial report of the Commission appointed to examine the New York custom-house. I concur with the Commission in their recommendations. It is my wish that the collection of the revenues should be free from partisan control, and organized on a strictly business basis, with the same guarantees for efficiency and fidelity in the selection of the chief and subordinate officers that would be required by a prudent merchant. Party leaders should have no more influence in appointments than other equally respectable citizens. No assessment for political purposes, on officers or subordinates, should be allowed. No useless officer or employé should be retained. No officer should be required or permitted to take part in the management of political organizations, caucuses, conventions, or election campaigns. Their right to vote, and to express their views on public questions, either orally or through the press, is not denied, provided it does not interfere with the discharge of their official duties.

Respectfully,

R. B. HAYES.

Hon. JOHN SHERMAN, &c.

EXECUTIVE ORDER,

No. 1.

JUNE 22, 1877.

EXECUTIVE ORDER.

Executive Mansion,
Washington, June 22, 1877.

Sir: I desire to call your attention to the following paragraph in a letter addressed by me to the Secretary of the Treasury, on the conduct to be observed by officers of the General Government in relation to the elections:

"No officer should be required or permitted to take part in the management of political organizations, caucuses, conventions, or election campaigns. Their right to vote and to express their views on public questions, either orally or through the press, is not denied, provided it does not interfere with the discharge of their official duties. No assessment for political purposes, on officers or subordinates, should be allowed."

This rule is applicable to every department of the civil service. It should be understood by every officer of the General Government that he is expected to conform his conduct to its requirements.

Very respectfully,

R. B. HAYES.

To the ——— ———.

PROCLAMATION.

RAILROAD RIOT IN WEST VIRGINIA.

JULY 18, 1877.

PROCLAMATION.

BY THE PRESIDENT OF THE UNITED STATES OF AMERICA.

A PROCLAMATION.

Whereas it is provided in the Constitution of the United States that the United States shall protect every State in this Union, on application of the Legislature, or of the Executive, (when the Legislature cannot be convened,) against domestic violence;

And whereas the Governor of the State of West Virginia has represented that domestic violence exists in said State, at Martinsburg, and at various other points along the line of the Baltimore and Ohio Railroad, in said State, which the authorities of said State are unable to suppress;

And whereas the laws of the United States require that in all cases of insurrection in any State or of obstruction to the laws thereof, whenever it may be necessary, in the judgment of the President, he shall forthwith, by proclamation, command such insurgents to disperse and retire peaceably to their respective abodes within a limited time:

Now, therefore, I, RUTHERFORD B. HAYES, President of the United States, do hereby admonish all good citizens of the United States, and all persons within the territory and jurisdiction of the United States, against aiding, countenancing, abetting, or taking part in such unlawful proceedings; and I do hereby warn all persons engaged in or connected with said domestic violence and obstruction of the laws to disperse and retire peaceably to their respective abodes on or before twelve o'clock noon of the 19th day of July instant.

In testimony whereof I have hereunto set my hand, and caused the seal of the United States to be affixed.

Done at the city of Washington this eighteenth day of July, in the year of our Lord one thousand eight hundred and seventy-
[SEAL.] seven, and of the Independence of the United States of America the one hundred and second.

R. B. HAYES.

By the President:
   F. W. SEWARD,
      Acting Secretary of State.

PROCLAMATION.

RAILROAD RIOT IN MARYLAND.

JULY 21, 1877.

PROCLAMATION.

BY THE PRESIDENT OF THE UNITED STATES OF AMERICA.

A PROCLAMATION.

Whereas it is provided in the Constitution of the United States that the United States shall protect every State in this Union, on application of the Legislature, or of the Executive, (when the Legislature cannot be convened,) against domestic violence;

And whereas the Governor of the State of Maryland has represented that domestic violence exists in said State, at Cumberland, and along the line of the Baltimore and Ohio Railroad, in said State, which the authorities of said State are unable to suppress;

And whereas the laws of the United States require that in all cases of insurrection in any State or of obstruction to the laws thereof, whenever in the judgment of the President it becomes necessary to use the military forces to suppress such insurrection or obstruction to the laws, he shall forthwith, by proclamation, command such insurgents to disperse and retire peaceably to their respective abodes within a limited time:

Now, therefore, I, RUTHERFORD B. HAYES, President of the United States, do hereby admonish all good citizens of the United States, and all persons within the territory and jurisdiction of the United States, against aiding, countenancing, abetting, or taking part in such unlawful proceedings; and I do hereby warn all persons engaged in or connected with said domestic violence and obstruction of the laws to disperse and retire peaceably to their respective abodes on or before noon of the twenty-second day of July instant.

In testimony whereof I have hereunto set my hand, and caused the seal of the United States to be affixed.

Done at the city of Washington this twenty-first day of July, in the year of our Lord one thousand eight hundred and seventy-
[SEAL.] seven, and of the Independence of the United States of America the one hundred and second.

R. B. HAYES.

By the President:
  WM. M. EVARTS,
    Secretary of State.

PROCLAMATION.

RAILROAD RIOT IN PENNSYLVANIA.

JULY 23, 1877.

PROCLAMATION.

BY THE PRESIDENT OF THE UNITED STATES OF AMERICA.

A PROCLAMATION.

Whereas it is provided in the Constitution of the United States that the United States shall protect every State in this Union, on application of the Legislature, or of the Executive, (when the Legislature cannot be convened,) against domestic violence;

And whereas the Governor of the State of Pennsylvania has represented that domestic violence exists in said State which the authorities of said State are unable to suppress;

And whereas the laws of the United States require that in all cases of insurrection in any State or of obstruction to the laws thereof, whenever in the judgment of the President it becomes necessary to use the military forces to suppress such insurrection or obstruction to the laws, he shall forthwith, by proclamation, command such insurgents to disperse and retire peaceably to their respective abodes within a limited time:

Now, therefore, I, RUTHERFORD B. HAYES, President of the United States, do hereby admonish all good citizens of the United States, and all persons within the territory and jurisdiction of the United States, against aiding, countenancing, abetting, or taking part in such unlawful proceedings; and I do hereby warn all persons engaged in or connected with said domestic violence and obstruction of the laws to disperse and retire peaceably to their respective abodes on or before twelve o'clock noon of the 24th day of July instant.

In testimony whereof I have hereunto set my hand, and caused the seal of the United States to be affixed.

Done at the city of Washington this twenty-third day of July, in the year of our Lord one thousand eight hundred and seventy-
[SEAL.] seven, and of the Independence of the United States of America the one hundred and second.

R. B. HAYES.

By the President:
  WM. M. EVARTS,
    Secretary of State.

MESSAGE

TO THE

TWO HOUSES OF CONGRESS AT THE COMMENCEMENT OF THE FIRST SESSION OF THE FORTY-FIFTH CONGRESS.

OCTOBER 15, 1877.

MESSAGE.

FELLOW-CITIZENS OF THE SENATE
AND HOUSE OF REPRESENTATIVES:

The adjournment of the last Congress, without making appropriations for the support of the Army for the present fiscal year, has rendered necessary a suspension of payments to the officers and men of the sums due them for services rendered after the 30th day of June last. The Army exists by virtue of statutes which prescribe its numbers, regulate its organization and employment, and which fix the pay of its officers and men, and declare their right to receive the same at stated periods. These statutes, however, do not authorize the payment of the troops in the absence of specific appropriations therefor. The Constitution has wisely provided that "no money shall be drawn from the Treasury but in consequence of appropriations made by law;" and it has also been declared by statute that "no department of the Government shall expend in any one fiscal year any sum in excess of appropriations made by Congress for that fiscal year." We have, therefore, an Army in service, authorized by law and entitled to be paid, but no funds available for that purpose. It may also be said, as an additional incentive to prompt action by Congress, that, since the commencement of the fiscal year, the Army, though without pay, has been constantly and actively employed in arduous and dangerous service, in the performance of which both officers and men have discharged their duty with fidelity and courage, and without complaint. These circumstances, in my judgment, constitute an extraordinary occasion, requiring that Congress be convened in advance of the time prescribed by law for your meeting in regular session. The importance of speedy action upon this subject on the part of Congress, is so manifest, that I venture to suggest the propriety of making the necessary appropriations for the support of the Army for the current year, at its present maximum numerical strength of twenty-five thousand men; leaving for future consideration all questions relating to an increase or decrease of the number of enlisted men. In the event of the reduction of the Army by subsequent legislation during the fiscal year, the excess of the appropriation could not be expended; and in the event of its enlargement, the additional sum required for the payment of the extra force could be provided in due time. It would be unjust to the troops now in service, and whose pay is already largely in arrears, if payment to them should be further postponed until after Congress shall have considered all the questions likely to arise in the effort to fix the proper limit to the strength of the Army.

Estimates of appropriations for the support of the military establishment for the fiscal year ending June 30, 1878, were transmitted to Congress by the former Secretary of the Treasury at the opening of its session in December last. These estimates, modified by the present Secretary so as to conform to present requirements, are now renewed—amounting to $32,436,764.98—and, having been transmitted to both Houses of Congress, are submitted for your consideration.

There is also required by the Navy Department $2,003,861.27. This sum is made up of $1,446,688.16 due to officers and enlisted men for the last quarter of the last fiscal year; $311,953.50 due for advances made by the fiscal agent of the Government in London for the support of the foreign service; $50,000 due to the Naval-Hospital fund; $150,000 due for arrearages of pay to officers; and $45,219.58 for the support of the Marine Corps.

There will also be needed an appropriation of $262,535.22 to defray the unsettled expenses of the United States courts for the fiscal year ending June 30, last, now due to attorneys, clerks, commissioners, and marshals, and for rent of court-rooms, the support of prisoners, and other deficiencies.

A part of the building of the Interior Department was destroyed by fire on the 24th of last month. Some immediate repairs and temporary structures have in consequence become necessary, estimates for which will be transmitted to Congress immediately, and an appropriation of the requisite funds is respectfully recommended.

The Secretary of the Treasury will communicate to Congress, in connection with the estimates for the appropriations for the support of the Army for the current fiscal year, estimates for such other deficiencies in the different branches of the public service as require immediate action, and cannot, without inconvenience, be postponed until the regular session.

I take this opportunity, also, to invite your attention to the propriety of adopting at your present session the necessary legislation to enable the people of the United States to participate in the advantages of the International Exhibition of Agriculture, Industry, and the Fine Arts, which is to be held at Paris in 1878, and in which this Government has been invited by the Government of France to take part.

This invitation was communicated to this Government in May, 1876, by the Minister of France at this Capital, and a copy thereof was submitted to the proper committees of Congress at its last session, but no action was taken upon the subject.

The Department of State has received many letters from various parts of the country expressing a desire to participate in the Exhibition, and numerous applications of a similar nature have also been made at the United States Legation at Paris.

The Department of State has also received official advice of the strong desire on the part of the French Government that the United States should participate in this enterprise, and space has hitherto been, and still is, reserved in the Exhibition buildings for the use of exhibitors from the United States, to the exclusion of other parties who have been applicants therefor.

In order that our industries may be properly represented at the Exhibition, an appropriation will be needed for the payment of salaries and expenses of commissioners for the transportation of goods, and for other purposes in connection with the object in view, and as May next is the time fixed for the opening of the Exhibition, if our citizens are to share the advantages of this international competition for the trade of other nations, the necessity of immediate action is apparent.

To enable the United States to co-operate in the International Exhibition which was held at Vienna in 1873, Congress then passed a joint resolution making an appropriation of two hundred thousand dollars, and authorizing the President to appoint a certain number of practical artisans and scientific men who should attend the Exhibition and report their proceedings and observations to him. Provision was also made for the appointment of a number of honorary commissioners.

I have felt that prompt action by Congress in accepting the invitation of the Government of France is of so much interest to the people of this country, and so suitable to the cordial relations between the Governments of the two countries, that the subject might properly be presented for attention at your present session.

The Government of Sweden and Norway has addressed an official invitation to this Government to take part in the International Prison Congress, to be held at Stockholm next year. The problem which the congress proposes to study—how to diminish crime—is one in which all civilized nations have an interest in common; and the congress of Stockholm seems likely to prove the most important convention ever held for the study of this grave question. Under authority of a joint resolution of Congress, approved February 16, 1875, a commissioner was appointed by my predecessor to represent the United States upon that occasion, and the prison congress having been, at the earnest desire of the Swedish Government, postponed to 1878, his commission was renewed by me. An appropriation of eight thousand dollars was made in the sundry civil-service act of 1875 to meet the expenses of the commissioner. I recommend the reappropriation of that sum for the same purpose, the former appropriation having been covered into the Treasury, and being no longer available for the purpose without further action by Congress. The subject is brought to your attention at this time in view of circumstances which render it highly desirable that the commissioner should proceed to the discharge of his important duties immediately.

As the several acts of Congress providing for detailed reports from the different departments of the Government, require their submission at the beginning of the regular annual session, I defer until that time any further reference to subjects of public interest.

R. B. HAYES.

WASHINGTON, *October* 15, 1877.

THANKSGIVING PROCLAMATION.

OCTOBER 29, 1877.

PROCLAMATION.

BY THE PRESIDENT OF THE UNITED STATES OF AMERICA.

A PROCLAMATION.

The completed circle of summer and winter, seed-time and harvest, has brought us to the accustomed season at which a religious people celebrates with praise and thanksgiving the enduring mercy of Almighty God. This devout and public confession of the constant dependence of man upon the Divine favor for all the good gifts of life and health, and peace and happiness, so early in our history made the habit of our people, finds in the survey of the past year new grounds for its joyful and grateful manifestation.

In all the blessings which depend upon benignant seasons this has indeed been a memorable year. Over the wide territory of our country, with all its diversity of soil and climate and products, the earth has yielded a bountiful return to the labor of the husbandman. The health of the people has been blighted by no prevalent or wide-spread diseases. No great disasters of shipwreck upon our coasts, or to our commerce on the seas, have brought loss and hardship to merchants or mariners, and clouded the happiness of the community with sympathetic sorrow.

In all that concerns our strength and peace and greatness as a Nation; in all that touches the permanence and security of our Government, and the beneficent institutions on which it rests; in all that affects the character and dispositions of our people, and tests our capacity to enjoy and uphold the equal and free condition of society, now permanent and universal throughout the land, the experience of the last year is conspicuously marked by the protecting providence of God, and is full of promise and hope for the coming generations.

Under a sense of these infinite obligations to the great Ruler of times and seasons and events, let us humbly ascribe it to our own faults and frailties if, in any degree, that perfect concord and happiness, peace and justice, which such great mercies should diffuse through the hearts and lives of our people, do not altogether and always and everywhere prevail. Let us with one spirit and with one voice lift up praise and thanksgiving to God for his manifold goodness to our land, his manifest care for our Nation.

Now, therefore, I, RUTHERFORD B. HAYES, President of the United States, do appoint Thursday, the twenty-ninth day of November next, as a Day of National Thanksgiving and Prayer; and I earnestly recommend that, withdrawing themselves from secular cares and labors, the people of the United States do meet together on that day in their respective places of worship, there to give thanks and praise to Almighty God for his mercies, and to devoutly beseech their continuance.

In witness whereof I have hereunto set my hand, and caused the seal of the United States to be affixed.

Done at the city of Washington this twenty-ninth day of October, in the year of our Lord one thousand eight hundred and seventy-[SEAL.] seven, and of the Independence of the United States the one hundred and second.

              R. B. HAYES.

By the President:
 WM. M. EVARTS,
  Secretary of State.

EXECUTIVE ORDER.

DEATH OF SENATOR OLIVER P. MORTON.

NOVEMBER 2, 1877.

EXECUTIVE ORDER.

Executive Mansion,
Washington, D. C., November 2, 1877.

I lament the sad occasion which makes it my duty to testify the public respect for the eminent citizen and distinguished statesman whose death yesterday, at his home in Indianapolis, has been made known to the people by telegraphic announcement.

The services of Oliver P. Morton to the Nation in the difficult and responsible administration of the affairs of the State of Indiana, as its Governor, at a critical juncture of the civil war, can never be overvalued by his countrymen. His long service in the Senate has shown his great powers as a legislator, and as a leader and chief counsellor of the political party charged with the conduct of the Government during that period.

In all things and at all times he has been able, strenuous, and faithful in the public service, and his fame with his countrymen rests upon secure foundations.

The several Executive Departments will be closed on the day of his funeral, and appropriate honors should be paid to the memory of the deceased statesman by the whole Nation.

R. B. HAYES.

MESSAGE

TO THE

TWO HOUSES OF CONGRESS AT THE COMMENCEMENT OF THE SECOND SESSION OF THE FORTY-FIFTH CONGRESS.

DECEMBER 3, 1877.

MESSAGE.

FELLOW-CITIZENS OF THE SENATE
AND HOUSE OF REPRESENTATIVES:

With devout gratitude to the bountiful Giver of all good, I congratulate you that, at the beginning of your first regular session, you find our country blessed with health and peace and abundant harvests, and with encouraging prospects of an early return of general prosperity.

To complete and make permanent the pacification of the country continues to be, and, until it is fully accomplished, must remain, the most important of all our national interests. The earnest purpose of good citizens generally, to unite their efforts in this endeavor, is evident. It found decided expression in the resolutions announced in 1876 by the national conventions of the leading political parties of the country. There was a wide-spread apprehension that the momentous results in our progress as a Nation, marked by the recent amendments to the Constitution, were in imminent jeopardy; that the good understanding which prompted their adoption, in the interest of a loyal devotion to the general welfare, might prove a barren truce, and that the two sections of the country, once engaged in civil strife, might be again almost as widely severed and disunited as they were when arrayed in arms against each other.

The course to be pursued which in my judgment seemed wisest, in the presence of this emergency, was plainly indicated in my inaugural address. It pointed to the time which all our people desire to see, when a genuine love of our whole country, and of all that concerns its true welfare, shall supplant the destructive forces of the mutual animosity of races and of sectional hostility. Opinions have differed widely as to the measures best calculated to secure this great end. This was to be expected. The measures adopted by the Administration have been subjected to severe and varied criticism. Any course whatever which might have been entered upon would certainly have encountered distrust and opposition. These measures were, in my judgment, such as were most in harmony with the Constitution and with the genius of our people, and best adapted, under all the circumstances, to attain the end in view. Beneficent results, already apparent, prove that these endeavors are not to be regarded as a mere experiment, and should sustain and encourage us in our efforts. Already, in the brief period which has elapsed, the immediate effectiveness, no less than the justice of the course pursued, is demonstrated, and I have an abiding faith that time will furnish its ample vindication in the minds of the great majority of my fellow-citizens. The discontinuance of the use of the Army for the purpose of upholding local governments in two States of the Union was no less a constitutional duty and requirement, under the circumstances existing at the time, than it was a much-needed measure for the restoration of local self-government and the promotion of national harmony. The withdrawal of the troops from such employment was effected deliberately, and with solicitous care for the peace and good order of society, and the protection of the property and persons and every right of all classes of citizens.

The results that have followed are indeed significant and encouraging. All apprehension of danger from remitting those States to local self-government is dispelled, and a most salutary change in the minds of the people has begun and is in progress in every part of that section of the country once the theatre of unhappy civil strife, substituting for suspicion, distrust, and aversion, concord, friendship, and patriotic attachment to the Union. No unprejudiced mind will deny that the terrible and often fatal collisions which for several years have been of frequent occurrence, and have agitated and alarmed the public mind, have almost entirely ceased, and that a spirit of mutual forbearance and hearty national interest has succeeded. There has been a general re-establishment of order, and of the orderly administration of justice; instances of remaining lawlessness have become of rare occurrence; political turmoil and turbulence have disappeared; useful industries have been resumed; public credit in the Southern States has been greatly strengthened; and the encouraging benefits of a revival of commerce between the sections of the country lately embroiled in civil war are fully enjoyed. Such are some of the results already attained, upon which the country is to be congratulated. They are of such importance, that we may with confidence patiently await the desired consummation that will surely come with the natural progress of events.

It may not be improper here to say that it should be our fixed and unalterable determination to protect, by all available and proper means, under the Constitution and the laws, the lately-emancipated race in the enjoyment of their rights and privileges; and I urge upon those to whom heretofore the colored people have sustained the relation of bondmen, the wisdom and justice of humane and liberal local legislation with respect to their education and general welfare. A firm adherence to the laws, both National and State, as to the civil and political rights of the colored people, now advanced to full and equal citizenship; the immediate repression and sure punishment by the National and local authorities, within their respective jurisdictions, of every instance of lawlessness and violence toward them, is required for the security alike of both races, and is justly demanded by the public opinion of the country and the age. In this way the restoration of harmony and good will, and the complete protection of every citizen in the full enjoyment of every constitutional right, will surely be attained. Whatever authority rests with me to this end, I shall not hesitate to put forth. Whatever belongs to the power of Congress and the jurisdiction of the courts of the Union, they may confidently be relied upon to provide and perform. And to the legislatures, the courts, and the executive authorities of the several States, I earnestly appeal to secure, by adequate, appropriate, and seasonable means, within their borders, these common and uniform rights of a united people which loves liberty, abhors oppression, and reveres justice. These objects are very dear to my heart. I shall continue most earnestly to strive for their attainment. The cordial co-operation of all classes—of all sections of the country and of both races—is required for this purpose; and with these blessings assured, and not otherwise, we may safely hope to hand down our free institutions of government unimpaired to the generations that will succeed us.

Among the other subjects of great and general importance to the people of this country I cannot be mistaken, I think, in regarding as pre-eminent the policy and measures which are designed to secure the restoration of the currency to that normal and healthful condition in which, by the resumption of specie payments, our internal trade and foreign commerce may be brought into harmony with the system of exchanges which is based upon the precious metals as the intrinsic money of the world. In the public judgment that this end should be sought and compassed as speedily and securely as the resources of the people and the wisdom of their Government can accomplish, there is a much greater degree of unanimity than is found to concur in the specific measures which will bring the country to this desired end, or the rapidity of the steps by which it can be safely reached.

Upon a most anxious and deliberate examination which I have felt it my duty to give to the subject, I am but the more confirmed in the opinion which I expressed in accepting the nomination for the Presidency and again upon my inauguration, that the policy of resumption should be pursued by every suitable means, and that no legislation would be wise that should disparage the importance or retard the attainment of that result. I have no disposition, and certainly no right, to question the sincerity or the intelligence of opposing opinions, and would neither conceal nor undervalue the considerable difficulties, and even occasional distresses, which may attend the progress of the Nation towards this primary condition to its general and permanent prosperity. I must, however, adhere to my most earnest conviction that any wavering in purpose or unsteadiness in methods, so far from avoiding or reducing the inconvenience inseparable from the transition from an irredeemable to a redeemable paper currency, would only tend to increased and prolonged disturbance in values, and, unless retrieved, must end in serious disorder, dishonor, and disaster in the financial affairs of the Government and of the people. The mischiefs which I apprehend, and urgently deprecate, are confined to no class of the people indeed, but seem to me most certainly to threaten the industrious masses, whether their occupations are of skilled or common labor. To them, it seems to me, it is of prime importance that their labor should be compensated in money which is itself fixed in exchangeable value by being irrevocably measured by the labor necessary to its production. This permanent quality of the money of the people is sought for, and can only be gained by the resumption of specie payments. The rich, the speculative, the operating, the money-dealing classes, may not always feel the mischiefs of, or may find casual profits in, a variable currency, but the misfortunes of such a currency to those who are paid salaries or wages are inevitable and remediless.

Closely connected with this general subject of the resumption of specie payments, is one of subordinate, but still of grave importance—I mean the readjustment of our coinage system, by the renewal of the silver dollar, as an element in our specie currency, endowed by legislation with the quality of legal-tender to a greater or less extent.

As there is no doubt of the power of Congress, under the Constitution, "to coin money and regulate the value thereof," and as this power covers the whole range of authority applicable to the metal, the rated value, and the legal-tender quality which shall be adopted for the coinage, the considerations which should induce or discourage a particular measure connected with the coinage belong clearly to the province of legislative discretion, and of public expediency. Without intruding upon this province of legislation in the least, I have yet thought the subject of such critical importance in the actual condition of our affairs, as to present an occasion for the exercise of the duty imposed by the Constitution on the President, of recommending to the consideration of Congress "such measures as he shall judge necessary and expedient."

Holding the opinion, as I do, that neither the interests of the Government nor of the people of the United States would be promoted by disparaging silver as one of the two precious metals which furnish the coinage of the world; and that legislation which looks to maintaining the volume of intrinsic money to as full a measure of both metals as their relative commercial values will permit, would be neither unjust nor inexpedient. I must ask your indulgence to a brief and definite statement of certain essential features in any such legislative measure which I feel it my duty to recommend.

I do not propose to enter the debate, represented on both sides by such able disputants in Congress and before the people and in the press, as to the extent to which the legislation of any one nation can control this question, even within its own borders, against the unwritten laws of trade, or the positive laws of other governments. The wisdom of Congress, in shaping any particular law that may be presented for my approval, may wholly supersede the necessity of my entering into these considerations, and I willingly avoid either vague or intricate inquiries. It is only certain plain and practical traits of such legislation that I desire to recommend to your attention.

In any legislation providing for a silver coinage, regulating its value and imparting to it the quality of legal-tender, it seems to me of great importance that Congress should not lose sight of its action as operating in a twofold capacity, and in two distinct directions. If the United States Government were free from a public debt, its legislative dealing with the question of silver coinage would be purely sovereign and governmental, under no restraints but those of constitutional power and the public good as affected by the proposed legislation. But, in the actual circumstances of the Nation, with a vast public debt distributed very widely among our own citizens, and held in great amounts also abroad, the nature of the silver-coinage measure, as affecting this relation of the Government to the holders of the public debt, becomes an element, in any proposed legislation, of the highest concern. The obligation of the public faith transcends all questions of profit or public advantage otherwise. Its unquestionable maintenance is the dictate as well as of the highest expediency, as of the most necessary duty, and will ever be carefully guarded by Congress and people alike.

The public debt of the United States, to the amount of $729,000,000, bears interest at the rate of six per cent., and $708,000,000 at the rate of five per cent., and the only way in which the country can be relieved from the payment of these high rates of interest is by advantageously refunding the indebtedness. Whether the debt is ultimately paid in gold or in silver coin is of but little moment compared with the possible reduction of interest one-third, by refunding it at such reduced rate. If the United States had the unquestioned right to pay its bonds in silver coin, the little benefit from that process would be greatly overbalanced by the injurious effect of such payment, if made or proposed against the honest convictions of the public creditors. All the bonds that have been issued since February 12, 1873, when gold became the only unlimited legal-tender metallic currency of the country, are justly payable in gold coin or in coin of equal value. During the time of these issues, the only dollar that could be or was received by the Government in exchange for bonds was the gold dollar. To require the public creditors to take, in repayment, any dollar of less commercial value, would be regarded by them as a repudiation of the full obligation assumed. The bonds issued prior to 1873 were issued at a time when the gold dollar was the only coin in circulation or contemplated by either the Government or the holders of the bonds as the coin in which they were to be paid. It is far better to pay these bonds in that coin than to seem to take advantage of the unforeseen fall in silver bullion to pay in a new issue of silver coin, thus made so much less valuable. The power of the United States to coin money and to regulate the value thereof ought never to be exercised for the purpose of enabling the Government to pay its obligations in a coin of less value than that contemplated by the parties when the bonds were issued. Any attempt to pay the national indebtedness in a coinage of less commercial value than the money of the world, would involve a violation of the public faith, and work irreparable injury to the public credit.

It was the great merit of the act of March, 1869, in strengthening the public credit, that it removed all doubt as to the purpose of the United States to pay their bonded debt in coin. That act was accepted as a pledge of public faith. The Government has derived great benefit from it in the progress thus far made in refunding the public debt at low rates of interest. An adherence to the wise and just policy of an exact observance of the public faith will enable the Government rapidly to reduce the burden of interest on the national debt to an amount exceeding $20,000,000 per annum, and effect an aggregate saving to the United States of more than $300,000,000 before the bonds can be fully paid.

In adapting the new silver coinage to the ordinary uses of currency in the every-day transactions of life and prescribing the quality of legal-tender to be assigned to it, a consideration of the first importance should be so to adjust the ratio between the silver and the gold coinage, which now constitutes our specie currency, as to accomplish the desired end of maintaining the circulation of the two metallic currencies, and keeping up the volume of the two precious metals as our intrinsic money. It is a mixed question for scientific reasoning and historical experience to determine how far, and by what methods, a practical equilibrium can be maintained which will keep both metals in circulation in their appropriate spheres of common use. An absolute equality of commercial value, free from disturbing fluctuations, is hardly attainable, and without it an unlimited legal-tender for private transactions assigned to both metals would irresistibly tend to drive out of circulation the dearer coinage, and disappoint the principal object proposed by the legislation in view. I apprehend, therefore, that the two conditions of a near approach to equality of commercial value between the gold and silver coinage of the same denomination, and of a limitation of the amounts for which the silver coinage is to be a legal-tender, are essential to maintaining both in circulation. If these conditions can be successfully observed, the issue from the mint of silver dollars would afford material assistance to the community in the transition to redeemable paper money, and would facilitate the resumption of specie payment and its permanent establishment. Without these conditions, I fear that only mischief and misfortune would flow from a coinage of silver dollars with the quality of unlimited legal-tender, even in private transactions.

Any expectation of temporary ease from an issue of silver coinage to pass as a legal-tender, at a rate materially above its commercial value, is, I am persuaded, a delusion. Nor can I think that there is any substantial distinction between an original issue of silver dollars at a nominal value materially above their commercial value, and the restoration of the silver dollar at a rate which once was, but has ceased to be, its commercial value. Certainly the issue of our gold coinage, reduced in weight materially below its legal-tender value, would not be any the less a present debasement of the coinage by reason of its equalling or even exceeding in weight a gold coinage which at some past time had been commercially equal to the legal-tender value assigned to the new issue.

In recommending that the regulation of any silver coinage which may be authorized by Congress should observe these conditions of commercial value and limited legal-tender, I am governed by the feeling that every possible increase should be given to the volume of metallic money which can be kept in circulation, and thereby every possible aid afforded to the people in the process of resuming specie payments. It is because of my firm conviction that a disregard of these conditions would frustrate the good results which are desired from the proposed coinage, and embarrass with new elements of confusion and uncertainty the business of the country, that I urge upon your attention these considerations.

I respectfully recommend to Congress that in any legislation providing for a silver coinage, and imparting to it the quality of legal-tender, there be impressed upon the measure a firm provision exempting the public debt, heretofore issued and now outstanding, from payment, either of principal or interest, in any coinage of less commercial value than the present gold coinage of the country.

The organization of the civil service of the country has for a number of years attracted more and more of the public attention. So general has become the opinion that the methods of admission to it, and the conditions of remaining in it, are unsound, that both the great political parties have agreed in the most explicit declarations of the necessity of reform, and in the most emphatic demands for it. I have fully believed these declarations and demands to be the expression of a sincere conviction of the intelligent masses of the people upon the subject, and that they should be recognized and followed by earnest and prompt action on the part of the Legislative and Executive Departments of the Government, in pursuance of the purpose indicated.

Before my accession to office I endeavored to have my own views distinctly understood, and upon my inauguration my accord with the public opinion was stated in terms believed to be plain and unambiguous. My experience in the executive duties has strongly confirmed the belief in the great advantage the country would find in observing strictly the plan of the Constitution, which imposes upon the Executive the sole duty and responsibility of the selection of those Federal officers who, by law, are appointed, not elected; and which, in like manner, assigns to the Senate the complete right to advise and consent to, or to reject, the nominations so made; whilst the House of Representatives stands as the public censor of the performance of official duties, with the prerogative of investigation and prosecution in all cases of dereliction. The blemishes and imperfections in the civil service may, as I think, be traced, in most cases, to a practical confusion of the duties assigned to the several departments of the Government. My purpose, in this respect, has been to return to the system established by the fundamental law, and to do this with the heartiest co-operation and most cordial understanding with the Senate and House of Representatives.

The practical difficulties in the selection of numerous officers for posts of widely-varying responsibilities and duties are acknowledged to be very great. No system can be expected to secure absolute freedom from mistakes, and the beginning of any attempted change of custom is quite likely to be more embarrassed in this respect than any subsequent period. It is here that the Constitution seems to me to prove its claim to the great wisdom accorded to it. It gives to the Executive the assistance of the knowledge and experience of the Senate, which, when acting upon nominations as to which they may be disinterested and impartial judges, secures as strong a guaranty of freedom from errors of importance as is perhaps possible in human affairs.

In addition to this, I recognize the public advantage of making all nominations, as nearly as possible, impersonal, in the sense of being free from mere caprice or favor in the selection; and in those offices in which special training is of greatly increased value, I believe such a rule as to the tenure of office should obtain as may induce men of proper qualifications to apply themselves industriously to the task of becoming proficients. Bearing these things in mind, I have endeavored to reduce the number of changes in subordinate places usually made upon the change of the general administration, and shall most heartily co-operate with Congress in the better systematizing of such methods and rules of admission to the public service, and of promotion within it, as may promise to be most successful in making thorough competency, efficiency, and character the decisive tests in these matters.

I ask the renewed attention of Congress to what has already been done by the Civil-Service Commission, appointed in pursuance of an act of Congress by my predecessor, to prepare and revise civil-service rules. In regard to much of the departmental service, especially at Washington, it may be difficult to organize a better system than that which has thus been provided, and it is now being used to a considerable extent under my direction. The commission has still a legal existence, although for several years no appropriation has been made for defraying its expenses. Believing that this commission has rendered valuable service, and will be a most useful agency in improving the administration of the civil service, I respectfully recommend that a suitable appropriation, to be immediately available, be made to enable it to continue its labors.

It is my purpose to transmit to Congress as early as practicable a report by the chairman of the commission, and to ask your attention to such measures on this subject as in my opinion will further promote the improvement of the civil service.

During the past year the United States have continued to maintain peaceful relations with foreign Powers.

The outbreak of war between Russia and Turkey, though at one time attended by grave apprehension as to its effect upon other European nations, has had no tendency to disturb the amicable relations existing between the United States and each of the two contending Powers. An attitude of just and impartial neutrality has been preserved, and I am gratified to state that, in the midst of their hostilities, both the Russian and the Turkish Governments have shown an earnest disposition to adhere to the obligations of all treaties with the United States, and to give due regard to the rights of American citizens.

By the terms of the treaty, defining the rights, immunities, and privileges of consuls, between Italy and the United States, ratified in 1868, either Government may, after the lapse of ten years, terminate the existence of the treaty by giving twelve months' notice of its intention. The Government of Italy, availing itself of this faculty, has now given the required notice, and the treaty will, accordingly, end on the 17th of September, 1878. It is understood, however, that the Italian Government wishes to renew it, in its general scope, desiring only certain modifications in some of its articles. In this disposition I concur, and shall hope that no serious obstacles may intervene to prevent or delay the negotiation of a satisfactory treaty.

Numerous questions in regard to passports, naturalization, and exemption from military service, have continued to arise in cases of emigrants from Germany who have returned to their native country. The provisions of the treaty of February 22, 1868, however, have proved to be so ample and so judicious, that the Legation of the United States at Berlin has been able to adjust all claims arising under it, not only without detriment to the amicable relations existing between the two Governments, but it is believed without injury or injustice to any duly-naturalized American citizen. It is desirable that the treaty originally made with the North German Union in 1868 should now be extended, so as to apply equally to all the States of the Empire of Germany.

The invitation of the Government of France to participate in the exposition of the products of agriculture, industry, and the fine arts, to be held at Paris during the coming year, was submitted for your consideration at the extra session. It is not doubted that its acceptance by the United States, and a well-selected exhibition of the products of American industry on that occasion, will tend to stimulate international commerce and emigration, as well as to promote the traditional friendship between the two countries.

A question arose, sometime since, as to the proper meaning of the extradition articles of the treaty of 1842 between the United States and Great Britain. Both Governments, however, are now in accord in the belief that the question is not one that should be allowed to frustrate the ends of justice, or to disturb the friendship between the two Nations. No serious difficulty has arisen in accomplishing the extradition of criminals when necessary. It is probable that all points of disagreement will, in due time, be settled, and, if need be, more explicit declarations be made in a new treaty.

The Fishery Commission, under Articles XVIII to XXV of the Treaty of Washington, has concluded its session at Halifax. The result of the deliberations of the commission, as made public by the commissioners, will be communicated to Congress.

A treaty for the protection of trade-marks has been negotiated with Great Britain, which has been submitted to the Senate for its consideration.

The revolution which recently occurred in Mexico was followed by the accession of the successful party to power, and the installation of its chief, General Porfirio Diaz, in the presidential office. It has been the custom of the United States, when such changes of government have heretofore occurred in Mexico, to recognize and enter into official relations with the *de facto* government as soon as it should appear to have the approval of the Mexican people, and should manifest a disposition to adhere to the obligations of treaties and international friendship. In the present case, the official recognition has been deferred by the occurrences on the Rio Grande border, the records of which have already been communicated to each House of Congress, in answer to their respective resolutions of inquiry. Assurances have been received that the authorities at the seat of the Mexican Government have both the disposition and the power to prevent and punish such unlawful invasions and depredations. It is earnestly to be hoped that events may prove these assurances to be well founded. The best interests of both countries require the maintenance of peace upon the border, and the development of commerce between the two Republics.

It is gratifying to add that this temporary interruption of official relations has not prevented due attention by the representatives of the United States in Mexico to the protection of American citizens, so far as practicable. Nor has it interfered with the prompt payment of the amounts due from Mexico to the United States under the treaty of July 4, 1868, and the awards of the Joint Commission. While I do not anticipate an interruption of friendly relations with Mexico, yet I cannot but look with some solicitude upon a continuance of border disorders as exposing the two countries to initiations of popular feeling and mischances of action which are naturally unfavorable to complete amity. Firmly determined that nothing shall be wanting on my part to promote a good understanding between the two Nations, I yet must ask the attention of Congress to the actual occurrences on the border, that the lives and property of our citizens may be adequately protected and peace preserved.

Another year has passed without bringing to a close the protracted contest between the Spanish Government and the insurrection in the Island of Cuba. While the United States have sedulously abstained from any intervention in this contest, it is impossible not to feel that it is attended with incidents affecting the rights and interests of American citizens. Apart from the effect of the hostilities upon trade between the United States and Cuba, their progress is inevitably accompanied by complaints, having more or less foundation, of searches, arrests, embargoes, and oppressive taxes upon the property of American residents, and of unprovoked interference with American vessels and commerce. It is due to the Government of Spain to say that, during the past year, it has promptly disavowed and offered reparation for any unauthorized acts of unduly zealous subordinates, whenever such acts have been brought to its attention. Nevertheless such occurrences cannot but tend to excite feelings of annoyance, suspicion, and resentment, which are greatly to be deprecated between the respective subjects and citizens of two friendly Powers.

Much delay (consequent upon accusations of fraud in some of the awards) has occurred in respect to the distribution of the limited amounts received from Venezuela under the treaty of April 25, 1866, applicable to the awards of the Joint Commission created by that treaty. So long as these matters are pending in Congress, the Executive cannot assume either to pass upon the questions presented, or to distribute the fund received. It is eminently desirable that definite legislative action should be taken, either affirming the awards to be final or providing some method for re-examination of the claims.

Our relations with the Republics of Central and South America, and with the Empire of Brazil, have continued without serious change, further than the temporary interruption of diplomatic intercourse with Venezuela and with Guatemala. Amicable relations have already been fully restored with Venezuela, and it is not doubted that all grounds of misunderstanding with Guatemala will speedily be removed. From all these countries there are favorable indications of a disposition on the part of their Governments and people to reciprocate our efforts in the direction of increased commercial intercourse.

The Government of the Samoan Islands has sent an envoy in the person of its Secretary of State to invite the Government of the United States to recognize and protect their independence, to establish commercial relations with their people, and to assist them in their steps toward regulated and responsible government. The inhabitants of these islands, having made considerable progress in Christian civilization and the development of trade, are doubtful of their ability to maintain peace and independence without the aid of some stronger power. The subject is deemed worthy of respectful attention, and the claims upon our assistance by this distant community will be carefully considered.

The long commercial depression in the United States has directed attention to the subject of the possible increase of our foreign trade and the methods for its development, not only with Europe, but with other countries, and especially with the States and sovereignties of the western hemisphere. Instructions from the Department of State were issued to the various diplomatic and consular officers of the Government, asking them to devote attention to the question of methods by which trade between the respective countries of their official residence and the United States could be most judiciously fostered. In obedience to these instructions, examinations and reports upon this subject have been made by many of these officers and transmitted to the Department, and the same are submitted to the consideration of Congress.

The annual report of the Secretary of the Treasury on the state of the finances presents important questions for the action of Congress, upon some of which I have already remarked.

The revenues of the Government during the fiscal year ending June 30, 1877, were $269,000,586.62. The total expenditures for the same period were $238,660,008.93, leaving a surplus revenue of $30,340,577.69. This has substantially supplied the requirements of the sinking-fund for that year. The estimated revenues of the current fiscal year are $265,500,000, and the estimated expenditures for the same period are $232,430,643.72. If these estimates prove to be correct, there will be a surplus revenue of $33,069,356.28, an amount nearly sufficient for the sinking-fund for that year. The estimated revenues for the next fiscal year are $269,250,000.

It appears from the report that during the last fiscal year the revenues of the Government, compared with the previous year, have largely decreased. This decrease, amounting to the sum of $18,481,452.54, was mainly in customs duties, caused partly by a large falling off of the amount of imported dutiable goods, and partly by the general fall of prices in the markets of production of such articles as pay *ad-valorem* taxes. While this is felt injuriously in the diminution of the revenue, it has been accompanied with a very large increase of exportations. The total exports during the last fiscal year, including coin, have been $658,637,457, and the imports have been $492,097,540—leaving a balance of trade in favor of the United States amounting to the sum of $166,539,917; the beneficial effects of which extend to all branches of business.

The estimated revenue for the next fiscal year will impose upon Congress the duty of strictly limiting appropriations, including the requisite sum for the maintenance of the sinking-fund, within the aggregated estimated receipts.

While the aggregate of taxes should not be increased, amendments might be made to the revenue laws that would, without diminishing the revenue, relieve the people from unnecessary burdens. A tax on tea and coffee is shown by the experience not only of our own country, but of other countries, to be easily collected, without loss by undervaluation or fraud, and largely borne in the country of production. A tax of ten cents a pound on tea and two cents a pound on coffee would produce a revenue exceeding $12,000,000, and thus enable Congress to repeal a multitude of annoying taxes yielding a revenue not exceeding that sum. The internal-revenue system grew out of the necessities of the war, and most of the legislation imposing taxes upon domestic products, under this system, has been repealed. By the substitution of a tax on tea and coffee, all forms of internal taxation may be repealed, except that on whiskey, spirits, tobacco, and beer. Attention is also called to the necessity of enacting more rigorous laws for the protection of the revenue and for the punishment of frauds and smuggling. This can best be done by judicious provisions that will induce the disclosure of attempted fraud by undervaluation and smuggling. All revenue laws should be simple in their provisions and easily understood. So far as practicable, the rates of taxation should be in the form of specific duties, and not *ad valorem*, requiring the judgment of experienced men to ascertain values, and exposing the revenue to the temptation of fraud.

My attention has been called during the recess of Congress to abuses existing in the collection of the customs, and strenuous efforts have been made for their correction by Executive orders. The recommendation submitted to the Secretary of the Treasury by a commission appointed to examine into the collection of customs duties at the port of New York, contain many suggestions for the modification of the customs laws, to which the attention of Congress is invited.

It is matter of congratulation that, notwithstanding the severe burdens caused by the war, the public faith with all creditors has been preserved, and that, as the result of this policy, the public credit has continuously advanced, and our public securities are regarded with the highest favor in the markets of the world. I trust that no act of the Government will cast a shadow upon its credit.

The progress of refunding the public debt has been rapid and satisfactory. Under the contract existing when I entered upon the discharge of the duties of my office, bonds bearing interest at the rate of 4½ per cent. were being rapidly sold, and within three months the aggregate sales of these bonds had reached the sum of $200,000,000. With my sanction the Secretary of the Treasury entered into a new contract for the sale of four per cent. bonds, and within thirty days after the popular subscription for such bonds was opened subscriptions were had amounting to $75,496,550, which were paid for within ninety days after the date of subscription. By this process, within but little more than one year, the annual interest on the public debt was reduced in the sum of $3,775,000. I recommend that suitable provision be made to enable the people to easily convert their savings into Government securities, as the best mode in which small savings may be well secured and yield a moderate interest. It is an object of public policy to retain among our own people the securities of the United States. In this way our country is guarded against their sudden return from foreign countries, caused by war or other disturbances beyond our limits.

The commerce of the United States with foreign Nations, and especially the export of domestic productions, has of late years largely increased; but the greater portion of this trade is conducted in foreign vessels. The importance of enlarging our foreign trade, and especially by direct and speedy interchange, with countries on this continent, cannot be over-estimated; and it is a matter of great moment that our own shipping interest should receive, to the utmost practical extent, the benefit of our commerce with other lands. These considerations are forcibly urged by all the large commercial cities of the country, and public attention is generally and wisely attracted to the solution of the problems they present. It is not doubted that Congress will take them up in the broadest spirit of liberality, and respond to the public demand, by practical legislation, upon this important subject.

The report of the Secretary of War shows that the Army has been actively employed during the year, and has rendered very important service in suppressing hostilities in the Indian country, and in preserving peace, and protecting life and property in the interior as well as along the Mexican border. A long and arduous campaign has been prosecuted, with final complete success, against a portion of the Nez Percés tribe of Indians. A full account of this campaign will be found in the report of the General of the Army. It will be seen that in its course several severe battles were fought, in which a number of gallant officers and men lost their lives. I join with the Secretary of War and the General of the Army in awarding to the officers and men employed in the long and toilsome pursuit, and in the final capture of these Indians, the honor and praise which are so justly their due.

The very serious riots which occurred in several of the States in July last rendered necessary the employment of a considerable portion of the Army to preserve the peace and maintain order. In the States of West Virginia, Maryland, Pennsylvania, and Illinois these disturbances were so formidable as to defy the local and State authorities, and the National Executive was called upon, in the mode provided by the Constitution and laws, to furnish military aid. I am gratified to be able to state that the troops sent, in response to these calls for aid in the suppression of domestic violence, were able, by the influence of their presence in the disturbed regions, to preserve the peace and restore order without the use of force. In the discharge of this delicate and important duty, both officers and men acted with great prudence and courage, and for their services deserve the thanks of the country.

Disturbances along the Rio Grande, in Texas, to which I have already referred, have rendered necessary the constant employment of a military force in that vicinity. A full report of all recent military operations in that quarter has been transmitted to the House of Representatives, in answer to a resolution of that body, and it will, therefore, not be necessary to enter into details. I regret to say that these lawless incursions into our territory by armed bands from the Mexican side of the line, for the purpose of robbery, have been of frequent occurrence, and, in spite of the most vigilant efforts of the commander of our forces, the marauders have generally succeeded in escaping into Mexico with their plunder. In May last I gave orders for the exercise of the utmost vigilance on the part of our troops for the suppression of these raids, and the punishment of the guilty parties, as well as the recapture of property stolen by them. General Ord, commanding in Texas, was directed to invite the co-operation of the Mexican authorities in efforts to this end, and to assure them that I was anxious to avoid giving the least offence to Mexico. At the same time, he was directed to give notice of my determination to put an end to the invasion of our territory by lawless bands, intent upon the plunder of our peaceful citizens, even if the effectual punishment of the outlaws should make the crossing of the border by our troops in their pursuit necessary. It is believed that this policy has had the effect to check somewhat these depredations, and that, with a considerable increase of our force upon that frontier, and the establishment of several additional military posts along the Rio Grande, so as more effectually to guard that extensive border, peace may be preserved, and the lives and property of our citizens in Texas fully protected.

Prior to the 1st day of July last the Army was, in accordance with law, reduced to the maximum of 25,000 enlisted men, being a reduction of 2,500 below the force previously authorized. This reduction was made, as required by law, entirely from the infantry and artillery branches of the service, without any reduction of the cavalry. Under the law, as it now stands, it is necessary that the cavalry regiments be recruited to one hundred men in each company for service on the Mexican and Indian frontiers. The necessary effect of this legislation is to reduce the infantry and artillery arms of the service below the number required for efficiency; and I concur with the Secretary of War in recommending that authority be given to recruit all companies of infantry to at least fifty men, and all batteries of artillery to at least seventy-five men, with the power, in case of emergency, to increase the former to one hundred, and the latter to one hundred and twenty-two men each.

I invite your special attention to the following recommendations of the Secretary of War:

First. That provision be made for supplying to the Army a more abundant and better supply of reading-matter.

Second. That early action be taken by Congress looking to a complete revision and republication of the Army Regulations.

Third. That section 1258 of the Revised Statutes, limiting the number of officers on the retired list, be repealed.

Fourth. That the claims arising under the act of July 4, 1864, for supplies taken by the Army during the war, be taken from the offices of the Quartermaster and Commissary-General, and transferred to the Southern Claims Commission, or some other tribunal having more time and better facilities for their prompt investigation and decision than are possessed by these officers.

Fifth. That Congress provide for an annuity-fund for the families of deceased soldiers, as recommended by the Paymaster-General of the Army.

The report of the Secretary of the Navy shows that we have six squadrons now engaged in the protection of our foreign commerce, and other duties pertaining to the naval service. The condition and operations of the Department are also shown. The total expenditures for the fiscal year ending June 30, 1877, were $16,077,974.54. There are unpaid claims against the Department chargeable to the last year, which are presented to the consideration of Congress by the report of the Secretary. The estimates for the fiscal year commencing July 1, 1878, are $16,233,234.40, exclusive of the sum of $2,314,231, submitted for new buildings, repairs, and improvements at the several navy-yards. The appropriations for the present fiscal year, commencing July 1, 1877, are $13,592,932.90. The amount drawn from the Treasury from July 1 to November 1, 1877, is $5,343,037.40, of which there is estimated to be yet available $1,029,528.30, showing the amount of actual expenditure during the first four months of the present fiscal year to have been $4,313,509.10.

The report of the Postmaster-General contains a full and clear statement of the operations and condition of the Post-Office Department. The ordinary revenues of the Department for the fiscal year ending June 30, 1877, including receipts from the money-order business and from official stamps and stamped envelopes, amounted to the sum of $27,531,585.26. The additional sum of $7,013,000 was realized from appropriations from the general treasury for various purposes, making the receipts from all sources $34,544,885.26. The total expenditures during the fiscal year amounted to $33,486,322.44, leaving an excess of total receipts over total expenditures of $1,058,562.82, and an excess of total expenditures over ordinary receipts of $5,954,737.18. Deducting from the total receipts the sum of $63,261.84, received from international money-orders of the preceding fiscal year, and deducting from the total expenditures the sum of $1,163,818.20, paid on liabilities incurred in previous fiscal years, the expenditures and receipts appertaining to the business of the last fiscal year were as follows:

Expenditures $32,322,504 24
Receipts, (ordinary, from money-order business and from
    official postage-stamps)........................... 27,468,323 42

    Excess of expenditures 4,854,180 82

The ordinary revenues of the Post-Office Department for the year ending June 30, 1879, are estimated at an increase of three per cent. over those of 1877, making $29,054,098.28, and the expenditures for the same year are estimated at $36,427,771, leaving an estimated deficiency for the year 1879 of $7,393,672.72. The additional legislation recommended by the Postmaster-General for improvements of the mail service, and to protect the postal revenues from the abuses practised under existing laws, is respectfully recommended to the careful consideration of Congress.

The report of the Attorney-General contains several suggestions as to the administration of justice, to which I invite your attention. The pressure of business in the Supreme Court and in certain circuit courts of the United States is now such that serious delays, to the great injury, and even oppression, of suitors occur, and a remedy should be sought for this condition of affairs. Whether it will be found in the plan briefly sketched in the report, of increasing the number of judges of the circuit courts, and by means of this addition to the judicial force of creating an intermediate court of errors and appeals, or whether some other mode can be devised for obviating the difficulties which now exist, I leave to your mature consideration.

The present condition of the Indian tribes on the territory of the United States, and our relations with them, are fully set forth in the reports of the Secretary of the Interior and the Commissioner of Indian Affairs. After a series of most deplorable conflicts—the successful termination of which, while reflecting honor upon the brave soldiers who accomplished it, cannot lessen our regret at their occurrence—we are now at peace with all the Indian tribes within our borders. To preserve that peace by a just and humane policy will be the object of my earnest endeavors. Whatever may be said of their character and savage propensities, of the difficulties of introducing among them the habits of civilized life, and of the obstacles they have offered to the progress of settlement and enterprise in certain parts of the country, the Indians are certainly entitled to our sympathy, and to a conscientious respect on our part for their claims upon our sense of justice. They were the aboriginal occupants of the land we now possess. They have been driven from place to place; the purchase-money paid to them, in some cases, for what they called their own, has still left them poor. In many instances, when they had settled down upon land assigned to them by compact, and began to support themselves by their own labor, they were rudely jostled off and thrust into the wilderness again. Many, if not most, of our Indian wars have had their origin in broken promises and acts of injustice upon our part; and the advance of the Indians in civilization has been slow, because the treatment they received did not permit it to be faster and more general. We cannot expect them to improve and to follow our guidance unless we keep faith with them in respecting the rights they possess, and unless, instead of depriving them of their opportunities, we lend them a helping-hand.

I cordially approve the policy regarding the management of Indian Affairs outlined in the reports of the Secretary of the Interior and of the Commissioner of Indian Affairs. The faithful performance of our promises is the first condition of a good understanding with the Indians. I cannot too urgently recommend to Congress that prompt and liberal provision be made for the conscientious fulfilment of all engagements entered into by the Government with Indian tribes. To withhold the means necessary for the performance of a promise is always a false economy, and is apt to prove disastrous in its consequences. Especial care is recommended to provide for Indians settled on their reservations cattle and agricultural implements, to aid them in whatever efforts they may make to support themselves; and by the establishment and maintenance of schools to bring them under the control of civilized influences. I see no reason why Indians who can give satisfactory proof of having by their own labor supported their families for a number of years, and who are willing to detach themselves from their tribal relations, should not be admitted to the benefit of the homestead act and the privileges of citizenship ; and I recommend the passage of a law to that effect. It will be an act of justice, as well as a measure of encouragement. Earnest efforts are being made to purify the Indian Service, so that every dollar appropriated by Congress shall redound to the benefit of the Indians, as intended. Those efforts shall have my firm support. With an improved service, and every possible encouragement held out to the Indians to better their condition and to elevate themselves in the scale of civilization, we may hope to accomplish, at the same time, a good work for them and for ourselves.

I invite the attention of Congress to the importance of the statements and suggestions made by the Secretary of the Interior concerning the depredations committed on the timber-lands of the United States, and the necessity for the preservation of forests. It is believed that the measures taken in pursuance of existing law to arrest those depredations will be entirely successful if Congress, by an appropriation for that purpose, renders their continued enforcement possible. The experience of other nations teaches us that a country cannot be stripped of its forests with impunity, and we shall expose ourselves to the gravest consequences unless the wasteful and improvident manner in which the forests of the United are destroyed be effectually checked. I earnestly recommend that the measures suggested by the Secretary of the Interior for the suppression of depredations on the public timber-lands of the United States, for the selling of timber from the public lands, and for the preservation of forests, be embodied in a law; and that, considering the urgent necessity of enabling the people of certain States and Territories to purchase timber from the public lands in a legal manner, which at present they cannot do, such a law be passed without unavoidable delay. I would also call the attention of Congress to the statements made by the Secretary of the Interior concerning the disposition that might be made of the desert lands not irrigable west of the 100th meridian. These lands are practically unsalable under existing laws, and the suggestion is worthy of consideration that a system of leasehold tenure would make them a source of profit to the United States, while at the same time legalizing the business of cattle-raising, which is at present carried on upon them.

The report of the Commissioner of Agriculture contains the gratifying announcement of the extraordinary success which has rewarded the agricultural industry of the country for the past year. With the fair prices which obtain for the products of the soil, especially for the surplus which our people have to export, we may confidently turn to this as the most important of all our resources for the revival of the depressed industries of the country. The report shows our agricultural progress during the year, and contains a statement of the work done by this department for the advancement of agricultural industry, upon which the prosperity of our people so largely depends. Matters of information are included of great interest to all who seek, by the experience of others, to improve their own methods of cultivation. The efforts of the Department to increase the production of important articles of consumption will, it is hoped, improve the demand for labor, and advance the business of the country, and eventually result in saving some of the many millions that are now annually paid to foreign Nations for sugar and other staple products which habitual use has made necessary in our domestic every-day life.

The Board on behalf the United States Executive Departments at the International Exhibition of 1876 has concluded its labors. The final report of the Board was transmitted to Congress by the President near the close of the last session. As these papers are understood to contain interesting and valuable information, and will constitute the only report emanating from the Government on the subject of the Exhibition, I invite attention to the matter and recommend that the report be published for general information.

Congress is empowered by the Constitution with the authority of exclusive legislation over the District of Columbia, in which the seat of Government of the Nation is located. The interests of the District having no direct representation in Congress, are entitled to especial consideration and care at the hands of the General Government. The capital of the United States belongs to the Nation, and it is natural that the American people should take pride in the seat of their National Government, and desire it to be an ornament to the country. Much has been done to render it healthful, convenient, and attractive, but much remains to be done, which its permanent inhabitants are not able and ought not to be expected to do. To impose upon them a large proportion of the cost required for public improvements, which are in a great measure planned and executed for the convenience of the Government, and of the many thousands of visitors from all parts of the country, who temporarily reside at the capital of the Nation, is an evident injustice. Special attention is asked by the Commissioners of the District in their report, which is herewith transmitted, to the importance of a permanent adjustment by Congress of the financial relations between the United States and the District, involving the regular annual contribution by the United States of its just proportion of the expenses of the District government, and of the outlay for all needed public improvements, and such measure of relief from the burden of taxation now resting upon the people of the District as in the wisdom of Congress may be deemed just.

The report of the Commissioners shows that the affairs of the District are in a condition as satisfactory as could be expected, in view of the heavy burden of debt resting upon it, and its very limited means for necessary expenses.

The debt of the District is as follows:

Old funded debt	$8,379,691 96
3.65 bonds, guaranteed by the United States	13,743,250 00
Total bonded debt	22,122,941 96
To which should be added certain outstanding claims, as explained in the report of the Commissioners	1,187,204 52
Making the total debt of the District	23,310,146 48

The Commissioners also ask attention to the importance of the improvement of the Potomac river, and the reclamation of the marshes bordering the city of Washington; and their views upon this subject are concurred in by the members of the Board of Health, whose report is also herewith transmitted. Both the commercial and sanitary interests of the District will be greatly promoted, I doubt not, by this improvement.

Your attention is invited to the suggestion of the Commissioners, and of the Board of Health, for the organization of a Board of Charities, to have supervision and control of the disbursement of all moneys for charitable purposes from the District treasury. I desire, also, to ask your special attention to the need of adding to the efficiency of the public schools of the District, by supplemental aid from the National Treasury. This is especially just, since so large a number of those attending these schools are children of employés of the Government. I earnestly commend to your care the interests of the people of the District, who are so intimately associated with the Government establishments, and to whose enterprise the good order and attractiveness of the capital are largely due; and I ask your attention to the request of the Commissioners for legislation in behalf of the interests intrusted to their care. The appropriations asked, for the care of the reservations belonging to the Government within the city, by the Commissioner of Public Buildings and Grounds, are also commended to your favorable consideration.

The report of the Joint Commission created by the act approved August 2, 1876, entitled "An act providing for the completion of the Washington Monument," is also herewith transmitted, with accompanying documents. The board of engineer officers detailed to examine the monument, in compliance with the second section of the act, have reported that the foundation is insufficient. No authority exists for making the expenditure necessary to secure its stability. I therefore recommend that the commission be authorized to expend such portion of the sum appropriated by the act as may be necessary for the purpose. The present unfinished condition of the monument, begun so long ago, is a reproach to the Nation. It cannot be doubted that the patriotic sense of the country will warmly respond to such prompt provision as may be made for its completion at an early day, and I urge upon Congress the propriety and necessity of immediate legislation for this purpose.

The wisdom of legislation upon the part of Congress in aid of the States, for the education of the whole people in those branches of study which are taught in the common schools of the country, is no longer a question. The intelligent judgment of the country goes still further, regarding it as also both constitutional and expedient for the General Government to extend to technical and higher education, such aid as is deemed essential to the general welfare and to our due prominence among the enlightened and cultured Nations of the world. The ultimate settlement of all questions of the future, whether of administration or finance, or of true nationality of sentiment, depends upon the virtue and intelligence of the people. It is vain to hope for the success of a free government without the means of insuring the intelligence of those who are the source of power. No less than one-seventh of the entire voting population of our country are yet unable to read and write.

It is encouraging to observe, in connection with the growth of fraternal feeling in those States in which slavery formerly existed, evidences of increasing interest in universal education, and I shall be glad to give my approval to any appropriate measures which may be enacted by Congress for the purpose of supplementing with national aid the local systems of education in those States, and in all the States; and having already invited your attention to the needs of the District of Columbia with respect to its public-school system, I here add that I believe it desirable, not so much with reference to the local wants of the District, but to the great and lasting benefit of the entire country, that this system should be crowned with a university in all respects in keeping with the National Capital, and thereby realize the cherished hopes of Washington on this subject.

I also earnestly commend the request of the Regents of the Smithsonian Institution that an adequate appropriation be made for the establishment and conduct of a national museum under their supervision.

The question of providing for the preservation and growth of the Library of Congress is also one of national importance. As the depository of all copyright publications and records, this library has outgrown the provisions for its accommodation; and the erection, on such site as the judgment of Congress may approve, of a fire-proof library-building, to preserve the treasures and enlarge the usefulness of this valuable collection, is recommended. I recommend also such legislation as will render available and efficient, for the purposes of instruction, so far as is consistent with the public service, the cabinets or museums of invention, of surgery, of education, and of agriculture, and other collections, the property of the National Government.

The capital of the Nation should be something more than a mere political centre. We should avail ourselves of all the opportunities which Providence has here placed at our command, to promote the general intelligence of the people and increase the conditions most favorable to the success and perpetuity of our institutions.

R. B. HAYES.

DECEMBER 3, 1877.

MESSAGE

RETURNING TO

THE HOUSE OF REPRESENTATIVES THE BILL ENTITLED "AN ACT TO AUTHORIZE THE COINAGE OF THE STANDARD SILVER DOLLAR AND TO RESTORE ITS LEGAL-TENDER CHARACTER.

FEBRUARY 28, 1878.

MESSAGE.

To the House of Representatives:

After a very careful consideration of the House bill No. 1093, entitled "An act to authorize the coinage of the standard silver dollar and to restore its legal-tender character," I feel compelled to return it to the House of Representatives, in which it originated, with my objections to its passage.

Holding the opinion which I expressed in my annual message, that "neither the interests of the Government nor of the people of the United States would be promoted by disparaging silver as one of the two precious metals which furnish the coinage of the world, and that legislation which looks to maintaining the volume of intrinsic money to as full a measure of both metals as their relative commercial values will permit would be neither unjust nor inexpedient," it has been my earnest desire to concur with Congress in the adoption of such measures to increase the silver coinage of the country as would not impair the obligation of contracts, either public or private, nor injuriously affect the public credit. It is only upon the conviction that this bill does not meet these essential requirements that I feel it my duty to withhold from it my approval.

My present official duty as to this bill permits only an attention to the specific objections to its passage which seem to me so important as to justify me in asking from the wisdom and duty of Congress that further consideration of the bill for which the Constitution has, in such cases, provided.

The bill provides for the coinage of silver dollars of the weight of 412½ grains each, of standard silver, to be a legal-tender at their nominal value for all debts and dues, public and private, except where otherwise expressly stipulated in the contract. It is well known that the market value of that number of grains of standard silver during the past year has been from ninety to ninety-two cents as compared with the standard gold dollar. Thus the silver dollar authorized by this bill is worth 8 to 10 per cent. less than it purports to be worth, and is made a legal-tender for debts contracted when the law did not recognize such coins as lawful money.

The right to pay duties in silver or certificates for silver deposits will, when they are issued in sufficient amount to circulate, put an end to the receipt of revenue in gold, and thus compel the payment of silver for both the principal and interest of the public debt. One thousand one hundred and forty-three million four hundred and ninety-three thousand four hundred dollars of the bonded debt, now outstanding, was issued prior to February, 1873, when the silver dollar was unknown in circulation in this country, and was only a convenient form of silver bullion for exportation; $583,440,350 of the funded debt has been issued since February, 1873, when gold alone was the coin for which the bonds were sold, and gold alone was the coin in which both parties to the contract understood that the bonds would be paid. These bonds entered into the markets of the world. They were paid for in gold when silver had greatly depreciated, and when no one would have bought them if it had been understood that they would be paid in silver. The sum of $225,000,000 of these bonds has been sold during my administration for gold coin, and the United States received the benefit of these sales by a reduction of the rate of interest to 4 and 4½ per cent. During the progress of these sales a doubt was suggested as to the coin in which payment of these bonds would be made. The public announcement was thereupon authorized that it was "not to be anticipated that any future legislation of Congress, or any action of any Department of the Government, would sanction or tolerate the redemption of the principal of these bonds, or the payment of the interest thereon, in coin of less value than the coin authorized by law at the time of the issue of the bonds, being the coin exacted by the Government in exchange for the same."

In view of these facts it will be justly regarded as a grave breach of the public faith to undertake to pay these bonds, principal or interest, in silver coin worth in the market less than the coin received for them. It is said that the silver dollar made a legal-tender by this bill will, under its operation, be equivalent in value to the gold dollar. Many supporters of the bill believe this, and would not justify an attempt to pay debts, either public or private, in coin of inferior value to the money of the world. The capital defect of the bill is that it contains no provision protecting from its operation pre-existing debts in case the coinage which it creates shall continue to be of less value than that which was the sole legal-tender when they were contracted. If it is now proposed for the purpose of taking advantage of the depreciation of silver in the payment of debts to coin and make a legal-tender a silver dollar of less commercial value than any dollar, whether of gold or paper, which is now lawful money in this country, such measure, it will hardly be questioned, will, in the judgment of mankind, be an act of bad faith. As to all debts heretofore contracted, the silver dollar should be made a legal-tender only at its market value. The standard of value should not be changed without the consent of both parties to the contract. National promises should be kept with unflinching fidelity. There is no power to compel a Nation to pay its just debts. Its credit depends on its honor. The Nation owes what it has led or allowed its creditors to expect. I cannot approve a bill which in my judgment authorizes the violation of sacred obligations. The obligation of the public faith transcends all questions of profit or public advantage. Its unquestionable maintenance is the dictate as well of the highest expediency as of the most necessary duty, and should ever be carefully guarded by the Executive, by Congress, and by the people.

It is my firm conviction that, if the country is to be benefited by a silver coinage, it can be done only by the issue of silver dollars of full value, which will defraud no man. A currency worth less than it purports to be worth will in the end defraud not only creditors, but all who are engaged in legitimate business, and none more surely than those who are dependent on their daily labor for their daily bread.

R. B. HAYES.

EXECUTIVE MANSION, *February 28, 1878.*

MESSAGE

RETURNING TO

THE HOUSE OF REPRESENTATIVES THE BILL ENTITLED "AN ACT TO AUTHORIZE A SPECIAL TERM OF THE CIRCUIT COURT OF THE UNITED STATES FOR THE SOUTHERN DISTRICT OF MISSISSIPPI, TO BE HELD AT SCRANTON, IN JACKSON COUNTY."

MARCH 6, 1878.

MESSAGE.

To the House of Representatives:

I return herewith House bill No. 3072, entitled "An act to authorize a special term of the circuit court of the United States for the southern district of Mississippi, to be held at Scranton, in Jackson County," with the following objections to its becoming a law:

The act provides that a special term of the circuit court of the United States for the southern district of Mississippi shall be held at Scranton, in Jackson County, Mississippi, to begin on the second Monday in March, 1878, and directs the clerk of said court to "cause notice of said special term of said court to be published in a newspaper in Jackson, Mississippi, and also in a newspaper in Scranton, at least ten days before the beginning thereof."

The act cannot be executed, inasmuch as there is not sufficient time to give the notice of the holding of the special term, which Congress thought proper to require.

The number of suits to be tried at the special term, in which the United States is interested, is forty-nine, and the amount involved exceeds $200,000. The Government cannot prepare for trial at said special term, because no fund appropriated by Congress can be made available for that purpose. If, therefore, the Government is compelled to go to trial at the special term provided for by this bill, the United States must be defeated for want of time and means to make preparation for the proper vindication of its rights.

The bill is therefore returned for the further consideration of Congress.

R. B. HAYES.

Executive Mansion, *March 6, 1878.*

I certify that this act originated in the House of Representatives.

Attest:

GEO. M. ADAMS,
Clerk.

AN ACT to authorize a special term of the circuit court of the United States for the southern district of Mississippi, to be held at Scranton, in Jackson County.

Be it enacted by the Senate and House of Representatives of the United States of America in Congress assembled, That a special term of the circuit court of the United States for the southern district of Mississippi shall be holden at Scranton, in Jackson County, Mississippi, to begin on the second Monday in March, eighteen hundred and seventy-eight; and the clerk of said court shall cause notice of said special term of said court to be published in a newspaper in Jackson, Mississippi, and also in a newspaper in Scranton, at least ten days before the beginning thereof. And all process, writs, bonds, and recognizances which relate to any suit or suits pending, or which may be instituted in said court in behalf of the United States against any party or parties for or on account of any lumber, logs, charcoal, or turpentine, or growing out of or on account of any alleged depredation upon, or timber cut or taken from, any of the public lands of the United States in said district shall be considered as belonging to such special term; and such suits shall be then and there tried and determined as if they had been brought, and such writs, process, bonds, and recognizances had been opened and taken with reference and made returnable to such special term. And the presiding judge of said court shall have power to continue such special term from time to time until said suits shall be determined, if, in his judgment, the ends of justice may so require.

SAM. J. RANDALL,
Speaker of the House of Representatives.
W. A. WHEELER,
Vice-President of the United States and President of the Senate.

PROCLAMATION.

MARTIAL LAW IN NEW MEXICO.

OCTOBER 7, 1878.

PROCLAMATION.

BY THE PRESIDENT OF THE UNITED STATES OF AMERICA.

A PROCLAMATION.

Whereas it is provided in the laws of the United States that whenever, by reason of unlawful obstructions, combinations or assemblages of persons, or rebellion against the authority of the Government of the United States, it shall become impracticable, in the judgment of the President, to enforce by the ordinary course of judicial proceedings the laws of the United States within any State or Territory, it shall be lawful for the President to call forth the militia of any or all the States, and to employ such parts of the land and naval forces of the United States as he may deem necessary to enforce the faithful execution of the laws of the United States, or to suppress such rebellion, in whatever State or Territory thereof the laws of the United States may be forcibly opposed or the execution thereof forcibly obstructed;

And whereas it has been made to appear to me that by reason of unlawful combinations and assemblages of persons in arms, it has become impracticable to enforce, by the ordinary course of judicial proceedings, the laws of the United States within the Territory of New Mexico, and especially within Lincoln County therein; and that the laws of the United States have been therein forcibly opposed and the execution thereof forcibly resisted;

And whereas the laws of the United States require that whenever it may be necessary, in the judgment of the President, to use the military force for the purpose of enforcing the faithful execution of the laws of the United States, he shall forthwith, by proclamation, command such insurgents to disperse and retire peaceably to their respective abodes, within a limited time:

Now, therefore, I, RUTHERFORD B. HAYES, President of the United States, do hereby admonish all good citizens of the United States, and especially of the Territory of New Mexico, against aiding, countenancing, abetting, or taking part in any such unlawful proceedings, and I do hereby warn all persons engaged in or connected with said obstruction of the laws, to disperse and retire peaceably to their respective abodes on or before noon of the thirteenth day of October, instant.

In witness whereof I have hereunto set my hand, and caused the seal of the United States to be affixed.

Done at the city of Washington this seventh day of October, in the year of our Lord eighteen hundred and seventy-eight, and of [SEAL.] the Independence of the United States the one hundred and third.

R. B. HAYES.

By the President:
   F. W. SEWARD,
     Acting Secretary of State.

THANKSGIVING PROCLAMATION.

OCTOBER 30, 1878.

PROCLAMATION.

BY THE PRESIDENT OF THE UNITED STATES OF AMERICA.

A PROCLAMATION.

The recurrence of that season at which it is the habit of our people to make devout and public confession of their constant dependence upon the Divine favor for all the good gifts of life and happiness and of public peace and prosperity, exhibits, in the record of the year, abundant reasons for our gratitude and thanksgiving.

Exuberant harvests, productive mines, ample crops of the staples of trade and manufactures, have enriched the country.

The resources, thus furnished to our reviving industry and expanding commerce, are hastening the day when discords and distresses, through the length and breadth of the land, will, under the continued favor of Providence, have given way to confidence, and energy and assured prosperity.

Peace with all Nations has been maintained unbroken, domestic tranquillity has prevailed, and the institutions of liberty and justice which the wisdom and virtue of our fathers established, remain the glory and defence of their children.

The general prevalence of the blessings of health through our wide land, has made more conspicuous the sufferings and sorrows, which the dark shadow of pestilence has cast upon a portion of our people. This heavy affliction, even, the Divine Ruler has tempered to the suffering communities in the universal sympathy and succor which have flowed to their relief, and the whole Nation may rejoice in the unity of spirit in our people by which they cheerfully share one another's burdens.

Now, therefore, I, RUTHERFORD B. HAYES, President of the United States, do appoint Thursday, the 28th day of November, next, as a Day of National Thanksgiving and Prayer; and I earnestly recommend that, withdrawing themselves from secular cares and labors, the people of the United States do meet together on that day in their respective places of worship, there to give thanks and praise to Almighty God for His mercies, and to devoutly beseech their continuance.

In witness whereof I have hereunto set my hand, and caused the seal of the United States to be affixed.

Done at the city of Washington this thirtieth day of October, in the year of our Lord one thousand eight hundred and seventy-eight, and of the Independence of the United States the one hundred and third.

[SEAL.]

R. B. HAYES.

By the President:
  WM. M. EVARTS,
    Secretary of State.

MESSAGE

TO THE

TWO HOUSES OF CONGRESS AT THE COMMENCEMENT OF THE THIRD SESSION OF THE FORTY-FIFTH CONGRESS.

DECEMBER 2, 1878.

MESSAGE.

FELLOW-CITIZENS OF THE SENATE
AND HOUSE OF REPRESENTATIVES:

Our heartfelt gratitude is due to the Divine Being, who holds in His hands the destinies of Nations, for the continued bestowal, during the last year, of countless blessings upon our country.

We are at peace with all other Nations. Our public credit has greatly improved, and is, perhaps, now stronger than ever before. Abundant harvests have rewarded the labors of those who till the soil, our manufacturing industries are reviving, and it is believed that general prosperity, which has been so long anxiously looked for, is at last within our reach.

The enjoyment of health by our people generally has, however, been interrupted, during the past season, by the prevalence of a fatal pestilence, the yellow-fever, in some portions of the Southern States, creating an emergency which called for prompt and extraordinary measures of relief. The disease appeared as an epidemic, at New Orleans and at other places on the lower Mississippi, soon after midsummer. It was rapidly spread by fugitives from the infected cities and towns, and did not disappear until early in November. The States of Louisiana, Mississippi, and Tennessee have suffered severely. About one hundred thousand cases are believed to have occurred, of which about twenty thousand, according to intelligent estimates, proved fatal. It is impossible to estimate with any approach to accuracy the loss to the country occasioned by this epidemic. It is to be reckoned by the hundred millions of dollars. The suffering and destitution that resulted excited the deepest sympathy in all parts of the Union. Physicians and nurses hastened from every quarter to the assistance of the afflicted communities. Voluntary contributions of money and supplies, in every needed form, were speedily and generously furnished. The Government was able to respond in some measure to the call for help, by providing tents, medicines, and food for the sick and destitute, the requisite directions for the purpose being given, in the confident expectation that this action of the Executive would receive the sanction of Congress. About eighteen hundred tents, and rations of the value of about twenty-five thousand dollars, were sent to cities and towns which applied for them, full details of which will be furnished to Congress by the proper Department.

The fearful spread of this pestilence has awakened a very general public sentiment in favor of national sanitary administration, which shall not only control quarantine, but have the sanitary supervision of internal commerce in times of epidemics, and hold an advisory relation to the State and municipal health authorities, with power to deal with whatever endangers the public health, and which the municipal and State authorities are unable to regulate. The national quarantine act approved April 29, 1878, which was passed too late in the last session of Congress to provide the means for carrying it into practical operation, during the past season, is a step in the direction here indicated. In view of the necessity for the most effective measures, by quarantine and otherwise, for the protection of our seaports, and the country generally, from this and other epidemics, it is recommended that Congress give to the whole subject early and careful consideration.

'The permanent pacification of the country by the complete protection of all citizens in every civil and political right continues to be of paramount interest with the great body of our people. Every step in this direction is welcomed with public approval, and every interruption of steady and uniform progress to the desired consummation awakens general uneasiness and wide-spread condemnation. The recent Congressional elections have furnished a direct and trustworthy test of the advance thus far made in the practical establishment of the right of suffrage, secured by the Constitution to the liberated race in the Southern States. All disturbing influences, real or imaginary, had been removed from all of these States.

The three constitutional amendments, which conferred freedom and equality of civil and political rights upon the colored people of the South, were adopted by the concurrent action of the great body of good citizens who maintained the authority of the National Government and the integrity and perpetuity of the Union at such a cost of treasure and life, as a wise and necessary embodiment in the organic law of the just results of the war. The people of the former slaveholding States accepted these results, and gave, in every practicable form, assurances that the thirteenth, fourteenth, and fifteenth amendments, and laws passed in pursuance thereof, should, in good faith, be enforced, rigidly and impartially, in letter and spirit, to the end that the humblest citizen, without distinction of race or color, should, under them, receive full and equal protection in person and property and in political rights and privileges. By these constitutional amendments, the southern section of the Union obtained a large increase of political power in Congress and in the Electoral College, and the country justly expected that elections would proceed, as to the enfranchised race, upon the same circumstances of legal and constitutional freedom and protection which obtained in all the other States of the Union. The friends of law and order looked forward to the conduct of these elections, as offering to the general judgment of the country an important opportunity to measure the degree in which the right of suffrage could be exercised by the colored people, and would be respected by their fellow-citizens; but a more general enjoyment of freedom of suffrage by the colored people, and a more just and generous protection of that freedom by the communities of which they form a part, were generally anticipated than the record of the elections discloses. In some of those States in which the colored people have been unable to make their opinions felt in the elections, the result is mainly due to influences not easily measured or remedied by legal protection; but in the States of Louisiana and South Carolina at large, and in some particular congressional districts outside of those States, the records of the elections seem to compel the conclusion that the rights of the colored voters have been overridden, and their participation in the elections not permitted to be either general or free.

It will be for the Congress for which these elections were held, to make such examinations into their conduct as may be appropriate to determine the validity of the claims of members to their seats. In the meanwhile it becomes the duty of the Executive and Judicial Departments of the Government, each in its province, to inquire into and punish violations of the laws of the United States which have occurred. I can but repeat what I said in this connection in my last message, that whatever authority rests with me to this end I shall not hesitate to put forth, and I am unwilling to forego a renewed appeal to the legislatures, the courts, the executive authorities, and the people of the States where these wrongs have been perpetrated, to give their assistance towards bringing to justice the offenders and preventing a repetition of the crimes. No means within my power will be spared to obtain a full and fair investigation of the alleged crimes, and to secure the conviction and just punishment of the guilty.

It is to be observed that the principal appropriation made for the Department of Justice at the last session contained the following clause: "And for defraying the expenses which may be incurred in the enforcement of the act approved February twenty-eighth, eighteen hundred and seventy-one, entitled 'An act to amend an act approved May thirtieth, eighteen hundred and seventy, entitled An act to enforce the rights of citizens of the United States to vote in the several States of the Union, and for other purposes,' or any acts amendatory thereof or supplementary thereto."

It is the opinion of the Attorney-General that the expenses of these proceedings will largely exceed the amount which was thus provided, and I rely confidently upon Congress to make adequate appropriations to enable the Executive Department to enforce the laws.

I respectfully urge upon your attention that the Congressional elections, in every district, in a very important sense, are justly a matter of political interest and concern throughout the whole country. Each State, every political party, is entitled to the share of power which is conferred by the legal and constitutional suffrage. It is the right of every citizen, possessing the qualifications prescribed by law, to cast one unintimidated ballot, and to have his ballot honestly counted. So long as the exercise of this power and the enjoyment of this right are common and equal, practically as well as formally, submission to the results of the suffrage will be accorded loyally and cheerfully, and all the departments of Government will feel the true vigor of the popular will thus expressed. No temporary or administrative interests of Government, however urgent or weighty, will ever displace the zeal of our people in defence of the primary rights of citizenship. They understand that the protection of liberty requires the maintenance, in full vigor, of the manly methods of free speech, free press, and free suffrage, and will sustain the full authority of Government to enforce the laws which are framed to preserve these inestimable rights. The material progress and welfare of the States depend on the protection afforded to their citizens. There can be no peace without such protection, no prosperity without peace, and the whole country is deeply interested in the growth and prosperity of all its parts.

While the country has not yet reached complete unity of feeling and reciprocal confidence between the communities so lately and so seriously estranged, I feel an absolute assurance that the tendencies are in that direction, and with increasing force. The power of public opinion will override all political prejudices, and all sectional or State attachments, in demanding that all over our wide territory the name and character of citizen of the United States shall mean one and the same thing, and carry with them unchallenged security and respect.

Our relations with other countries continue peaceful. Our neutrality in contests between foreign Powers has been maintained and respected.

The Universal Exposition held at Paris during the past summer has been attended by large numbers of our citizens. The brief period allowed for the preparation and arrangement of the contributions of our citizens to this great Exposition was well employed in energetic and judicious efforts to overcome this disadvantage. These efforts, led and directed by the Commissioner-General, were remarkably successful, and the exhibition of the products of American industry was creditable and gratifying in scope and character. The reports of the United States Commissioners, giving its results in detail, will be duly laid before you. Our participation in this international competition for the favor and the trade of the world may be expected to produce useful and important results in promoting intercourse, friendship, and commerce with other Nations.

In accordance with the provisions of the act of February 28, 1878, three commissioners were appointed to an international conference on the subject of adopting a common ratio between gold and silver, for the purpose of establishing internationally the use of bimetallic money, and securing fixity of relative value between those metals.

Invitations were addressed to the various Governments which had expressed a willingness to participate in its deliberations. The conference held its meetings in Paris in August last. The report of the Commissioners, herewith submitted, will show its results. No common ratio between gold and silver could be agreed upon by the conference. The general conclusion was reached that it is necessary to maintain in the world the monetary functions of silver as well as of gold, leaving the selection of the use of one or the other of these two metals, or of both, to be made by each State.

Congress having appropriated at its last session the sum of $5,500,000 to pay the award of the Joint Commission at Halifax, if, after correspondence with the British Government on the subject of the conformity of the award to the requirements of the treaty and to the terms of the question thereby submitted to the Commission, the President shall deem it his duty to make the payment, communications upon these points were addressed to the British Government through the Legation of the United States at London. Failing to obtain the concurrence of the British Government in the views of this Government respecting the award, I have deemed it my duty to tender the sum named, within the year fixed by the treaty, accompanied by a notice of the grounds of the payment, and a protest against any other construction of the same. The correspondence upon this subject will be laid before you.

The Spanish Government has officially announced the termination of the insurrection in Cuba, and the restoration of peace throughout that Island. Confident expectations are expressed of a revival of trade and prosperity, which it is earnestly hoped may prove well founded. Numerous claims of American citizens for relief for injuries or restoration of property have been among the incidents of the long-continued hostilities. Some of these claims are in process of adjustment by Spain, and the others are promised early and careful consideration.

The treaty made with Italy in regard to reciprocal consular privileges has been duly ratified and proclaimed.

No questions of grave importance have arisen with any other of the European Powers.

The Japanese Government has been desirous of a revision of such parts of its treaties with foreign Powers as relate to commerce, and, it is understood, has addressed to each of the treaty Powers a request to open negotiations with that view. The United States Government has been inclined to regard the matter favorably. Whatever restrictions upon trade with Japan are found injurious to that people cannot but affect injuriously Nations holding commercial intercourse with them. Japan, after a long period of seclusion, has within the past few years made rapid strides in the path of enlightenment and progress, and, not unreasonably, is looking forward to the time when her relations with the Nations of Europe and America shall be assimilated to those which they hold with each other. A treaty looking to this end has been made, which will be submitted for the consideration of the Senate.

After an interval of several years, the Chinese Government has again sent envoys to the United States. They have been received, and a permanent Legation is now established here by that Government. It is not doubted that this step will be of advantage to both Nations in promoting friendly relations and removing causes of difference.

The treaty with the Samoan Islands, having been duly ratified and accepted on the part of both Governments, is now in operation, and a survey and soundings of the harbor of Pago-Pago have been made by a naval vessel of the United States, with a view of its occupation as a naval station, if found desirable to the service.

Since the resumption of diplomatic relations with Mexico, correspondence has been opened and still continues between the two Governments upon the various questions which at one time seemed to endanger their relations. While no formal agreement has been reached as to the troubles on the border, much has been done to repress and diminish them. The effective force of United States troops on the Rio

Grande, by a strict and faithful compliance with instructions, has done much to remove the sources of dispute, and it is now understood that a like force of Mexican troops on the other side of the river is also making an energetic movement against the marauding Indian tribes.

This Government looks with the greatest satisfaction upon every evidence of strength in the National authority of Mexico, and upon every effort put forth to prevent or to punish incursions upon our territory. Reluctant to assume any action or attitude in the control of these incursions by military movements across the border not imperatively demanded for the protection of the lives and property of our own citizens, I shall take the earliest opportunity, consistent with the proper discharge of this plain duty, to recognize the ability of the Mexican Government to restrain effectively violations of our territory. It is proposed to hold next year an International Exhibition in Mexico, and it is believed that the display of the agricultural and manufacturing products of the two Nations will tend to better understanding and increased commercial intercourse between their people.

With Brazil, and the Republics of Central and South America, some steps have been taken toward the development of closer commercial intercourse. Diplomatic relations have been resumed with Colombia and with Bolivia. A boundary question between the Argentine Republic and Paraguay has been submitted by those governments for arbitration to the President of the United States, and I have, after a careful examination, given a decision upon it.

A naval expedition up the Amazon and Madeira rivers has brought back information valuable both for scientific and commercial purposes. A like expedition is about visiting the coast of Africa and the Indian Ocean. The reports of diplomatic and consular officers in relation to the development of our foreign commerce have furnished many facts that have proved of public interest, and have stimulated to practical exertion the enterprise of our people.

The report of the Secretary of the Treasury furnishes a detailed statement of the operations of that Department of the Government, and of the condition of the public finances.

The ordinary revenues from all sources for the fiscal year ended June 30, 1878, were $257,763,878.70; the ordinary expenditures for the same period were $236,964,326.80—leaving a surplus revenue for the year of $20,799,551.90.

The receipts for the present fiscal year, ending June 30, 1879, actual and estimated, are as follows: Actual receipts for the first quarter commencing July 1, 1878, $73,389,743.43; estimated receipts for the remaining three-quarters of the year, $191,110,256.57; total receipts for the current fiscal year, actual and estimated, $264,500,000. The expenditures for the same period will be, actual and estimated, as follows: For the quarter commencing July 1, 1878, actual expenditures, $73,344,573.27; and for the remaining three-quarters of the year the expenditures are estimated at $166,755,426.73—making the total expenditures $240,100,000; and leaving an estimated surplus revenue for the year ending June 30, 1879, of $24,400,000.

The total receipts during the next fiscal year, ending June 30, 1880, estimated according to existing laws, will be $264,500,000; and the estimated ordinary expenditures for the same period will be $236,320,412.68; leaving a surplus of $28,179,587.32 for that year.

In the foregoing statements of expenditures, actual and estimated, no amount is allowed for the sinking-fund provided for by the act approved February 25, 1862, which requires that one per cent. of the entire debt of the United States shall be purchased or paid within each fiscal year, to be set apart as a sinking-fund. There has been, however, a substantial compliance with the conditions of the law. By its terms the public debt should have been reduced, between 1862 and the close of the last fiscal year, $518,361,806.28; the actual reduction of the ascertained debt, in that period, has been $720,644,739.61; being in excess of the reduction required by the sinking-fund act—$202,282,933.33.

The amount of the public debt, less cash in the Treasury, November 1, 1878, was $2,024,200,083.18—a reduction, since the same date last year, of $23,150,617.39.

The progress made during the last year in refunding the public debt at lower rates of interest is very gratifying. The amount of four per cent. bonds sold during the present year prior to November 23, 1878, is $100,270,900, and six per cent. bonds, commonly known as five-twenties, to an equal amount, have been or will be redeemed as calls mature.

It has been the policy of the Department to place the four per cent. bonds within easy reach of every citizen who desires to invest his savings, whether small or great, in these securities. The Secretary of the Treasury recommends that the law be so modified that small sums may be invested, and that through the post offices or other agents of the Government, the freest opportunity may be given in all parts of the country for such investments.

The best mode suggested is, that the Department be authorized to issue certificates of deposit, of the denomination of ten dollars, bearing interest at the rate of 3.65 per cent. per annum, and convertible at any time within one year after their issue into the four per cent. bonds authorized by the refunding act, and to be issued only in exchange for United States notes sent to the Treasury by mail or otherwise. Such a provision of law, supported by suitable regulations, would enable any person readily, without cost or risk, to convert his money into an interest-bearing security of the United States, and the money so received could be applied to the redemption of six per cent. bonds.

The coinage of gold during the last fiscal year was $52,798,980. The coinage of silver dollars, under the act passed February 28, 1878, amounted on the 23d of November, 1878, to $19,814,550; of which amount $4,984,947 are in circulation, and the balance, $14,829,603, is still in the possession of the Government.

With views unchanged with regard to the act under which the coinage of silver proceeds, it has been the purpose of the Secretary faithfully to execute the law, and to afford a fair trial to the measure.

In the present financial condition of the country, I am persuaded that the welfare of legitimate business and industry of every description will be best promoted by abstaining from all attempts to make radical changes in the existing financial legislation. Let it be understood that during the coming year the business of the country will be undisturbed by governmental interference with laws affecting it, and we may confidently expect that the resumption of specie payments, which will take place at the appointed time, will be successfully and easily maintained, and that it will be followed by a healthful and enduring revival of business prosperity.

Let the healing influence of time, the inherent energies of our people, and the boundless resources of our country, have a fair opportunity, and relief from present difficulties will surely follow.

The report of the Secretary of War shows that the Army has been well and economically supplied, that our small force has been actively employed, and has faithfully performed all the service required of it. The *morale* of the Army has improved, and the number of desertions has materially decreased during the year.

The Secretary recommends—

1. That a pension be granted to the widow of the late Lieutenant Henry H. Benner, 18th Infantry, who lost his life by yellow-fever while in command of the steamer "J. M. Chambers," sent with supplies for the relief of sufferers in the South from that disease.

2. The establishment of the annuity scheme for the benefit of the heirs of deceased officers, as suggested by the Paymaster-General.

3. The adoption by Congress of a plan for the publication of the records of the War of the Rebellion, now being prepared for that purpose.

4. The increase of the extra *per diem* of soldier-teachers employed in post-schools, and liberal appropriations for the erection of buildings for schools and libraries at the different posts.

5. The repeal or amendment of the act of June 18, 1878, forbidding the "use of the Army as a *posse comitatus*, or otherwise, for the purpose of executing the laws, except in such cases and under such circumstances as may be expressly authorized by the Constitution or by act of Congress."

6. The passage of a joint resolution of Congress legalizing the issues of rations, tents, and medicines which were made for the relief of sufferers from yellow-fever.

7. That provision be made for the erection of a fire-proof building for the preservation of certain valuable records, now constantly exposed to destruction by fire.

These recommendations are all commended to your favorable consideration.

The report of the Secretary of the Navy shows that the Navy has improved during the last fiscal year. Work has been done on seventy-five vessels, ten of which have been thoroughly repaired and made ready for sea. Two others are in rapid progress towards completion. The total expenditures of the year, including the amount appropriated for the deficiencies of the previous year, were $17,468,392.65. The actual expenses chargeable to the year, exclusive of these deficiencies, were $13,306,914.09, or $767,199.18 less than those of the previous year, and $4,928,677.74 less than the expenses, including the deficiencies. The estimates for the fiscal year ending June 30, 1880, are $14,562,381.45—exceeding the appropriations of the present year only $33,949.75; which excess is occasioned by the demands of the Naval Academy and the Marine Corps, as explained in the Secretary's report. The appropriations for the present fiscal year are $14,528,431.70, which, in the opinion of the Secretary, will be ample for all the current expenses of the Department during the year. The amount drawn from the Treasury from July 1 to November 1, 1878, is $4,740,544.14, of which $70,980.75 has been refunded, leaving as the expenditure for that period $4,669,563.39, or $520,899.24 less than the corresponding period of the last fiscal year.

The report of the Postmaster-General embraces a detailed statement of the operations of the Post-Office Department. The expenditures of that Department for the fiscal year ended June 30, 1878, were $34,165,084.49. The receipts, including sales of stamps, money-order business, and official stamps, were $29,277,516.95. The sum of

$290,436.90, included in the foregoing statement of expenditures, is chargeable to preceding years, so that the actual expenditures for the fiscal year ended June 30, 1878, are $33,874,647.50. The amount drawn from the Treasury on appropriations, in addition to the revenues of the Department, was $5,307,652.82. The expenditures for the fiscal year ending June 30, 1880, are estimated at $36,571,900, and the receipts from all sources at $30,664,023.90, leaving a deficiency to be appropriated out of the Treasury of $5,907,876.10. The report calls attention to the fact that the compensation of postmasters and of railroads for carrying the mail is regulated by law, and that the failure of Congress to appropriate the amounts required for these purposes does not relieve the Government of responsibility, but necessarily increases the deficiency bills which Congress will be called upon to pass.

In providing for the postal service, the following questions are presented: Should Congress annually appropriate a sum for its expenses largely in excess of its revenues, or should such rates of postage be established as will make the Department self-sustaining? Should the postal service be reduced by excluding from the mails matter which does not pay its way? Should the number of post-routes be diminished? Should other methods be adopted which will increase the revenues or diminish the expenses of the postal service?

The International Postal Congress, which met at Paris May 1, 1878, and continued in session until June 4 of the same year, was composed of delegates from nearly all the civilized countries of the world. It adopted a new convention to take the place of the treaty concluded at Berne October 9, 1874; which goes into effect on the 1st of April, 1879, between the countries whose delegates have signed it. It was ratified and approved, by and with the consent of the President, August 13, 1878. A synopsis of this Universal Postal Convention will be found in the report of the Postmaster-General, and the full text in the appendix thereto. In its origin the Postal Union comprised twenty-three countries, having a population of three hundred and fifty millions of people. On the 1st of April next it will comprise forty-three countries and colonies, with a population of more than six hundred and fifty millions of people, and will soon, by the accession of the few remaining countries and colonies which maintain organized postal services, constitute, in fact as well as in name, as its new title indicates, a Universal Union, regulating, upon a uniform basis of cheap postage-rates, the postal intercourse between all civilized Nations.

Some embarrassment has arisen out of the conflict between the customs laws of this country and the provisions of the Postal Convention in regard to the transmission of foreign books and newspapers to this country by mail. It is hoped that Congress will be able to devise some means of reconciling the difficulties which have thus been created, so as to do justice to all parties involved.

The business of the Supreme Court, and of the courts in many of the circuits, has increased to such an extent during the past years that additional legislation is imperative to relieve and prevent the delay of justice, and possible oppression, to suitors, which is thus occasioned. The encumbered condition of these dockets is presented anew in the report of the Attorney-General, and the remedy suggested is earnestly urged for Congressional action. The creation of additional circuit judges, as proposed, would afford a complete remedy, and would involve an expense—at the present rate of salaries—of not more than $60,000 a year.

The annual reports of the Secretary of the Interior and of the Commissioner of Indian Affairs present an elaborate account of the present condition of the Indian tribes, and of that branch of the public service which ministers to their interests. While the conduct of the Indians, generally, has been orderly, and their relations with their neighbors friendly and peaceful, two local disturbances have occurred, which were deplorable in their character, but remained, happily, confined to a comparatively small number of Indians. The discontent among the Bannocks, which led first to some acts of violence on the part of some members of the tribe, and finally to the outbreak, appears to have been caused by an insufficiency of food on the reservation, and this insufficiency to have been owing to the inadequacy of the appropriations made by Congress to the wants of the Indians at a time when the Indians were prevented from supplying the deficiency by hunting. After an arduous pursuit by the troops of the United States, and several engagements, the hostile Indians were reduced to subjection, and the larger part of them surrendered themselves as prisoners. In this connection, I desire to call attention to the recommendation made by the Secretary of the Interior that a sufficient fund be placed at the disposal of the Executive, to be used, with proper accountability, at discretion, in sudden emergencies of the Indian service.

The other case of disturbance was that of a band of Northern Cheyennes, who suddenly left their reservation in the Indian Territory and marched rapidly through the States of Kansas and Nebraska, in the direction of their old hunting-grounds, committing murders and other crimes on their way. From documents accompanying the report of the Secretary of the Interior, it appears that this disorderly band was as fully supplied with the necessaries of life as the four thousand seven hundred other Indians who remained quietly on the reservation, and that the disturbance was caused by men of a restless and mischievous disposition among the Indians themselves. Almost the whole of this band have surrendered to the military authorities, and it is a gratifying fact that, when some of them had taken refuge in the camp of the Red Cloud Sioux, with whom they had been in friendly relations, the Sioux held them as prisoners, and readily gave them up to the officers of the United States, thus giving new proof of the loyal spirit which, alarming rumors to the contrary notwithstanding, they have uniformly shown ever since the wishes they expressed at the council of September, 1877, had been complied with.

Both the Secretary of the Interior and the Secretary of War unite in the recommendation that provision be made by Congress for the organization of a corps of mounted "Indian auxiliaries," to be under the control of the Army, and to be used for the purpose of keeping the Indians on their reservations and preventing or repressing disturbance on their part. I earnestly concur in this recommendation. It is believed that the organization of such a body of Indian cavalry, receiving a moderate pay from the Government, would considerably weaken the restless element among the Indians by withdrawing from it a number of young men, and giving them congenial employment under the Government, it being a matter of experience that Indians in our service, almost without exception, are faithful in the performance of the duties assigned to them. Such an organization would materially aid the Army in the accomplishment of a task for which its numerical strength is sometimes found insufficient.

But, while the employment of force for the prevention or repression of Indian troubles is of occasional necessity, and wise preparation should be made to that end, greater reliance must be placed on humane and civilizing agencies for the ultimate solution of what is called the Indian problem. It may be very difficult, and require much patient effort, to curb the unruly spirit of the savage Indian to the restraints of civilized life, but experience shows that it is not impossible. Many of the tribes which are now quiet and orderly and self-supporting were once as savage as any that at present roam over the plains or in the mountains of the far West, and were then considered inaccessible to civilizing influences. It may be impossible to raise them fully up to the level of the white population of the United States; but we should not forget that they are the aborigines of the country, and called the soil their own on which our people have grown rich, powerful, and happy.

We owe it to them as a moral duty to help them in attaining at least that degree of civilization which they may be able to reach. It is not only our duty—it is also our interest to do so. Indians who have become agriculturists or herdsmen, and feel an interest in property, will thenceforth cease to be a warlike and disturbing element. It is also a well-authenticated fact that Indians are apt to be peaceable and quiet when their children are at school, and I am gratified to know, from the expressions of Indians themselves and from many concurring reports, that there is a steadily increasing desire, even among Indians belonging to comparatively wild tribes, to have their children educated. I invite attention to the reports of the Secretary of the Interior and the Commissioner of Indian Affairs, touching the experiment recently inaugurated, in taking fifty Indian children, boys and girls, from different tribes, to the Hampton Normal Agricultural Institute, in Virginia, where they are to receive an elementary English education and training in agriculture and other useful work, to be returned to their tribes, after the completed course, as interpreters, instructors, and examples. It is reported that the officer charged with the selection of those children might have had thousands of young Indians sent with him had it been possible to make provision for them. I agree with the Secretary of the Interior in saying that "the result of this interesting experiment, if favorable, may be destined to become an important factor in the advancement of civilization among the Indians."

The question, whether a change in the control of the Indian service should be made, was, at the last session of Congress, referred to a committee for inquiry and report. Without desiring to anticipate that report, I venture to express the hope that in the decision of so important a question, the views expressed above may not be lost sight of, and that the decision, whatever it may be, will arrest further agitation of this subject, such agitation being apt to produce a disturbing effect upon the service as well as on the Indians themselves.

In the enrolment of the bill making appropriations for sundry civil expenses, at the last session of Congress, that portion which provided for the continuation of the Hot Springs Commission was omitted. As the commission had completed the work of taking testimony on the many conflicting claims, the suspension of their labors, before determining the rights of claimants, threatened, for a time, to embarrass the interests, not only of the Government, but also of a large number of the citizens of Hot Springs, who were waiting for final action on their claims before beginning contemplated improvements. In order to prevent serious difficulties, which were apprehended, and at the solicitation of many leading citizens of Hot Springs, and others interested in the welfare of the town, the Secretary of the Interior was authorized to request the late commissioners to take charge of the records of their proceedings, and to perform such work as could properly be done by them under such circumstances, to facilitate the future adjudication of the claims at an early day, and to preserve the status of the claimants until their rights shall be finally determined. The late commissioners complied with that request, and report that the testimony, in all the cases, has been written out, examined, briefed, and so arranged as to facilitate an early settlement when authorized by law. It is recommended that the requisite authority be given at as early a day in the session as possible, and that a fair compensation be allowed the late commissioners for the expense incurred and the labor performed by them since the 25th of June last.

I invite the attention of Congress to the recommendations made by the Secretary of the Interior with regard to the preservation of the timber on the public lands of the United States. The protection of the public property is one of the first duties of the Government. The Department of the Interior should, therefore, be enabled, by sufficient appropriations, to enforce the laws in that respect. But this matter appears still more important as a question of public economy. The rapid destruction of our forests is an evil fraught with the gravest consequences, especially in the mountainous districts, where the rocky slopes, once denuded of their trees, will remain so forever. There the injury, once done, cannot be repaired. I fully concur with the Secretary of the Interior in the opinion that, for this reason, legislation touching the public timber in the mountainous States and Territories of the West, should be especially well considered, and that existing laws, in which the destruction of the forests is not sufficiently guarded against, should be speedily modified. A general law concerning this important subject appears to me to be a matter of urgent public necessity.

From the organization of the Government, the importance of encouraging, by all possible means, the increase of our agricultural productions has been acknowledged and urged upon the attention of Congress and the people as the surest and readiest means of increasing our substantial and enduring prosperity.

The words of Washington are as applicable to-day as when, in his eighth annual message, he said: "It is not to be doubted that, with reference either to individual or national welfare, agriculture is of primary importance. In proportion as Nations advance in population and other circumstances of maturity, this truth becomes more apparent, and renders the cultivation of the soil more and more an object of public patronage. Institutions for promoting it grow up, supported by the public purse—and to what object can it be dedicated with greater propriety? Among the means which have been employed to this end, none have been attended with greater success than the establishment of boards composed of proper characters, charged with collecting and diffusing information, and enabled, by premiums and small pecuniary aids, to encourage and assist the spirit of discovery and improvement, this species of establishment contributing doubly to the increase of improvement by stimulating to enterprise and experiment, and by drawing to a common centre the results everywhere of individual skill and observation, and spreading them thence over the whole Nation. Experience accordingly hath shown that they are very cheap instruments of immense national benefit."

The great preponderance of the agricultural over any other interest in the United States, entitles it to all the consideration claimed for it by Washington. About one-half of the population of the United States is engaged in agriculture. The value of the agricultural products of the United States for the year 1878 is estimated at three thousand millions of dollars. The exports of agricultural products for the year 1877, as appears from the report of the Bureau of Statistics, were five hundred and twenty-four millions of dollars. The great extent of our country, with its diversity of soil and climate, enables us to produce within our own borders, and by our own labor, not only the necessaries but most of the luxuries that are consumed in civilized countries. Yet, notwithstanding our advantages of soil, climate, and intercommunication, it appears from the statistical statements in the report of the Commissioner of Agriculture, that we import annually from foreign lands many millions of dollars' worth of agricultural products which could be raised in our own country.

Numerous questions arise in the practice of advanced agriculture which can only be answered by experiments, often costly and sometimes fruitless, which are beyond the means of private individuals, and are a just and proper charge on the whole Nation for the benefit of the Nation. It is good policy, especially in times of depression and uncertainty in other business pursuits, with a vast area of uncultivated, and hence unproductive territory, wisely opened to homestead settlement, to encourage, by every proper and legitimate means, the occupation and tillage of the soil. The efforts of the Department of Agriculture to stimulate old and introduce new agricultural industries, to improve the quality and increase the quantity of our products, to determine the value of old or establish the importance of new methods of culture, are worthy of your careful and favorable consideration, and assistance by such appropriations of money and enlargement of facilities as may seem to be demanded by the present favorable conditions for the growth and rapid development of this important interest.

The abuse of animals in transit is widely attracting public attention. A national convention of societies specially interested in the subject has recently met at Baltimore, and the facts developed, both in regard to cruelties to animals and the effect of such cruelties upon the public health, would seem to demand the careful consideration of Congress, and the enactment of more efficient laws for the prevention of these abuses.

The report of the Commissioner of the Bureau of Education shows very gratifying progress throughout the country, in all the interests committed to the care of this important office. The report is especially encouraging with respect to the extension of the advantages of the common-school system, in sections of the country where the general enjoyment of the privilege of free schools is not yet attained.

To education more than to any other agency we are to look, as the resource for the advancement of the people in the requisite knowledge and appreciation of their rights and responsibilities as citizens, and I desire to repeat the suggestion contained in my former message in behalf of the enactment of appropriate measures by Congress for the purpose of supplementing, with national aid, the local systems of education in the several States.

Adequate accommodations for the great library, which is overgrowing the capacity of the rooms now occupied at the Capitol, should be provided without further delay. This invaluable collection of books, manuscripts, and illustrative art, has grown to such proportions, in connection with the copyright system of the country, as to demand the prompt and careful attention of Congress, to save it from injury in its present crowded and insufficient quarters. As this library is national in its character, and must, from the nature of the case, increase even more rapidly in the future than in the past, it cannot be doubted that the people will sanction any wise expenditure to preserve it and to enlarge its usefulness.

The appeal of the Regents of the Smithsonian Institution for the means to organize, exhibit, and make available for the public benefit the articles now stored away belonging to the National Museum, I heartily recommend to your favorable consideration.

The attention of Congress is again invited to the condition of the river-front of the city of Washington. It is a matter of vital importance to the health of the residents of the National Capital, both temporary and permanent, that the low lands in front of the city, now subject to tidal overflow, should be reclaimed. In their present condition these flats obstruct the drainage of the city, and are a dangerous source of malarial poison. The reclamation will improve the navigation of the river by restricting and consequently deepening its channel, and is also of importance, when considered in connection with the extension of the public ground and the enlargement of the park west and south of the Washington Monument. The report of the board of survey, heretofore ordered by act of Congress, on the improvement of the harbor of Washington and Georgetown, is respectfully commended to consideration.

The report of the Commissioners of the District of Columbia presents a detailed statement of the affairs of the District.

The relative expenditures by the United States and the District for local purposes is contrasted, showing that the expenditures by the people of the District greatly exceed those of the General Government. The exhibit is made in connection with estimates for the requisite repair of the defective pavements and sewers of the city, which is a work of immediate necessity; and, in the same connection, a plan is presented for the permanent funding of the outstanding securities of the District.

The benevolent, reformatory, and penal institutions of the District are all entitled to the favorable attention of Congress. The Reform School needs additional buildings and teachers. Appropriations which will place all of these institutions in a condition to become models of usefulness and beneficence, will be regarded by the country as liberality wisely bestowed.

The Commissioners, with evident justice, request attention to the discrimination made by Congress against the District in the donation of land for the support of the public schools, and ask that the same liberality that has been shown to the inhabitants of the various States and Territories of the United States may be extended to the District of Columbia.

The Commissioners also invite attention to the damage inflicted upon public and private interests by the present location of the depots and switching-tracks of the several railroads entering the city, and ask for legislation looking to their removal. The recommendations and suggestions contained in the report will, I trust, receive the careful consideration of Congress.

Sufficient time has, perhaps, not elapsed since the reorganization of government of the District, under the recent legislation of Congress, for the expression of a confident opinion as to its successful operation; but the practical results already attained are so satisfactory that the friends of the new government may well urge upon Congress the wisdom of its continuance, without essential modification, until, by actual experience, its advantages and defects may be more fully ascertained.

R. B. HAYES.

EXECUTIVE MANSION, *December* 2, 1878.

MESSAGE

TO THE

SENATE OF THE UNITED STATES, TRANSMITTING INFORMATION CONCERNING POSTAL AND COMMERCIAL INTERCOURSE BETWEEN THE UNITED STATES AND SOUTH AMERICAN COUNTRIES.

DECEMBER 17, 1878.

MESSAGE.

To the Senate of the United States:

In answer to the resolution of the Senate of the 5th instant, requesting the transmission to the Senate of "any information which may have been received by the Departments concerning postal and commercial intercourse between the United States and South American countries, together with any recommendations desirable to be submitted of measures to be adopted for facilitating and improving such intercourse," I transmit herewith reports from the Secretary of State and the Postmaster-General, with accompanying papers.

The external commerce of the United States has for many years been the subject of solicitude, because of the outward drain of the precious metals it has caused. For fully twenty years previous to 1877, the shipment of gold was constant and heavy, so heavy during the entire period of the suspension of specie payments as to preclude the hope of resumption safely during its continuance. In 1876, however, vigorous efforts were made by enterprising citizens of the country, and have since been continued, to extend our general commerce with foreign lands, especially in manufactured articles, and these efforts have been attended with very marked success.

The importation of manufactured goods was at the same time reduced in an equal degree, and the result has been an extraordinary reversal of the conditions so long prevailing, and a complete cessation of the outward drain of gold. The official statement of the values represented in foreign commerce will show the unprecedented magnitude to which the movement has attained, and the protection thus secured to the public interests at the time when commercial security has become indispensable.

The agencies through which this change has been effected must be maintained and strengthened, if the future is to be made secure. A return to excessive imports, or to a material decline in export trade, would render possible a return to the former condition of adverse balances, with the inevitable outward drain of gold as a necessary consequence. Every element of aid to the introduction of the products of our soil and manufactures into new markets should be made available.

At present, such is the favor in which many of the products of the United States are held, that they obtain a remunerative distribution, notwithstanding positive differences of cost resulting from our defective shipping, and the imperfection of our arrangements in every respect, in comparison with those of our competitors, for conducting trade with foreign markets.

If we have equal commercial facilities we need not fear competition anywhere.

The laws have now directed a resumption of financial equality with other Nations, and have ordered a return to the basis of coin values. It is of the greatest importance that the commercial condition now fortunately attained shall be made permanent, and that our rapidly increasing export trade shall not be allowed to suffer for want of the ordinary means of communication with other countries.

The accompanying reports contain a valuable and instructive summary of information with respect to our commercial interests in South America, where an inviting field for the enterprise of our people is presented. They are transmitted with the assurance that any measures that may be enacted in furtherance of these important interests will meet with my cordial approval.

R. B. HAYES.

EXECUTIVE MANSION, *December* 17, 1878.

TO THE PRESIDENT:

The Secretary of State, to whom was referred the resolution of the Senate of the 5th instant, requesting the President to transmit to the Senate "any information which may have been received by the Departments concerning postal and commercial intercourse between the United States and South American countries, together with any recommendations desirable to be adopted for facilitating and improving such intercourse," has the honor to lay before the President copies of despatches from the diplomatic agents of the United States accredited to the Governments of South America, touching the subject-matter of the resolution; and also, as coming within the purview thereof, copies of a report and its annexes, presented to this Department by Mr. J. W. Fralick, upon his return from an extended journey through the leading States of South America. * * *

With reference to the request of the Senate for "any recommendations desirable to be submitted of measures to be adopted for facilitating and improving" postal and commercial intercourse, the Secretary of State, without entering into an extended discussion of the very important and interesting topics suggested by the papers submitted, respectfully calls attention to certain manifest conclusions which all these reports tend to support.

I. It seems to be very evident that the provision of regular steam postal communication, by aid from Government, has been the forerunner of the commercial predominance of Great Britain in the great marts of Central and South America, both on the Pacific and Atlantic coasts of the continent. It is no less apparent that the efforts of other European Nations, Germany, France, and Italy, to share in this profitable trade have been successful in proportion with their adoption of regular steam postal communication with the several markets whose trade they sought.

II. These papers show, also, that the enterprise and sagacity thus shown by European Nations have actually *reversed* the advantage which our geographical position gives us in relation to this extensive commerce of the American hemisphere. The commercial correspondence of our merchants with the trading points on the east and west coasts crosses the Atlantic twice to make a postal connection in a circuit of trade which has its beginning and its end on our own continent. The statistics of our limited trade under this extraordinary disadvantage, show that the growing preference for our products in these South American markets insist upon being gratified, even at the cost of a circuit of importation which carries our merchandise to Europe and incorporates it as a contribution to the volume and the profits of European South American trade. No stronger demonstration of the tendency of commerce to follow in the train of postal communication can be conceived than this vast and expensive circuit of importation resorted to in default of direct opportunities between the countries of demand and supply.

III. It would seem from these reports that the merchants and the communities, no less than the Governments, of these countries strongly desire an enlargement of direct trade with the United States. With all the advantages of foreign commerce supplied by the existing European arrangements for its prosecution, these markets perceive that this unnatural circuit, when the resources of the United States could supply a direct trade in its place, must be at the expense of the party subjected to the system and the profit of the party which administers and controls it. Everywhere there is shown a great desire to expand their trade with the United States, and even the least prosperous exchequers of these Governments are ready to be opened to share in the expenses of steam postal communications, of whose value in promoting foreign commerce their own experience furnishes irrefragable proof.

IV. While many less immediate and less simple measures, about which judgments may not readily concur, may properly be canvassed by our people, now eager for a restoration and extension of foreign commerce, upon this one simple and first step of direct, regular, and frequent steam postal communication between the United States and the principal commercial ports of Central and South America there would seem to be no room for doubt.

If this be so, it is obviously the dictate of interest and duty, on the part of the Government, to promote by every just and appropriate means the attainment of this first and principal agency for the desired expansion of our foreign commerce. It is difficult to understand how this commencement and development of an ocean postal system, to be a forerunner of the expected trade, can be wholly trusted to the mere interests of mercantile combinations.

The Governments of the foreign States with which this commerce is to be opened are ready to take their part in the public expense of this postal communication with us, and the participation or non-participation by the United States in this public expense seems to be the turning-point in the acceptance or rejection of the reciprocal trade now proffered us.

WM. M. EVARTS.

DEPARTMENT OF STATE,
Washington, December 17, 1878.

MESSAGE

TO THE

SENATE OF THE UNITED STATES, TRANSMITTING A LETTER FROM THE SECRETARY OF THE TREASURY, WITH ACCOMPANYING DOCUMENTS, RELATING TO THE NEW YORK CUSTOM-HOUSE.

JANUARY 31, 1879.

MESSAGE.

To the Senate:

I transmit herewith a letter of the Secretary of the Treasury, in relation to the suspension of the late collector and naval officer of the port of New York, with accompanying documents.

In addition thereto I respectfully submit the following observations: The custom-house in New York collects more than two-thirds of all the customs revenues of the Government. Its administration is a matter not of local interest merely, but is of great importance to the people of the whole country. For a long period of time it has been used to manage and control political affairs. The officers suspended by me are, and for several years have been, engaged in the active personal management of the party politics of the city and State of New York. The duties of the offices held by them have been regarded as of subordinate importance to their partisan work. Their offices have been conducted as part of the political machinery under their control. They have made the custom-house a centre of partisan political management.

The custom-house should be a business office. It should be conducted on business principles. General James, the postmaster of New York city, writing on the subject, says: "The post office is a business institution, and should be run as such. It is my deliberate judgment that I and my subordinates can do more for the party of our choice by giving the people of this city a good and efficient postal service than by controlling primaries or dictating nominations." The New York custom-house should be placed on the same footing with the New York post office. But under the suspended officers the custom-house would be one of the principal political agencies in the State of New York. To change this, they profess to believe, would be, in the language of Mr. Cornell, in his response, "to surrender their personal and political rights."

Convinced that the people of New York, and of the country generally, wish the New York custom-house to be administered solely with a view to the public interest, it is my purpose to do all in my power to introduce into this great office the reforms which the country desires.

With my information of the facts in the case, and with a deep sense of the responsible obligation imposed upon me by the Constitution, to "take care that the laws be faithfully executed," I regard it as my plain duty to suspend the officers in question, and to make the nominations now before the Senate, in order that this important office may be honestly and efficiently administered.

R. B. HAYES.

EXECUTIVE MANSION, *January* 31, 1879.

LETTER

TO

GENERAL E. A. MERRITT, COLLECTOR OF CUSTOMS,
NEW YORK CITY.

FEBRUARY 4, 1879.

LETTER.

EXECUTIVE MANSION,
Washington, February 4, 1879.

DEAR GENERAL: I congratulate you on your confirmation. It is a great gratification to your friends, very honorable to you, and will prove, I believe, of signal service to the country.

My desire is that your office shall be conducted on strictly business principles, and according to the rules which were adopted, on the recommendation of the Civil-Service Commission, by the administration of General Grant. In making appointments and removals of subordinates, you should be perfectly independent of mere influence. Neither my recommendation nor that of the Secretary of the Treasury, nor the recommendation of any member of Congress, or other influential person, should be specially regarded. Let appointments and removals be made on business principles, and by fixed rules. There must be, I assume, a few places the duties of which are confidential, and which should be filled by those whom you personally know to be trustworthy; but restrict the area of patronage to the narrowest possible limits. Let no man be put out merely because he is a friend of the late collector, and no man be put in merely because he is <u>our</u> friend. I am glad you approve of the message sent to the Senate. I wish you to see that all that is expressed in it, and all that is implied in it, is faithfully carried out.

With the assurance of my entire confidence,
I remain, sincerely,
R. B. HAYES.

General E. A. MERRITT,
Collector of Customs, New York.

MESSAGE

RETURNING TO

THE HOUSE OF REPRESENTATIVES THE BILL ENTITLED "AN ACT TO RESTRICT THE IMMIGRATION OF CHINESE TO THE UNITED STATES."

MARCH 1, 1879.

MESSAGE.

TO THE HOUSE OF REPRESENTATIVES:

After a very careful consideration of House bill No. 2423, entitled "An act to restrict the immigration of Chinese to the United States," I herewith return it to the House of Representatives, in which it originated, with my objections to its passage.

The bill, as it was sent to the Senate from the House of Representatives, was confined in its provisions to the object named in its title, which is that of "An act to restrict the immigration of Chinese to the United States." The only means adopted to secure the proposed object was a limitation on the number of Chinese passengers which might be brought to this country by any one vessel to fifteen, and as this number was not fixed in any proportion to the size or tonnage of the vessel, or by any consideration of the safety or the accommodation of these passengers, the simple purpose and effect of the enactment were to repress this immigration to an extent falling but little short of its absolute exclusion.

The bill, as amended in the Senate and now presented to me, includes an independent and additional provision which aims at, and in terms requires, the abrogation by this Government of articles 5 and 6 of the treaty with China, commonly called the Burlingame treaty, through the action of the Executive enjoined by this provision of the act.

The Burlingame treaty, of which the ratifications were exchanged at Peking, November 23, 1869, recites as the occasion and motive of its negotiation by the two Governments that "since the conclusion of the treaty between the United States of America and the Ta Tsing Empire (China) of the 18th of June, 1858, circumstances have arisen showing the necessity of additional articles thereto," and proceeds to an agreement as to said additional articles. These negotiations, therefore, ending by the signature of the additional articles July 28, 1868, had for their object the completion of our treaty rights and obligations toward the Government of China by the incorporation of these new articles as, thenceforth, parts of the principal treaty to which they are made supplemental. Upon the settled rules of interpretation applicable to such supplemental negotiations, the text of the principal treaty and of these "additional articles thereto" constitute one treaty, from the conclusion of the new negotiations, in all parts of equal and concurrent force and obligation between the two Governments, and to all intents and purposes as if embraced in one instrument.

The principal treaty, of which the ratifications were exchanged August 16, 1859, recites that "the United States of America and the Ta Tsing Empire desiring to maintain firm, lasting, and sincere friendship, have resolved to renew, in a manner clear and positive, by means of a treaty or general convention of peace, amity, and commerce, the rules of which shall in future be mutually observed in the intercourse of their respective countries," and proceeds, in its thirty articles, to lay out a careful and comprehensive system for the commercial relations of our people with China. The main substance of all the provisions of this treaty is to define and secure the rights of our people in respect of access to, residence and protection in, and trade with China. The actual provisions in our favor, in these respects, were framed to be, and have been found to be, adequate and appropriate to the interests of our commerce, and by the concluding article we receive the important guarantee, "that should at any time the Ta Tsing Empire grant to any Nation, or the merchants or citizens of any Nation, any right, privilege, or favor connected either with navigation, commerce, political or other intercourse which is not conferred by this treaty, such right, privilege, and favor shall at once freely inure to the benefit of the United States, its public officers, merchants, and citizens." Against this body of stipulations in our favor, and this permanent engagement of equality in respect of all future concessions to foreign Nations, the general promise of permanent peace and good offices on our part seems to be the only equivalent. For this the first article undertakes as follows: "There shall be, as there have always been, peace and friendship between the United States of America and the Ta Tsing Empire, and between their people respectively. They shall not insult or oppress each other for any trifling cause, so as to produce an estrangement between them; and if any other Nation should act unjustly or oppressively, the United States will exert their good offices, on being informed of the case, to bring about an amicable arrangement of the question, thus showing their friendly feelings."

At the date of the negotiation of this treaty our Pacific possessions had attracted a considerable Chinese immigration, and the advantages and the inconveniences felt or feared therefrom had become more or less manifest, but they dictated no stipulations on the subject to be incorporated in the treaty. The year 1868 was marked by the striking event of a spontaneous embassy from the Chinese Empire, headed by an American citizen, Anson Burlingame, who had relinquished his diplomatic representation of his own country in China to assume that of the Chinese Empire to the United States and the European Nations. By this time the facts of the Chinese immigration and its nature and influences, present and prospective, had become more noticeable, and were more observed by the population immediately affected, and by this Government. The principal feature of the Burlingame treaty was its attention to and its treatment of the Chinese immigration and the Chinese as forming, or as they should form, a part of our population. Up to this time our uncovenanted hospitality to immigration, our fearless liberality of citizenship, our equal and comprehensive justice to all inhabitants, whether they abjured their foreign nationality or not, our civil freedom and our religious toleration, had made all comers welcome, and under these protections the Chinese, in considerable numbers, had made their lodgment upon our soil.

The Burlingame treaty undertakes to deal with this situation, and its fifth and sixth articles embrace its most important provisions in this regard, and the main stipulations in which the Chinese Government has secured an obligatory protection of its subjects within our territory. They read as follows:

"ARTICLE V. The United States of America and the Emperor of China cordially recognize the inherent and inalienable right of man to change his home and allegiance, and also the mutual advantage of the free migration and emigration of their citizens and subjects respectively from the one country to the other for purposes of curiosity, of trade, or as permanent residents. The high contracting parties, therefore, join in reprobating any other than an entirely voluntary emigration for these purposes. They consequently agree to pass laws making it a penal offence for a citizen of the United States or Chinese subjects to take Chinese subjects either to the United States or to any other foreign country, or for a Chinese subject or citizen of the United States to take citizens of the United States to China or to any other foreign country without their free and voluntary consent, respectively.

"ARTICLE VI. Citizens of the United States visiting or residing in China shall enjoy the same privileges, immunities, or exemptions, in respect to travel or residence, as may there be enjoyed by the citizens or subjects of the most favored Nation; and, reciprocally, Chinese subjects visiting or residing in the United States shall enjoy the same privileges, immunities, and exemptions, in respect to travel or residence, as may there be enjoyed by the citizens or subjects of the most favored Nation. But nothing herein contained shall be held to confer naturalization upon citizens of the United States in China, nor upon the subjects of China in the United States."

An examination of these two articles, in the light of the experience then influential in suggesting their "necessity," will show that the fifth article was framed in hostility to what seemed the principal mischief to be guarded against, to wit, the introduction of Chinese laborers by methods which should have the character of a forced and servile importation, and not of a voluntary emigration of freemen seeking our shores upon motives and in a manner consonant with the system of our institutions and approved by the experience of the Nation. Unquestionably the adhesion of the Government of China to these liberal principles of freedom in emigration, with which we were so familiar, and with which we were so well satisfied, was a great advance toward opening that Empire to our civilization and religion, and gave promise in the future of greater and greater practical results in the diffusion throughout that great population of our arts and industries, our manufactures, our material improvements, and the sentiments of government and religion, which seem to us so important to the welfare of mankind. The first clause of this article secures this acceptance by China of the American doctrines of free migration to and fro among the peoples and races of the earth.

The second clause, however, in its reprobation of "any other than entirely voluntary emigration" by both the high contracting parties, and in the reciprocal obligations, whereby we secured the solemn and unqualified engagement on the part of the Government of China "to pass laws making it a penal offence for a citizen of the United States or Chinese subjects to take Chinese subjects either to the United States or to any other foreign country without their free and voluntary consent," constitutes the great force and value of this article. Its importance, both in principle and in its practical service toward our protection against servile importation in the guise of immigration, cannot be over-estimated. It commits the Chinese Government to active and efficient measures to suppress this iniquitous system where those measures are most necessary and can be most effectual. It gives to this Government the footing of a treaty right to such measures and the means and opportunity of insisting upon their adoption, and of complaint and resentment at their neglect. The fifth article, therefore, if it fall short of what the pressure of the later experience of our Pacific States may urge upon the attention of this Government as essential to the public welfare, seems to be in the right direction, and to contain important advantages, which, once relinquished, cannot be easily recovered.

The second topic which interested the two Governments under the actual condition of things which prompted the Burlingame treaty was adequate protection under the solemn and definite guarantees of a treaty of the Chinese already in this country and those who should seek our shores. This was the object and forms the subject of the sixth article, by whose reciprocal engagement the citizens and subjects of the two Governments, respectively, visiting or residing in the country of the other, are secured the same privileges, immunities, or exemptions, there enjoyed by the citizens or subjects of the most favored Nations. The treaty of 1858, to which these articles are made supplemental, provides for a great amount of privilege and protection, both of person and property, to American citizens in China; but it is upon this sixth article that the main body of the treaty-rights and securities of the Chinese already in this country depends. Its abrogation, were the rest of the treaty left in force, would leave them to such treatment as we should voluntarily accord them by our laws and customs. Any treaty obligation would be wanting to restrain our liberty of action toward them, or to measure or sustain the right of the Chinese Government to complaint or redress in their behalf.

The lapse of ten years since the negotiation of the Burlingame treaty has exhibited to the notice of the Chinese Government, as well as to our own people, the working of this experiment of immigration in great numbers of Chinese laborers to this country, and their maintenance here of all the traits of race, religion, manners and customs, habitations, mode of life, and segregation here, and the keeping up of the ties of their original home, which stamp them as strangers and sojourners, and not as incorporated elements of our national life and growth. This experience may naturally suggest the reconsideration of the subject, as dealt with by the Burlingame treaty, and may properly become the occasion of more direct and circumspect recognition, in renewed negotiations, of the difficulties surrounding this political and social problem. It may well be that, to the apprehension of the Chinese Government, no less than our own, the simple provisions of the Burlingame treaty may need to be replaced by more careful methods, securing the Chinese and ourselves against a larger and more rapid infusion of this foreign race than our system of industry and society can take up and assimilate with ease and safety. This ancient Government, ruling a polite and sensitive people, distinguished by a high sense of national pride, may properly desire an adjustment of their relations with us, which would in all things confirm, and in no degree endanger, the permanent peace and amity and the growing commerce and prosperity, which it has been the object and the effect of our existing treaties to cherish and perpetuate.

I regard the very grave discontents of the people of the Pacific

States with the present working of the Chinese immigration, and their still graver apprehensions therefrom in the future, as deserving the most serious attention of the people of the whole country, and a solicitous interest on the part of Congress and the Executive. If this were not my own judgment, the passage of this bill by both Houses of Congress would impress upon me the seriousness of the situation, when a majority of the representatives of the people of the whole country had thought it to justify so serious a measure of relief.

The authority of Congress to terminate a treaty with a foreign power by expressing the will of the Nation no longer to adhere to it, is as free from controversy under our Constitution as is the further proposition that the power of making new treaties or modifying existing treaties is not lodged by the Constitution in Congress, but in the President, by and with the advice and consent of the Senate, as shown by the concurrence of two-thirds of that body. A denunciation of a treaty by any Government is, confessedly, justifiable only upon some reason both of the highest justice and of the highest necessity. The action of Congress in the matter of the French treaties, in 1879, if it be regarded as an abrogation by this Nation of a subsisting treaty, strongly illustrates the character and degree of justification which was then thought suitable to such a proceeding. The preamble of the act recites that "the treaties concluded between the United States and France have been repeatedly violated on the part of the French Government, and the just claims of the United States for reparation of the injuries so committed have been refused, and their attempts to negotiate an amicable adjustment of all complaints between the two Nations have been repelled with indignity;" and that "under authority of the French Government there is yet pursued against the United States a system of predatory violence, infracting the said treaties, and hostile to the rights of a free and independent Nation."

The enactment, as a logical consequence of these recited facts, declares that the United States are of right freed and exonerated from the stipulations of the treaties and of the consular convention heretofore concluded between the United States and France, and that the same shall not henceforth be regarded as legally obligatory on the Government or citizens of the United States."

The history of the Government shows no other instance of an abrogation of a treaty by Congress.

Instances have sometimes occurred where the ordinary legislation of Congress has, by its conflict with some treaty obligation of the Government toward a foreign Power, taken effect as an infraction of the treaty, and been judicially declared to be operative to that result. But neither such legislation nor such judicial sanction of the same has been regarded as an abrogation, even for the moment, of the treaty. On the contrary, the treaty in such case still subsists between the Governments, and the casual infraction is repaired by appropriate satisfaction in maintenance of the treaty.

The bill before me does not enjoin upon the President the abrogation of the entire Burlingame treaty, much less of the principal treaty of which it is made the supplement. As the power of modifying an existing treaty, whether by adding or striking out provisions, is a part of the treaty-making power under the Constitution, its exercise is not competent for Congress; nor would the assent of China to this partial abrogation of the treaty make the action of Congress, in thus procuring an amendment of a treaty, a competent exercise of authority under the Constitution. The importance, however, of this special consideration seems superseded by the principle that a denunciation of a part of a treaty, not made by the terms of the treaty itself separable from the rest, is a denunciation of the whole treaty. As the other high contracting party has entered into no treaty obligations except such as include the part denounced, the denunciation by one party of the part necessarily liberates the other party from the whole treaty.

I am convinced that, whatever urgency might in any quarter or by any interest be supposed to require an instant suppression of further emigration from China, no reasons can require the immediate withdrawal of our treaty protection of the Chinese already in this country, and no circumstances can tolerate an exposure of our citizens in China, merchants or missionaries, to the consequences of so sudden an abrogation of their treaty protections. Fortunately, however, the actual recession in the flow of the emigration from China to the Pacific coast, shown by trustworthy statistics, relieves us from any apprehension that the treatment of the subject in the proper course of diplomatic negotiations will introduce any new features of discontent or disturbance among the communities directly affected. Were such delay fraught with more inconveniences than have ever been suggested by the interests most earnest in promoting this legislation, I cannot but regard the summary disturbance of our existing treaties with China as greatly more inconvenient to much wider and more permanent interests of the country.

I have no occasion to insist upon the more general considerations of interest and duty which sacredly regard the faith of the Nation in whatever form of obligation it may have been given. These sentiments animate the deliberations of Congress and pervade the minds of our whole people. Our history gives little occasion for any reproach in this regard, and in asking the renewed attention of Congress to this bill, I am persuaded that their action will maintain the public duty and the public honor.

R. B. HAYES.

EXECUTIVE MANSION, *March* 1, 1879.

After mature consideration of House bill No. 2423, entitled "An act to restrict the immigration of Chinese to the United States," I am constrained by my convictions of duty to return it, with my objections to its passage, to the House of Representatives, in which it originated.

The seventh section of the bill is as follows:

"That this act shall take effect from and after the 1st day of July, 1879; and the President of the United States shall, immediately on the approval of this act, give notice to the Government of China of the abrogation of the articles 5 and 6 of the additional articles of the treaty of June 18, 1858, between the United States and China, proclaimed February 5, 1870, commonly called the Burlingame treaty."

The following are the articles of the treaty between the United States and China named in the foregoing section of the bill, and which, by its approval, would be immediately abrogated, viz:

"ARTICLE V. The United States of America and the Emperor of China cordially recognize the inherent and inalienable right of man to change his home and allegiance, and also the mutual advantage of the free migration and emigration of their citizens and subjects, respectively, from the one country to the other, for purposes of curiosity, of trade, or as permanent residents. The high contracting parties, therefore, join in reprobating any other than an entirely voluntary emigration for these purposes. They consequently agree to pass laws making it a penal offence for a citizen of the United States or Chinese subjects to take Chinese subjects either to the United States or to any other foreign country, or for a Chinese subject or citizen of the United States to take citizens of the United States to China or to any other foreign country without their free and voluntary consent, respectively.

"ARTICLE VI. Citizens of the United States visiting or residing in China shall enjoy the same privileges, immunities, or exemptions, in respect to travel or residence, as may there be enjoyed by the citizens or subjects of the most favored Nation; and, reciprocally, Chinese subjects visiting or residing in the United States shall enjoy the same privileges, immunities, and exemptions, in respect to travel or residence, as may there be enjoyed by the citizens or subjects of the most favored Nation. But nothing herein contained shall be held to confer naturalization upon citizens of the United States in China, nor upon the subjects of China in the United States."

The Burlingame treaty of 1868, which contains the foregoing articles, was, as its title shows, an addition to the treaty of 1858, commonly known as the Read treaty, and, together with that treaty, establishes and regulates the present relations between this country and China. These treaty relations were not formed on the solicitation of that Empire. They are of our seeking, and are the work of our own statesmen. Mr. Burlingame was sent to China as minister of the United States in 1861. In 1867 he announced his purpose to resign his place as minister of the United States, in order to become the minister of China to the United States; and in 1868 he came to Washington as the representative of China, one of a commission of which he was the head, and over which he had control. In June, 1868, he, with the then Secretary of State, Mr. Seward, negotiated the present treaty between the United States and China. It was ratified by the Senate with the almost universal approval of the people of the United States, and, having been sent to China, was afterwards ratified by that Empire.

Under the guarantees of protection afforded by this treaty, subjects of China, to the number of probably not less than one hundred thousand, are now domiciled in the United States. In like manner, American citizens, in comparatively much smaller numbers, however, engaged as missionaries, merchants, and mechanics, are now in China, protected by the provisions of this treaty. Commercial and manufacturing enterprises, already of considerable magnitude and rapidly increasing in importance, are dependent on the continuance of favorable treaty relations between the United States and China. If these relations are now to be terminated by the abrogation of essential parts of the existing treaty by the sole action of the United States, on what ground is such action to be taken? The bill under consideration contains no recital of the causes which are believed by its supporters to justify the abrogation of solemn treaty stipulations. Every important fact in regard to the object of the bill which is now urged in its support existed and was perfectly well known in 1868, when the treaty was ratified by the United States. The immigration in question had continued for twenty years, and its character and tendency were fully understood, and had been considered and discussed by legislative bodies and by the people. No grave and sudden change of conditions has occurred. No unforeseen emergency exists. The case stands almost precisely as it has stood for nearly a quarter of a century. Let it be admitted that the dangers apprehended from a longer continuance of the Chinese immigration require consideration and action; they surely do not require a departure from the well-settled principles and usages of Nations in their intercourse with each other, and in regard to the observance of treaties. We should deal with China in this matter precisely as we would expect and wish other Nations to deal with us under similar circumstances. The peremptory abrogation of a part of this treaty without negotiation with China, and without her consent, is the abrogation of the whole. The abrogation of a treaty by one of the contracting parties is justifiable only upon reasons both of the highest justice and of the highest necessity. To do this without notice; without fixing a day in advance when the act shall take effect; without affording an opportunity to

China to be heard; and without the happening of any grave or unforeseen emergency, will be regarded by the enlightened judgment of mankind as the denial of the obligation of the national faith.

Entertaining this view of the bill before me, I am compelled to withhold from it my signature, and to return it to the House of Representatives, in which it originated, for that further consideration which the Constitution requires.

R. B. HAYES.

EXECUTIVE MANSION, *March* 1, 1879.

PROCLAMATION

CONVENING

THE TWO HOUSES OF CONGRESS.

MARCH 4, 1879.

PROCLAMATION.

BY THE PRESIDENT OF THE UNITED STATES OF AMERICA.

A PROCLAMATION.

Whereas the final adjournment of the Forty-fifth Congress without making the usual and necessary appropriations for the legislative, executive, and judicial expenses of the Government for the fiscal year ending June 30, 1880, and without making the usual and necessary appropriations for the support of the Army for the same fiscal year, presents an extraordinary occasion, requiring the President to exercise the power vested in him by the Constitution to convene the Houses of Congress in anticipation of the day fixed by law for their next meeting:

Now, therefore, I, RUTHERFORD B. HAYES, President of the United States, do, by virtue of the power to this end in me vested by the Constitution, convene both Houses of Congress to assemble at their respective Chambers at twelve o'clock noon on Tuesday, the 18th day of March, instant, then and there to consider and determine such measures as, in their wisdom, their duty and the welfare of the people may seem to demand.

In witness whereof I have hereunto set my hand, and caused the seal of the United States to be affixed.

Done at the city of Washington this 4th day of March, A. D. 1879, [SEAL.] and of the Independence of the United States of America the one hundred and third.

R. B. HAYES.

By the President:
  WM. M. EVARTS,
    Secretary of State.

MESSAGE

TO THE

TWO HOUSES OF CONGRESS AT THE COMMENCEMENT OF THE FIRST SESSION OF THE FORTY-SIXTH CONGRESS.

MARCH 19, 1879.

MESSAGE.

FELLOW-CITIZENS OF THE SENATE
AND HOUSE OF REPRESENTATIVES:

The failure of the last Congress to make the requisite appropriations for legislative and judicial purposes, for the expenses of the several Executive Departments of the Government, and for the support of the Army, has made it necessary to call a special session of the Forty-sixth Congress.

The estimates of the appropriations needed, which were sent to Congress by the Secretary of the Treasury at the opening of the last session, are renewed, and are herewith transmitted to both the Senate and the House of Representatives.

Regretting the existence of the emergency which requires a special session of Congress at a time when it is the general judgment of the country that the public welfare will be best promoted by permanency in our legislation and by peace and rest, I commend these few necessary measures to your considerate attention.

RUTHERFORD B. HAYES.

WASHINGTON, *March* 19, 1879.

PROCLAMATION

IN RELATION TO

ILLEGAL SETTLEMENTS IN THE INDIAN TERRITORY.

APRIL 26, 1879

PROCLAMATION.

BY THE PRESIDENT OF THE UNITED STATES OF AMERICA.

A PROCLAMATION.

Whereas it has become known to me that certain evil-disposed persons have, within the territory and jurisdiction of the United States, begun and set on foot preparations for an organized and forcible possession of and settlement upon the lands of what is known as the Indian Territory, west of the State of Arkansas, which Territory is designated, recognized, and described by the treaties and laws of the United States and by the Executive authorities as Indian country, and as such is only subject to occupation by Indian tribes, officers of the Indian Department, military posts, and such persons as may be privileged to reside and trade therein under the intercourse laws of the United States; and whereas those laws provide for the removal of all persons residing and trading therein without express permission of the Indian Department and agents, and also of all persons whom such agents may deem to be improper persons to reside in the Indian country:

Now, therefore, for the purpose of properly protecting the interests of the Indian nations and tribes, as well as of the United States in said Indian Territory, and of duly enforcing the laws governing the same, I, RUTHERFORD B. HAYES, President of the United States, do admonish and warn all such persons so intending or preparing to remove upon said lands or into said Territory, without permission of the proper agent of the Indian Department, against any attempt to so remove or settle upon any of the lands of said Territory; and I do further warn and notify any and all such persons who may so offend, that they will be speedily and immediately removed therefrom by the agent according to the laws made and provided; and if necessary the aid and assistance of the military forces of the United States will be invoked to carry into proper execution the laws of the United States herein referred to.

In testimony whereof I have hereunto set my hand, and caused the seal of the United States to be affixed.

Done at the city of Washington this twenty-sixth day of April, in the year of our Lord one thousand eight hundred and seventy-nine, and of the Independence of the United States the one hundred and third.

[SEAL.]

RUTHERFORD B. HAYES.

By the President:
    WM. M. EVARTS,
        Secretary of State.

MESSAGE

RETURNING TO

THE HOUSE OF REPRESENTATIVES THE BILL ENTITLED "AN ACT MAKING APPROPRIATIONS FOR THE SUPPORT OF THE ARMY FOR THE FISCAL YEAR ENDING JUNE 30, 1880, AND FOR OTHER PURPOSES."

APRIL 29, 1879.

MESSAGE.

To the House of Representatives:

I have maturely considered the important questions presented by the bill entitled "An act making appropriations for the support of the Army for the fiscal year ending June 30, 1880, and for other purposes," and I now return it to the House of Representatives, in which it originated, with my objections to its approval.

The bill provides in the usual form for the appropriations required for the support of the Army during the next fiscal year. If it contained no other provisions, it would receive my prompt approval. It includes, however, further legislation, which, attached as it is to appropriations which are requisite for the efficient performance of some of the most necessary duties of the Government, involves questions of the gravest character. The sixth section of the bill is amendatory of the statute now in force in regard to the authority of persons in the civil, military, and naval service of the United States, "at the place where any general or special election is held in any State." This statute was adopted February 25, 1865, after a protracted debate in the Senate, and almost without opposition in the House of Representatives, by the concurrent votes of both of the leading political parties of the country, and became a law by the approval of President Lincoln. It was reenacted in 1874 in the Revised Statutes of the United States—sections 2002 and 5528, which are as follows:

"SEC. 2002. No military or naval officer or other person engaged in the civil, military, or naval service of the United States shall order, bring, keep, or have under his authority or control any troops or armed men at the place where any general or special election is held in any State, unless it be necessary to repel the armed enemies of the United States, or to keep the peace at the polls."

"SEC. 5528. Every officer of the Army or Navy, or other person in the civil, military, or naval service of the United States, who orders, brings, keeps, or has under his authority or control any troops or armed men at any place where a general or special election is held in any State, unless such force be necessary to repel armed enemies of the United States or to keep the peace at the polls, shall be fined not more than $5,000, and suffer imprisonment at hard labor not less than three months nor more than five years."

The amendment proposed to this statute, in the bill before me, omits from both of the foregoing sections the words "or to keep the peace at the polls." The effect of the adoption of this amendment may be considered—

First. Upon the right of the United States Government to use military force to keep the peace at the elections for members of Congress; and—

Second. Upon the right of the Government, by civil authority, to protect these elections from violence and fraud.

In addition to the sections of the statute above quoted, the following provisions of law relating to the use of the military power at the elections are now in force:

"SEC. 2003. No officer of the Army or Navy of the United States shall prescribe or fix, or attempt to prescribe or fix, by proclamation, order, or otherwise, the qualifications of voters in any State, or in any manner interfere with the freedom of any election in any State, or with the exercise of the free right of suffrage in any State."

"SEC. 5529. Every officer or other person in the military or naval service who, by force, threat, intimidation, order, advice, or otherwise, prevents, or attempts to prevent, any qualified voter of any State from freely exercising the right of suffrage at any general or special election in such State, shall be fined not more than five thousand dollars, and imprisoned at hard labor not more than five years.

"SEC. 5530. Every officer of the Army or Navy who prescribes or fixes, or attempts to prescribe or fix, whether by proclamation, order, or otherwise, the qualifications of voters at any election in any State, shall be punished as provided in the preceding section.

"SEC. 5531. Every officer or other person in the military or naval service who, by force, threat, intimidation, order, or otherwise, compels, or attempts to compel, any officer holding an election in any State to receive a vote from a person not legally qualified to vote, or who imposes, or attempts to impose, any regulations for conducting any general or special election in a State different from those prescribed by law, or who interferes in any manner with any officer of an election in the discharge of his duty, shall be punished as provided in section fifty-five hundred and twenty-nine.

"SEC. 5532. Every person convicted of any of the offences specified in the five preceding sections shall, in addition to the punishments therein severally prescribed, be disqualified from holding any office of honor, profit, or trust under the United States; but nothing in those sections shall be construed to prevent any officer, soldier, sailor, or marine from exercising the right of suffrage in any election district to which he may belong, if otherwise qualified according to the laws of the State in which he offers to vote."

The foregoing enactments would seem to be sufficient to prevent military interference with the elections. But the last Congress, to remove all apprehension of such interference, added to this body of law:

Section 15 of an act entitled "An act making appropriations for the support of the Army for the fiscal year ending June 30, 1879, and for other purposes," approved June 18, 1878, which is as follows:

"SEC. 15. From and after the passage of this act it shall not be lawful to employ any part of the Army of the United States as a *posse comitatus*, or otherwise, for the purpose of executing the laws, except in such cases and under such circumstances as such employment of said force may be expressly authorized by the Constitution or by act of Congress; and no money appropriated by this act shall be used to pay any of the expenses incurred in the employment of any troops in violation of this section, and any person wilfully violating the provisions of this section shall be deemed guilty of a misdemeanor, and on conviction thereof shall be punished by fine not exceeding ten thousand dollars or imprisonment not exceeding two years, or by both such fine and imprisonment."

This act passed the Senate, after full consideration, without a single vote recorded against it on its final passage, and, by a majority of more than two-thirds, it was concurred in by the House of Representatives.

The purpose of the section quoted was stated in the Senate by one of its supporters as follows:

"Therefore I hope, without getting into any controversy about the past, but acting wisely for the future, that we shall take away the idea that the Army can be used by a general or special deputy marshal, or any marshal, merely for election purposes as a posse, ordering them about the polls or ordering them anywhere else, when there is no election going on, to prevent disorders or to suppress disturbances that should be suppressed by the peace officers of the State, or, if they must bring others to their aid, they should summon the unorganized citizens, and not summon the officers and men of the Army as a *posse comitatus* to quell disorders, and thus get up a feeling which will be disastrous to peace among the people of the country."

In the House of Representatives the object of the act of 1878 was stated by the gentleman who had it in charge in similar terms. He said:

"But these are all minor points and insignificant questions compared with the great principle which was incorporated by the House in the bill in reference to the use of the Army in time of peace. The Senate had already conceded what they called, and what we might accept, as the principle, but they had stricken out the penalty, and had stricken out the word '*expressly*,' so that the Army might be used in all cases where *implied* authority might be inferred. The House committee planted themselves firmly upon the doctrine that rather than yield this fundamental principle, for which for three years this House had struggled, they would allow the bill to fail—notwithstanding the reforms which we had secured—regarding these reforms as of but little consequence alongside the great principle that the Army of the United States, in time of peace, should be under the control of Congress, and obedient to its laws. After a long and protracted negotiation, the Senate committee have conceded that principle in all its length and breadth, including the penalty, which the Senate had stricken out. We bring you back, therefore, a report, with the alteration of a single word, which the lawyers assure me is proper to be made, restoring to this bill the principle for which we have contended so long, and which is so vital to secure the rights and liberties of the people.

* * * * * * * *

"Thus have we, this day, secured to the people of this country the same great protection against a standing army which cost a struggle of two hundred years for the Commons of England to secure for the British people."

From this brief review of the subject, it sufficiently appears that, under existing laws, there can be no military interference with the elections. No case of such interference has, in fact, occurred since the passage of the act last referred to. No soldier of the United States has appeared under orders at any place of election in any State. No complaint even of the presence of United States troops has been made in any quarter. It may, therefore, be confidently stated that there is no necessity for the enactment of section six of the bill before me, to prevent military interference with the elections. The laws already in force are all that is required for that end.

But that part of section six of this bill which is significant and vitally important, is the clause which, if adopted, will deprive the civil authorities of the United States of all power to keep the peace at the Congressional elections. The Congressional elections in every district, in a very important sense, are justly a matter of political interest and concern throughout the whole country. Each State, every political party, is entitled to the share of power which is conferred by the legal and constitutional suffrage. It is the right of every citizen, possessing the qualifications prescribed by law, to cast one unintimidated ballot, and to have his ballot honestly counted. So long as the exercise of this power and the enjoyment of this right are common and equal, practically as well as formally, submission to the results of the suffrage will be accorded loyally and cheerfully, and all the departments of Government will feel the true vigor of the popular will thus expressed.

Two provisions of the Constitution authorize legislation by Congress for the regulation of the Congressional elections.

Section 4 of Article 1 of the Constitution declares—

"The times, places, and manner of holding elections for Senators and Representatives shall be prescribed in each State by the Legislature thereof; but the Congress may at any time, by law, make or alter such regulations, except as to the places of choosing Senators."

The fifteenth amendment of the Constitution is as follows:

"SEC. 1. The right of citizens of the United States to vote shall not be denied or abridged by the United States, or by any State, on account of race, color, or previous condition of servitude.

"SEC. 2. The Congress shall have power to enforce this article by appropriate legislation."

The Supreme Court has held that this amendment invests the citizens of the United States with a new constitutional right which is within the protecting power of Congress. That right the court declares to be exemption from discrimination in the exercise of the elective franchise on account of race, color, or previous condition of servitude. The power of Congress to protect this right by appropriate legislation is expressly affirmed by the court.

National legislation to provide safeguards for free and honest elections is necessary, as experience has shown, not only to secure the right to vote to the enfranchised race at the South, but also to prevent fraudulent voting in the large cities of the North. Congress has therefore exercised the power conferred by the Constitution, and has enacted certain laws to prevent discriminations on account of race, color, or previous condition of servitude, and to punish fraud, violence, and intimidation at Federal elections. Attention is called to the following sections of the Revised Statutes of the United States, viz:

Section 2004, which guarantees to all citizens the right to vote without distinction on account of race, color, or previous condition of servitude.

Sections 2005 and 2006, which guarantee to all citizens equal opportunity, without discrimination, to perform all the acts required by law as a prerequisite or qualification for voting.

Section 2022, which authorizes the United States marshal and his deputies to keep the peace and preserve order at the Federal elections.

Section 2024, which expressly authorizes the United States marshal and his deputies to summon a *posse comitatus* whenever they or any of them are forcibly resisted in the execution of their duties under the law, or are prevented from executing such duties by violence.

Section 5522, which provides for the punishment of the crime of interfering with the supervisors of elections and deputy marshals in the discharge of their duties at the elections of Representatives in Congress.

These are some of the laws on this subject which it is the duty of the Executive Department of the Government to enforce. The intent and effect of the sixth section of this bill is to prohibit all the civil officers of the United States, under penalty of fine and imprisonment, from employing any adequate civil force for this purpose at the place where their enforcement is most necessary: namely, at the places where the Congressional elections are held. Among the most valuable enactments to which I have referred are those which protect the supervisors of Federal elections in the discharge of their duties at the polls. If the proposed legislation should become the law, there will be no power vested in any officer of the Government to protect from violence the officers of the United States engaged in the discharge of their duties. Their rights and duties under the law will remain, but the National Government will be powerless to enforce its own statutes. The States may employ both military and civil power to keep the peace, and to enforce the laws at State elections. It is now proposed to deny to the United States even the necessary civil authority to protect the National elections. No sufficient reason has been given for this discrimination in favor of the State and against the National authority. If well-founded objections exist against the present National election laws, all good citizens should unite in their amendment. The laws providing the safeguards of the elections should be impartial, just, and efficient. They should, if possible, be so non-partisan and fair in their operation that the minority—the party out of power—will have no just grounds to complain. The present laws have, in practice, unquestionably conduced to the prevention of fraud and violence at the elections. In several of the States, members of different political parties have applied for the safeguards which they furnish. It is the right and duty of the National Government to enact and enforce laws which will secure free and fair Congressional elections. The laws now in force should not be repealed except in connection with the enactment of measures which will better accomplish that important end. Believing that section six of the bill before me will weaken, if it does not altogether take away, the power of the National Government to protect the Federal elections by the civil authorities, I am forced to the conclusion that it ought not to receive my approval.

This section is, however, not presented to me as a separate and independent measure, but is, as has been stated, attached to the bill making the usual annual appropriations for the support of the Army. It makes a vital change in the election laws of the country, which is in no way connected with the use of the Army. It prohibits, under heavy penalties, any person engaged in the civil service of the United States from having any force at the place of any election prepared to preserve order, to make arrests, to keep the peace, or in any manner to enforce the laws. This is altogether foreign to the purpose of an Army appropriation bill. The practice of tacking to appropriation bills measures not pertinent to such bills did not prevail until more than forty years after the adoption of the Constitution. It has become a common practice. All parties when in power have adopted it. Many abuses and great waste of public money have in this way crept into appropriation bills. The public opinion of the country is against it. The States which have recently adopted constitutions have generally provided a remedy for the evil, by enacting that no law shall contain more than one subject, which shall be plainly expressed in its title. The constitutions of more than half of the States contain substantially this provision. The public welfare will be promoted in many ways by a return to the early practice of the Government, and to the true principle of legislation, which requires that every measure shall stand or fall according to its own merits. If it were understood that to attach to an appropriation bill a measure irrelevant to the general object of the bill would imperil and probably prevent its final passage and approval, a valuable reform in the parliamentary practice of Congress would be accomplished. The best justification that has been offered for attaching irrelevant riders to appropriation bills is that it is done for convenience sake, to facilitate the passage of measures which are deemed expedient by all the branches of Government which participate in legislation. It cannot be claimed that there is any such reason for attaching this amendment of the election laws to the Army appropriation bill. The history of the measure contradicts this assumption. A majority of the House of Representatives in the last Congress was in favor of section six of this bill. It was known that a majority of the Senate was opposed to it, and that as a separate measure it could not be adopted. It was attached to the Army appropriation bill to compel the Senate to assent to it. It was plainly announced to the Senate that the Army appropriation bill would not be allowed to pass unless the proposed amendments of the election laws were adopted with it. The Senate refused to assent to the bill on account of this irrelevant section. Congress thereupon adjourned without passing an appropriation bill for the Army, and the present extra session of the Forty-sixth Congress became necessary to furnish the means to carry on the Government.

The ground upon which the action of the House of Representatives is defended has been distinctly stated by many of its advocates. A week before the close of the last session of Congress the doctrine in question was stated by one of its ablest defenders, as follows:

"It is our duty to repeal these laws. It is not worth while to attempt the repeal except upon an appropriation bill. The Republican Senate would not agree to, nor the Republican President sign, a bill for such repeal. Whatever objection to legislation upon appropriation bills may be made in ordinary cases does not apply where free elections and the liberty of the citizen are concerned. * * * We have the power to vote money; let us annex conditions to it, and insist upon the redress of grievances."

By another distinguished member of the House it was said:

"The right of the representatives of the people to withhold supplies is as old as English liberty. History records numerous instances where the Commons, feeling that the people were oppressed by laws that the Lords would not consent to repeal by the ordinary methods of legislation, obtained redress at last by refusing appropriations unless accompanied by relief measures."

That a question of the gravest magnitude, and new in this country, was raised by this course of proceeding, was fully recognized also by its defenders in the Senate. It was said by a distinguished Senator:

"Perhaps no greater question in the form we are brought to consider it was ever considered by the American Congress in time of peace; for it involves not merely the merits or demerits of the laws which the House bill proposes to repeal, but involves the rights, the privileges, the powers, the duties of the two branches of Congress and of the President of the United States. It is a vast question; it is a question whose importance can scarcely be estimated; it is a question that never yet has been brought so sharply before the American Congress and the American people as it may be now. It is a question which sooner or later must be decided, and the decision must determine what are the powers of the House of Representatives under the Constitution, and what is the duty of that House in the view of the framers of that Constitution according to its letter and its spirit.

"Mr. President, I should approach this question, if I were in the best possible condition to speak and to argue it, with very grave diffidence, and certainly with the utmost anxiety, for no one can think of it as long and as carefully as I have thought of it without seeing that we are at the beginning perhaps of a struggle that may last as long in this country as a similar struggle lasted in what we are accustomed to call the mother-land. There the struggle lasted for two centuries before it was ultimately decided. It is not likely to last so long here, but it may last until every man in this chamber is in his grave. It is the question whether or no the House of Representatives has a right to say: 'We will grant supplies only upon condition that grievances are redressed. We are the representatives of the tax-payers of the Republic. We, the House of Representatives, alone have the right to originate money bills; we, the House of Representatives, have alone the right to originate bills which grant the money of the people; the Senate represents States; we represent the tax-payers of the Republic; we, therefore, by the very terms of the Constitution, are charged with the duty of originating the bills which grant the money of the people. We claim the right, which the House of Commons in England established, after two centuries of contest, to say that we will not grant the money of the people unless there is a redress of grievances.'"

Upon the assembling of this Congress, in pursuance of a call for an extra session, which was made necessary by the failure of the Forty-fifth Congress to make the needful appropriations for the support of the Government, the question was presented whether the attempt made in the last Congress to engraft by construction a new principle upon the Constitution should be persisted in or not. This Congress has ample opportunity and time to pass the appropriation bills, and also to enact any political measures which may be determined upon in separate bills by the usual and orderly methods of proceeding. But the majority of both Houses have deemed it wise to adhere to the principle asserted and maintained in the last Congress by the majority of the House of Representatives. That principle is, that the House of Representatives has the sole right to originate bills for raising revenue, and therefore has the right to withhold appropriations upon which the existence of the Government may depend unless the Senate and the President shall give their assent to any legislation which the House may see fit to attach to appropriation bills. To establish this principle is to make a radical, dangerous, and unconstitutional change in the character of our institutions. The various Departments of the Government, and the Army and the Navy, are established by the Constitution, or by laws passed in pursuance thereof. Their duties are clearly defined, and their support is carefully provided for by law. The money required for this purpose has been collected from the people, and is now in the Treasury, ready to be paid out as soon as the appropriation bills are passed. Whether appropriations are made or not the collection of the taxes will go on. The public money will accumulate in the Treasury. It was not the intention of the framers of the Constitution that any single branch of the Government should have the power to dictate conditions upon which this treasure should be applied to the purposes for which it was collected. Any such intention, if it had been entertained, would have been plainly expressed in the Constitution.

That a majority of the Senate now concurs in the claim of the House adds to the gravity of the situation, but does not alter the question at issue. The new doctrine, if maintained, will result in a consolidation of unchecked and despotic power in the House of Representatives. A bare majority of the House will become the Government. The Executive will no longer be what the framers of the Constitution intended, an equal and independent branch of the Government. It is clearly the constitutional duty of the President to exercise his discretion and judgment upon all bills presented to him without constraint or duress from any other branch of the Government. To say that a majority of either or both of the Houses of Congress may insist on the approval of a bill under the penalty of stopping all of the operations of the Government for want of the necessary supplies, is to deny to the Executive that share of the legislative power which is plainly conferred by the second section of the seventh article of the Constitution. It strikes from the Constitution the qualified negative of the President. It is said that this should be done because it is the peculiar function of the House of Representatives to represent the will of the people. But no single branch or department of the Government has exclusive authority to speak for the American people. The most authentic and solemn expression of their will is contained in the Constitution of the United States. By that Constitution they have ordained and established a Government whose powers are distributed among co-ordinate branches, which, as far as possible, consistently with a harmonious co-operation, are absolutely independent of each other. The people of this country are unwilling to see the supremacy of the Constitution replaced by the omnipotence of any department of the Government.

The enactment of this bill into a law will establish a precedent which will tend to destroy the equal independence of the several branches of the Government. Its principle places not merely the Senate and the Executive, but the judiciary also, under the coercive dictation of the House. The House alone will be the judge of what constitutes a grievance, and also of the means and measures of redress. An act of Congress to protect elections is now the grievance complained of. But the House may on the same principle determine that any other act of Congress, a treaty made by the President, with the advice and consent of the Senate, a nomination or appointment to office, or that a decision or opinion of the Supreme Court is a grievance, and that the measure of redress is to withhold the appropriations required for the support of the offending branch of the Government.

Believing that this bill is a dangerous violation of the spirit and meaning of the Constitution, I am compelled to return it to the House in which it originated without my approval. The qualified negative with which the Constitution invests the President is a trust that involves a duty which he cannot decline to perform. With a firm and conscientious purpose to do what I can to preserve, unimpaired, the constitutional powers and equal independence, not merely of the Executive, but of every branch of the Government, which will be imperilled by the adoption of the principle of this bill, I desire earnestly to urge upon the House of Representatives a return to the wise and wholesome usage of the earlier days of the Republic, which excluded from appropriation bills all irrelevant legislation. By this course you will inaugurate an important reform in the method of Congressional legislation; your action will be in harmony with the fundamental principles of the Constitution and the patriotic sentiment of nationality which is their firm support; and you will restore to the country that feeling of confidence and security and the repose which are so essential to the prosperity of all of our fellow-citizens.

RUTHERFORD B. HAYES.

EXECUTIVE MANSION, *April* 29, 1879.

MESSAGE

RETURNING TO

THE HOUSE OF REPRESENTATIVES THE BILL ENTITLED "AN ACT TO PROHIBIT MILITARY INTERFERENCE AT ELECTIONS."

MAY 12, 1879.

MESSAGE.

To the House of Representatives:

After careful consideration of the bill entitled "An act to prohibit military interference at elections," I return it to the House of Representatives, in which it originated, with the following objections to its approval:

In the communication sent to the House of Representatives on the 29th of last month, returning to the House without my approval the bill entitled "An act making appropriations for the support of the Army for the fiscal year ending June 30, 1880, and for other purposes," I endeavored to show by quotations from the statutes of the United States now in force, and by a brief statement of facts in regard to recent elections in the several States, that no additional legislation was necessary to prevent interference with the elections by the military or naval forces of the United States. The fact was presented in that communication that at the time of the passage of the act of June 18, 1878, in relation to the employment of the Army as a *posse comitatus* or otherwise, it was maintained by its friends that it would establish a vital and fundamental principle which would secure to the people protection against a standing army. The fact was also referred to that, since the passage of this act, Congressional, State, and municipal elections have been held throughout the Union, and that in no instance has complaint been made of the presence of United States soldiers at the polls.

Holding as I do the opinion that any military interference whatever at the polls is contrary to the spirit of our institutions, and would tend to destroy the freedom of elections, and sincerely desiring to concur with Congress in all of its measures, it is with very great regret that I am forced to the conclusion that the bill before me is not only unnecessary to prevent such interference, but is a dangerous departure from long-settled and important constitutional principles.

The true rule as to the employment of military force at the elections is not doubtful. No intimidation or coercion should be allowed to control or influence citizens in the exercise of their right to vote, whether it appears in the shape of combinations of evil-disposed persons, or of armed bodies of the militia of a State, or of the military force of the United States.

The elections should be free from all forcible interference, and, as far as practicable, from all apprehension of such interference. No soldiers, either of the Union or of the State militia, should be present at the polls to take the place or to perform the duties of the ordinary civil police force. There has been and will be no violation of this rule under orders from me during this administration. But there should be no denial of the right of the National Government to employ its military force on any day and at any place in case such employment is necessary to enforce the Constitution and laws of the United States.

The bill before me is as follows:

"*Be it enacted*, &c., That it shall not be lawful to bring to or employ, at any place where a general or special election is being held in a State, any part of the Army or Navy of the United States, unless such force be necessary to repel the armed enemies of the United States, or to enforce section 4, article 4, of the Constitution of the United States, and the laws made in pursuance thereof, on application of the Legislature or Executive of the State where such force is to be used; and so much of all laws as is inconsistent herewith is hereby repealed."

It will be observed that the bill exempts from the general prohibition against the employment of military force at the polls two specified cases. These exceptions recognize and concede the soundness of the principle that military force may properly and constitutionally be used at the place of elections, when such use is necessary to enforce the Constitution and the laws. But the excepted cases leave the prohibition so extensive and far-reaching that its adoption will seriously impair the efficiency of the Executive Department of the Government.

The first act expressly authorizing the use of military power to execute the laws was passed almost as early as the organization of the Government under the Constitution, and was approved by President Washington, May 2, 1792. It is as follows:

"SEC. 2. *And be it further enacted*, That whenever the laws of the United States shall be opposed, or the execution thereof obstructed, in any State, by combinations too powerful to be suppressed by the ordinary course of judicial proceedings, or by the powers vested in the marshals by this act, the same being notified to the President of the United States by an associate justice or the district judge, it shall be lawful for the President of the United States to call forth the militia of such State to suppress such combinations, and to cause the laws to be duly executed. And if the militia of a State where such combinations may happen shall refuse or be insufficient to suppress the same, it shall be lawful for the President, if the Legislature of the United States be not in session, to call forth and employ such numbers of the militia of any other State or States most convenient thereto as may be necessary; and the use of militia, so to be called forth, may be continued, if necessary, until the expiration of thirty days after the commencement of the ensuing session."

In 1795 this provision was substantially re-enacted in a law which repealed the act of 1792. In 1807 the following act became the law by the approval of President Jefferson:

"That in all cases of insurrection or obstruction to the laws, either of the United States or of any individual State or Territory, where it is lawful for the President of the United States to call forth the militia for the purpose of suppressing such insurrection, or of causing the laws to be duly executed, it shall be lawful for him to employ, for the same purposes, such part of the land or naval force of the United States as shall be judged necessary, having first observed all the prerequisites of the law in that respect."

By this act it will be seen that the scope of the law of 1795 was extended so as to authorize the National Government to use not only the militia but the Army and Navy of the United States in "causing the laws to be duly executed."

The important provision of the acts of 1792, 1795, and 1807, modified in its terms from time to time to adapt it to the existing emergency, remained in force until, by an act approved by President Lincoln July 29, 1861, it was re-enacted substantially in the same language in which it is now found in the Revised Statutes, viz:

"SEC. 5298. Whenever, by reason of unlawful obstructions, combinations, or assemblages of persons, or rebellion against the authority of the Government of the United States, it shall become impracticable, in the judgment of the President, to enforce, by the ordinary course of judicial proceedings, the laws of the United States within any State or Territory, it shall be lawful for the President to call forth the militia of any or all the States, and to employ such parts of the land and naval forces of the United States as he may deem necessary to enforce the faithful execution of the laws of the United States, or to suppress such rebellion, in whatever State or Territory thereof the laws of the United States may be forcibly opposed, or the execution thereof forcibly obstructed."

This ancient and fundamental law has been in force from the foundation of the Government. It is now proposed to abrogate it on certain days and at certain places. In my judgment no fact has been produced which tends to show that it ought to be repealed or suspended for a single hour at any place in any of the States or Territories of the Union. All the teachings of experience in the course of our history are in favor of sustaining its efficiency unimpaired. On every occasion when the supremacy of the Constitution has been resisted, and the perpetuity of our institutions imperilled, the principle of this statute, enacted by the fathers, has enabled the Government of the Union to maintain its authority and to preserve the integrity of the Nation.

At the most critical periods of our history, my predecessors in the

Executive office have relied on this great principle. It was on this principle that President Washington suppressed the whiskey rebellion in Pennsylvania in 1794. In 1806, on the same principle, President Jefferson broke up the Burr conspiracy by issuing "orders for the employment of such force, either of the regulars or of the militia, and by such proceedings of the civil authorities, * * * as might enable them to suppress effectually the further progress of the enterprise." And it was under the same authority that President Jackson crushed nullification in South Carolina, and that President Lincoln issued his call for troops to save the Union in 1861. On numerous other occasions of less significance, under probably every administration, and certainly under the present, this power has been usefully exerted to enforce the laws, without objection by any party in the country, and almost without attracting public attention.

The great elementary constitutional principle which was the foundation of the original statute of 1792, and which has been its essence in the various forms it has assumed since its first adoption, is, that the Government of the United States possesses under the Constitution, in full measure, the power of self-protection by its own agencies, altogether independent of State authority, and, if need be, against the hostility of State governments. It should remain embodied in our statutes, unimpaired, as it has been from the very origin of the Government. It should be regarded as hardly less valuable or less sacred than a provision of the Constitution itself.

There are many other important statutes containing provisions that are liable to be suspended or annulled at the times and places of holding elections, if the bill before me should become a law. I do not undertake to furnish a list of them. Many of them—perhaps the most of them—have been set forth in the debates on this measure. They relate to extradition, to crimes against the election laws, to quarantine regulations, to neutrality, to Indian reservations, to the civil rights of citizens, and to other subjects. In regard to them all, it may be safely said, that the meaning and effect of this bill is to take from the General Government an important part of its power to enforce the laws.

Another grave objection to the bill is its discrimination in favor of the State and against the National authority. The presence or employment of the Army or Navy of the United States is lawful under the terms of this bill at the place where an election is being held in a State to uphold the authority of a State government then and there in need of such military intervention, but unlawful to uphold the authority of the Government of the United States then and there in need of such military intervention. Under this bill the presence and employment of the Army or Navy of the United States would be lawful, and might be necessary to maintain the conduct of a State election against the domestic violence that would overthrow it, but would be unlawful to maintain the conduct of a National election against the same local violence that would overthrow it. This discrimination has never been attempted in any previous legislation by Congress, and is no more compatible with sound principles of the Constitution or the necessary maxims and methods of our system of government on occasions of elections than at other times. In the early legislation of 1792 and of 1795, by which the militia of the States was the only military power resorted to for the execution of the constitutional powers in support of State or National authority, both functions of the Government were put upon the same footing. By the act of 1807 the employment of the Army and Navy was authorized for the performance of both constitutional duties in the same terms.

In all later statutes on the same subject-matter the same measure of authority to the Government has been accorded for the performance of both these duties. No precedent has been found in any previous legislation, and no sufficient reason has been given for the discrimination in favor of the State and against the National authority which this bill contains.

Under the sweeping terms of the bill, the National Government is effectually shut out from the exercise of the right, and from the discharge of the imperative duty to use its whole Executive power whenever and wherever required for the enforcement of its laws at the places and times where and when its elections are held. The employment of its organized armed forces for any such purpose would be an offence against the law unless called for by, and therefore upon permission of, the authorities of the State in which the occasion arises. What is this but the substitution of the discretion of the State governments for the discretion of the Government of the United States as to the performance of its own duties? In my judgment, this is an abandonment of its obligations by the National Government—a subordination of National authority, and an intrusion of State supervision over National duties, which amounts, in spirit and tendency, to State supremacy.

Though I believe that the existing statutes are abundantly adequate to completely prevent military interference with the elections in the sense in which the phrase is used in the title of this bill and is employed by the people of this country, I shall find no difficulty in concurring in any additional legislation limited to that object which does not interfere with the indispensable exercise of the powers of the Government under the Constitution and laws.

RUTHERFORD B. HAYES.

EXECUTIVE MANSION, *May* 12, 1879.

MESSAGE

RETURNING TO

THE HOUSE OF REPRESENTATIVES THE BILL ENTITLED "AN ACT MAKING APPROPRIATIONS FOR THE LEGISLATIVE, EXECUTIVE, AND JUDICIAL EXPENSES OF THE GOVERNMENT, FOR THE FISCAL YEAR ENDING JUNE 30, 1880, AND FOR OTHER PURPOSES."

MAY 29, 1879

MESSAGE.

To the House of Representatives:

After mature consideration of the bill entitled "An act making appropriations for the legislative, executive, and judicial expenses of the Government for the fiscal year ending June thirtieth, eighteen hundred and eighty, and for other purposes," I herewith return it to the House of Representatives, in which it originated, with the following objections to its approval:

The main purpose of the bill is to appropriate the money required to support, during the next fiscal year, the several civil departments of the Government. The amount appropriated exceeds in the aggregate eighteen millions of dollars.

This money is needed to keep in operation the essential functions of all the great departments of the Government—legislative, executive, and judicial. If the bill contained no other provisions, no objection to its approval would be made. It embraces, however, a number of clauses relating to subjects of great general interest, which are wholly unconnected with the appropriations which it provides for. The objections to the practice of tacking general legislation to appropriation bills, especially when the object is to deprive a co-ordinate branch of the Government of its right to the free exercise of its own discretion and judgment touching such general legislation, were set forth in the special message in relation to House bill number one, which was returned to the House of Representatives on the 29th of last month. I regret that the objections which were then expressed to this method of legislation have not seemed to Congress of sufficient weight to dissuade from this renewed incorporation of general enactments in an appropriation bill, and that my constitutional duty in respect of the general legislation thus placed before me cannot be discharged without seeming to delay, however briefly, the necessary appropriations by Congress for the support of the Government. Without repeating those objections, I respectfully refer to that message for a statement of my views on the principle maintained in debate by the advocates of this bill, viz., that "to withhold appropriations is a constitutional means for the redress" of what the majority of the House of Representatives may regard as "a grievance."

The bill contains the following clauses, viz:

"*And provided further,* That the following sections of the Revised Statutes of the United States, namely, sections two thousand and sixteen, two thousand and eighteen, and two thousand and twenty, and all of the succeeding sections of said statutes down to and including section two thousand and twenty-seven, and also section fifty-five hundred and twenty-two, be, and the same are hereby, repealed;" * * * "and that all the other sections of the Revised Statutes, and all laws and parts of laws authorizing the appointment of chief supervisors of elections, special deputy marshals of elections, or general deputy marshals having any duties to perform in respect to any election and prescribing their duties and powers and allowing them compensation, be, and the same are hereby repealed."

It also contains clauses amending sections 2017, 2019, 2028, and 2031 of the Revised Statutes.

The sections of the Revised Statutes which the bill, if approved, would repeal or amend, are part of an act approved May 30, 1870, and amended February 28, 1871, entitled "An act to enforce the rights of citizens of the United States to vote in the several States of this Union, and for other purposes." All of the provisions of the above-named acts, which it is proposed in this bill to repeal or modify, relate to the Congressional elections. The remaining portion of the law, which will continue in force after the enactment of this measure, is that which provides for the appointment, by a judge of the circuit court of the United States, of two supervisors of election in each election district, at any Congressional election, on due application of citizens who desire, in the language of the law, "to have such election *guarded* and *scrutinized.*"

The duties of the supervisors will be to attend at the polls at all Congressional elections, and to remain after the polls are open until every vote cast has been counted, but they will "have no authority to make arrests, or to perform other duties than to be in the immediate presence of the officers holding the election, and to witness all their proceedings, including the counting of the votes, and the making of a return thereof." The part of the election law which will be repealed by the approval of this bill, includes those sections which give authority to the supervisors of election "to personally scrutinize, count, and canvass each ballot," and all the sections which confer authority upon the United States marshals and deputy marshals, in connection with the Congressional elections. The enactment of this bill will also repeal section 5522 of the Criminal Statutes of the United States, which was enacted for the protection of United States officers engaged in the discharge of their duties at the Congressional elections. This section protects supervisors and marshals in the performance of their duties by making the obstruction or the assaulting of these officers, or any interference with them by bribery or solicitation, or otherwise, crimes against the United States.

The true meaning and effect of the proposed legislation are plain. The supervisors, with the authority to observe and witness the proceedings at the Congressional elections, will be left; but there will be no power to protect them, or to prevent interference with their duties, or to punish any violation of the law from which their powers are derived. If this bill is approved, only the shadow of the authority of the United States at the National elections will remain—the substance will be gone. The supervision of the elections will be reduced to a mere inspection, without authority on the part of the supervisors to do any act whatever to make the election a fair one. All that will be left to the supervisors is the permission to have such oversight of the elections as political parties are in the habit of exercising without any authority of law, in order to prevent their opponents from obtaining unfair advantages. The object of the bill is to destroy any control whatever by the United States over the Congressional elections.

The passage of this bill has been urged upon the ground that the election of members of Congress is a matter which concerns the States alone; that these elections should be controlled exclusively by the States; that there are and can be no such elections as National elections; and that the existing law of the United States regulating the Congressional elections is without warrant in the Constitution.

It is evident, however, that the framers of the Constitution regarded the election of members of Congress in every State and in every district as, in a very important sense, justly a matter of political interest and concern to the whole country. The original provision of the Constitution on this subject is as follows:

SEC. 4, ARTICLE 1. "The times, places, and manner of holding elections for Senators and Representatives shall be prescribed in each State by the Legislature thereof; but the Congress may at any time, by law, make or alter such regulations, except as to the places of choosing Senators."

A further provision has been since added, which is embraced in the fifteenth amendment. It is as follows:

"SEC. 1. The right of citizens of the United States to vote shall not be denied or abridged by the United States, or by any State, on account of race, color, or previous condition of servitude.

"SEC. 2. The Congress shall have power to enforce this article by appropriate legislation."

Under the general provision of the Constitution, (section 4, article 1,)

Congress, in 1866, passed a comprehensive law which prescribed full and detailed regulations for the election of Senators by the Legislatures of the several States. This law has been in force almost thirteen years. In pursuance of it all of the members of the present Senate of the United States hold their seats. Its constitutionality is not called in question. It is confidently believed that no sound argument can be made in support of the constitutionality of National regulation of Senatorial elections which will not show that the elections of members of the House of Representatives may also be constitutionally regulated by the National authority.

The bill before me itself recognizes the principle that the Congressional elections are not State elections, but National elections. It leaves in full force the existing statute under which supervisors are still to be appointed by National authority, to "observe and witness" the Congressional elections whenever due application is made by citizens who desire said elections to be "guarded and scrutinized." If the power to supervise, in any respect whatever, the Congressional elections exists, under section 4, article 1, of the Constitution, it is a power which, like every other power belonging to the Government of the United States, is paramount and supreme, and includes the right to employ the necessary means to carry it into effect.

The statutes of the United States which regulate the election of members of the House of Representatives, an essential part of which it is proposed to repeal by this bill, have been in force about eight years. Four Congressional elections have been held under them, two of which were at the Presidential elections of 1872 and 1876. Numerous prosecutions, trials, and convictions have been had in the courts of the United States in all parts of the Union for violations of these laws. In no reported case has their constitutionality been called in question by any judge of the courts of the United States. The validity of these laws is sustained by the uniform course of judicial action and opinion.

If it is urged that the United States election laws are not necessary, an ample reply is furnished by the history of their origin and of their results. They were especially prompted by the investigation and exposure of the frauds committed in the city and State of New York at the elections of 1868. Committees representing both of the leading political parties of the country have submitted reports to the House of Representatives on the extent of those frauds. A committee of the Fortieth Congress, after a full investigation, reached the conclusion that the number of fraudulent votes cast in the city of New York alone in 1868 was not less than twenty-five thousand. A committee of the Forty-fourth Congress, in their report submitted in 1877, adopted the opinion that for every one hundred actual voters of the city of New York in 1868, one hundred and eight votes were cast; when, in fact, the number of lawful votes cast could not have exceeded eighty-eight per cent. of the actual voters of the city. By this statement the number of fraudulent votes at that election, in the city of New York alone, was between thirty and forty thousand. These frauds completely reversed the result of the election in the State of New York, both as to the choice of Governor and State officers, and as to the choice of electors of President and Vice-President of the United States. They attracted the attention of the whole country. It was plain that if they could be continued and repeated with impunity, free government was impossible. A distinguished Senator, in opposing the passage of the election laws, declared that he had "for a long time believed that our form of Government was a comparative failure in the larger cities." To meet these evils and to prevent these crimes the United States laws regulating Congressional elections were enacted.

The framers of these laws have not been disappointed in their results. In the large cities, under their provisions, the elections have been comparatively peaceable, orderly, and honest. Even the opponents of these laws have borne testimony to their value and efficiency, and to the necessity for their enactment. The Committee of the Forty-fourth Congress, composed of members a majority of whom were opposed to these laws, in their report on the New York election of 1876, said:

"The committtee would commend to other portions of the country and to other cities this remarkable system, developed through the agency of both local and Federal authorities acting in harmony for an honest purpose. In no portion of the world, and in no era of time, where there has been an expression of the popular will through the forms of law, has there been a more complete and thorough illustration of republican institutions. Whatever may have been the previous habit or conduct of elections in those cities, or howsoever they may conduct themselves in the future, this election of 1876 will stand as a monument of what good faith, honest endeavor, legal forms, and just authority may do for the protection of the electoral franchise."

This bill recognizes the authority and duty of the United States to appoint supervisors to guard and scrutinize the Congressional elections, but it denies to the Government of the United States all power to make its supervision effectual. The great body of the people of all parties want free and fair elections. They do not think that a free election means freedom from the wholesome restraints of law, or that the place of an election should be a sanctuary for lawlessness and crime. On the day of an election peace and good order are more necessary than on any other day of the year. On that day the humblest and feeblest citizens, the aged and the infirm, should be, and should have reason to feel that they are, safe in the exercise of their most responsible duty, and their most sacred right as members of society, their duty and their right to vote. The constitutional authority to regulate the Congressional elections which belongs to the Government of the United States, and which it is necessary to exert to secure the right to vote to every citizen possessing the requisite qualifications, ought to be enforced by appropriate legislation. So far from public opinion in any part of the country favoring any relaxation of the authority of the Government in the protection of elections from violence and corruption, I believe it demands greater vigor, both in the enactment and in the execution of laws framed for that purpose. Any oppression, any partisan partiality, which experience may have shown in the working of existing laws, may well engage the careful attention both of Congress and of the Executive, in their respective spheres of duty, for the correction of these mischiefs. As no Congressional elections occur until after the regular session of Congress will have been held, there seems to be no public exigency that would preclude a seasonable consideration at that session of any administrative details that might improve the present methods designed for the protection of all citizens in the complete and equal exercise of the right and power of the suffrage at such elections. But with my views, both of the constitutionality and of the value of the existing laws, I cannot approve any measure for their repeal except in connection with the enactment of other legislation which may reasonably be expected to afford wiser and more efficient safeguards for free and honest Congressional elections.

RUTHERFORD B. HAYES.

EXECUTIVE MANSION, *May* 29, 1879.

MESSAGE

RETURNING TO

THE HOUSE OF REPRESENTATIVES THE BILL ENTITLED "AN ACT MAKING APPROPRIATIONS FOR CERTAIN JUDICIAL EXPENSES."

JUNE 23, 1879.

MESSAGE.

To the House of Representatives:

After careful examination of the bill entitled "An act making appropriations for certain judicial expenses," I return it herewith to the House of Representatives, in which it originated, with the following objections to its approval:

The general purpose of the bill is to provide for certain judicial expenses of the Government for the fiscal year ending June thirtieth, eighteen hundred and eighty, for which the sum of two million six hundred and ninety thousand dollars is appropriated. These appropriations are required to keep in operation the general functions of the judicial department of the Government, and if this part of the bill stood alone there would be no objection to its approval. It contains, however, other provisions, to which I desire respectfully to ask your attention.

At the present session of Congress a majority of both Houses favoring a repeal of the Congressional-election laws, embraced in title twenty-six of the Revised Statutes, passed a measure for that purpose, as part of a bill entitled "An act making appropriations for the legislative, executive, and judicial expenses of the Government for the fiscal year ending June 30, 1880, and for other purposes." Unable to concur with Congress in that measure, on the 29th of May last I returned the bill to the House of Representatives, in which it originated, without my approval, for that further consideration for which the Constitution provides. On reconsideration the bill was approved by less than two-thirds of the House, and failed to become a law. The election laws, therefore, remain valid enactments, and the supreme law of the land, binding not only upon all private citizens, but also alike and equally binding upon all who are charged with the duties and responsibilities of the legislative, the executive, and the judicial departments of the Government.

It is not sought by the bill before me to repeal the election laws. Its object is to defeat their enforcement. The last clause of the first section is as follows:

"And no part of the money hereby appropriated is appropriated to pay any salaries, compensation, fees, or expenses under or in virtue of title twenty-six of the Revised Statutes, or of any provision of said title."

Title twenty-six of the Revised Statutes, referred to in the foregoing clause, relates to the elective franchise, and contains the laws now in force regulating the Congressional elections.

The second section of the bill reaches much further. It is as follows:

"SEC. 2. That the sums appropriated in this act for the persons and public service embraced in its provisions are in full for such persons and public service for the fiscal year ending June 30, 1880, and no Department or officer of the Government shall, during said fiscal year, make any contract or incur any liability for the future payment of money under any of the provisions of title twenty-six of the Revised Statutes of the United States authorizing the appointment or payment of general or special deputy marshals for service in connection with elections or on election day, until an appropriation sufficient to meet such contract or pay such liability shall have first been made by law."

This section of the bill is intended to make an extensive and essential change in the existing laws. The following are the provisions of the statutes on the same subject which are now in force:

"SEC. 2679. No Department of the Government shall expend, in any one fiscal year, any sum in excess of appropriations made by Congress for that fiscal year, or involve the Government in any contract for the future payment of money in excess of such appropriations."

"SEC. 2732. No contract or purchase on behalf of the United States shall be made unless the same is authorized by law, or is under an appropriation adequate to its fulfillment, except in the War and Navy Departments, for clothing, subsistence, forage, fuel, quarters, or transportation, which, however, shall not exceed the necessities of the current year."

The object of these sections of the Revised Statutes is plain. It is, first, to prevent any money from being expended unless appropriations have been made therefor; and, second, to prevent the Government from being bound by any contract not previously authorized by law, except for certain necessary purposes in the War and Navy Departments.

Under the existing laws, the failure of Congress to make the appropriations required for the execution of the provisions of the election laws would not prevent their enforcement. The right and duty to appoint the general and special deputy marshals which they provide for would still remain, and the Executive Department of the Government would also be empowered to incur the requisite liability for their compensation. But the second section of this bill contains a prohibition not found in any previous legislation. Its design is to render the election laws inoperative and a dead letter during the next fiscal year. It is sought to accomplish this by omitting to appropriate money for their enforcement, and by expressly prohibiting any Department or officer of the Government from incurring any liability under any of the provisions of title twenty-six of the Revised Statutes authorizing the appointment or payment of general or special deputy marshals for service on election days, until an appropriation sufficient to pay such liability shall have first been made.

The President is called upon to give his affirmative approval to positive enactments which in effect deprive him of the ordinary and necessary means of executing laws still left in the statute-book, and embraced within his constitutional duty to see that the laws are executed. If he approves the bill, and thus gives to such positive enactments the authority of law, he participates in the curtailment of his means of seeing that the law is faithfully executed while the obligation of the law and of his constitutional duty remains unimpaired.

The appointment of special deputy marshals is not made by the statute a spontaneous act of authority on the part of any executive or judicial officer of the Government, but is accorded as a popular right of the citizens to call into operation this agency for securing the purity and freedom of elections in any city or town having twenty thousand inhabitants or upward. Section 2021 of the Revised Statutes puts it in the power of any two citizens of such city or town to require of the marshal of the district the appointment of these special deputy marshals. Thereupon the duty of the marshal becomes imperative, and its non-performance would expose him to judicial mandate or punishment, or to removal from office by the President, as the circumstances of his conduct might require. The bill now before me neither revokes this popular right of the citizens nor relieves the marshal of the duty imposed by law, nor the President of his duty to see that this law is faithfully executed.

I forbear to enter again upon any general discussion of the wisdom and necessity of the election laws, or of the dangerous and unconstitutional principle of this bill, that the power vested in Congress to originate appropriations involves the right to compel the Executive to approve any legislation which Congress may see fit to attach to such bills, under the penalty of refusing the means needed to carry on essential functions of the Government. My views on these subjects have been sufficiently presented in the special messages sent by me to the House of Representatives during their present session. What was said in those messages I regard as conclusive as to my duty in respect to the bill before me. The arguments urged in those communications against the repeal of the election laws, and against the right of Congress to deprive the Executive of that separate and independent discretion and judgment which the Constitution confers and requires, are equally cogent in opposition to this bill. This measure leaves the powers and duties of the supervisors of elections untouched. The compensation of those officers is provided for under permanent laws, and no liability for which an appropriation is now required would, therefore, be incurred by their appointment. But the power of the National Government to protect them in the discharge of their duty at the polls would be taken away. The States may employ both civil and military power at the elections, but by this bill even the civil authority to protect the Congressional elections is denied to the United States. The object is to prevent any adequate control by the United States over the National elections by forbidding the payment of deputy marshals, the officers who are clothed with authority to enforce the election laws.

The fact that these laws are deemed objectionable by a majority of both Houses of Congress is urged as a sufficient warrant for this legislation.

There are two lawful ways to overturn legislative enactments: one is their repeal; the other is the decision of a competent tribunal against their validity. The effect of this bill is to deprive the Executive Department of the Government of the means to execute laws which are not repealed, which have not been declared invalid, and which it is, therefore, the duty of the Executive and of every other Department of the Government to obey and to enforce.

I have, in my former message on this subject, expressed a willingness to concur in suitable amendments for the improvement of the election laws; but I cannot consent to their absolute and entire repeal, and I cannot approve legislation which seeks to prevent their enforcement.

RUTHERFORD B. HAYES.

EXECUTIVE MANSION, *June* 23, 1879.

MESSAGE

RETURNING TO

THE HOUSE OF REPRESENTATIVES THE BILL ENTITLED "AN ACT MAKING APPROPRIATIONS TO PAY FEES OF UNITED STATES MARSHALS AND THEIR GENERAL DEPUTIES."

JUNE 30, 1879.

MESSAGE.

To the House of Representatives:

I return to the House of Representatives, in which it originated, the bill entitled "An act making appropriations to pay fees of United States marshals and their general deputies," with the following objections to its becoming a law:

The bill appropriates the sum of six hundred thousand dollars for the payment, during the fiscal year ending June thirtieth, eighteen hundred and eighty, of United States marshals and their general deputies. The offices thus provided for are essential to the faithful execution of the laws. They were created and their powers and duties defined by Congress at its first session after the adoption of the Constitution in the Judiciary Act, which was approved September 24, 1789. Their general duties, as defined in the act which originally established them, were substantially the same as those prescribed in the statutes now in force.

The principal provision on the subject in the Revised Statutes is as follows:

"SECTION 787. It shall be the duty of the marshal of each district to attend the district and circuit courts, when sitting therein, and to execute throughout the district all lawful precepts directed to him, and issued under the authority of the United States; and he shall have power to command all necessary assistance in the execution of his duty."

The original act was amended February 28, 1795, and the amendment is now found in the Revised Statutes in the following form:

"SECTION 788. The marshals and their deputies shall have in each State the same powers in executing the laws of the United States as the sheriffs and their deputies in such State may have by law in executing the laws thereof."

By subsequent statutes, additional duties have been from time to time imposed upon the marshals and their deputies, the due and regular performance of which are required for the efficiency of almost every branch of the public service. Without these officers there would be no means of executing the warrants, decrees, or other process of the courts, and the judicial system of the country would be fatally defective. The criminal jurisdiction of the courts of the United States is very extensive. The crimes committed within the maritime jurisdiction of the United States are all cognizable only in the courts of the United States. Crimes against public justice; crimes against the operations of the Government, such as forging or counterfeiting the money or securities of the United States; crimes against the postal laws; offences against the elective franchise, against the civil rights of citizens, against the existence of the Government; crimes against the internal-revenue laws, the customs laws, the neutrality laws; crimes against laws for the protection of Indians, and of the public lands—all of these crimes, and many others, can be punished only under United States laws—laws which, taken together, constitute a body of jurisprudence which is vital to the welfare of the whole country, and which can be enforced only by means of the marshals and deputy marshals of the United States. In the District of Columbia all of the process of the courts is executed by the officers in question. In short, the execution of the criminal laws of the United States, the service of all civil process in cases in which the United States is a party, and the execution of the revenue laws, the neutrality laws, and many other laws of large importance, depend on the maintenance of the marshals and their deputies. They are in effect the only police of the United States Government. Officers with corresponding powers and duties are found in every State of the Union and in every country which has a jurisprudence which is worthy of the name. To deprive the National Government of these officers would be as disastrous to society as to abolish the sheriffs, constables, and police officers in the several States. It would be a denial to the United States of the right to execute its laws—a denial of all authority which requires the use of civil force. The law entitles these officers to be paid. The funds needed for the purpose have been collected from the people, and are now in the Treasury. No objection is therefore made to that part of the bill before me which appropriates money for the support of the marshals and deputy marshals of the United States.

The bill contains, however, other provisions which are identical in tenor and effect with the second section of the bill entitled "An act making appropriations for certain judicial expenses," which, on the 23d of the present month, was returned to the House of Representatives with my objections to its approval. The provisions referred to are as follows:

"SEC. 2. That the sums appropriated in this act for the persons and public service embraced in its provisions are in full for such persons and public service for the fiscal year ending June thirtieth, eighteen hundred and eighty; and no Department or officer of the Government shall, during said fiscal year, make any contract or incur any liability for the future payment of money under any of the provisions of title twenty-six mentioned in section one of this act until an appropriation sufficient to meet such contract or pay such liability shall have first been made by law."

Upon a reconsideration, in the House of Representatives, of the bill which contained these provisions it lacked a constitutional majority, and therefore failed to become a law. In order to secure its enactment the same measure is again presented for my approval, coupled in the bill before me with appropriations for the support of marshals and their deputies during the next fiscal year. The object manifestly is to place before the Executive this alternative: either to allow necessary functions of the public service to be crippled or suspended for want of the appropriations required to keep them in operation, or to approve legislation which in official communications to Congress he has declared would be a violation of his constitutional duty. Thus, in this bill the principle is clearly embodied that, by virtue of the provision of the Constitution which requires that "all bills for raising revenue shall originate in the House of Representatives," a bare majority of the House of Representatives has the right to withhold appropriations for the support of the Government unless the Executive consents to approve any legislation which may be attached to appropriation bills. I respectfully refer to the communications on this subject which I have sent to Congress during its present session for a statement of the grounds of my conclusions, and desire here merely to repeat that, in my judgment, to establish the principle of this bill is to make a radical, dangerous, and unconstitutional change in the character of our institutions.

RUTHERFORD B. HAYES.
EXECUTIVE MANSION, *June* 30, 1879.

MESSAGE

TO

THE TWO HOUSES OF CONGRESS.

JUNE 30, 1879.

MESSAGE.

To the Senate and House of Representatives:

The bill making provision for the payment of the fees of United States marshals and their general deputies, which I have this day returned to the House of Representatives, in which it originated, with my objections, having upon its reconsideration by that body failed to become a law, I respectfully call your attention to the immediate necessity of making some adequate provision for the due and efficient execution by the marshals and deputy marshals of the United States of the constant and important duties enjoined upon them by the existing laws. All appropriations to provide for the performance of these indispensable duties expire to-day. Under the laws prohibiting public officers from involving the Government in contract liabilities beyond actual appropriations, it is apparent that the means at the disposal of the Executive Department for executing the laws through the regular ministerial officers will after to-day be left inadequate. The suspension of these necessary functions in the ordinary administration of the first duties of Government for the shortest period is inconsistent with the public interests, and at any moment may prove inconsistent with the public safety.

It is impossible for me to look without grave concern upon a state of things which will leave the public service thus unprovided for and the public interests thus unprotected, and I earnestly urge upon your attention the necessity of making immediate appropriations for the maintenance of the service of the marshals and deputy marshals for the fiscal year which commences to-morrow.

RUTHERFORD B. HAYES.

Executive Department, *June* 30, 1879.

ADDRESS

AT THE

ANNUAL REUNION OF THE TWENTY-THIRD REGIMENT, OHIO VETERAN VOLUNTEER INFANTRY, AT YOUNGSTOWN, OHIO.

SEPTEMBER 17, 1879.

ADDRESS.

COMRADES AND FELLOW CITIZENS:

After almost a year spent in Washington, engrossed in public affairs, it is a great pleasure to visit again my friends in Ohio, and especially to meet so many of my old comrades at this yearly reunion of the Twenty-third Regiment. Since we last met at Willoughby, a year ago, there has been a vast improvement in the business condition of our country. Whatever differences of opinion may be still found among the people of this part of Ohio as to the importance of the resumption of specie payments, and as to the methods by which it has been accomplished, there is one kind of resumption which is very noticeable in Youngstown, and which is making rapid progress in the whole country, about which I imagine we are all heartily agreed. When I last visited this beautiful valley of the Mahoning, four years ago, the financial crisis, and the gloomy outlook for business and labor and capital, occupied the thoughts and depressed the spirits of the people wherever I met them, whether in public assemblies, at their places of business, or at their hospitable homes. Now, however, how great and how gratifying is the change! All around us here, and throughout the country generally, we see cheering and hopeful indications of better times. Not only have specie payments been resumed, but business activity and profitable employment for capital and labor have come also. The chief industry and interest of this valley—the great iron interest—already begins to share largely in the benefit of our improved condition, and I therefore heartily congratulate all classes of citizens in this large assemblage on the present favorable business situation, and on the bright and encouraging prospect which the future holds out.

There is a subject interesting to every citizen, and especially to those who served in the Union Army, in regard to which I wish to say a few words:

Since our last reunion, in several of the States and in Congress, events have occurred which have revived the discussion of the question as to the objects for which we fought in the great conflict from 1861 to 1865, and as to what was accomplished by the final triumph of the Union cause. The question is, What was settled by the war? What may those who fought for the Union justly claim; and what ought those who fought for secession, faithfully to accept as the legitimate results of the war?

An eminent citizen of our State, Mr. Groesbeck, said some years ago, that "war legislates." He regarded the new constitutional amendments as part of the legislation of the war for the Union, and said, with significant emphasis, "and they will stand." The equal-rights amendments are the legislation of the war for the Union, and they ought to stand. Great wars always legislate. A little more than a hundred years ago, this land, where we now are, was claimed and held by France. General Wolfe, on the plains of Abraham, settled that claim, and the result was the transfer of the title and jurisdiction of this entire section of the country to England. For a few years its chief ruler was the English King. The Revolution followed, and the question of its ownership was again the subject of war legislation, and it became a part of the United States, no longer under a monarchy, but under a free Republican Government.

I need not enter into any discussion of the causes of our civil war. We all know that the men who planned the destruction of the Union and the establishment of the Confederate States, based their attempt on a construction of the Constitution called the State-rights doctrine, and on the interest of the people of those States in the extension and perpetuation of slavery. The doctrine of State-rights was, that each State was sovereign and supreme, and might nullify the laws of the Union or secede from the Union at pleasure. They held that slavery was the natural and normal condition of the colored man, and that, therefore, slavery in this country could and should be the corner-stone of a free government.

No man has ever stated the issues of the civil war more fully, more clearly, or more accurately than Mr. Lincoln. In any inquiry as to what may fairly be included among the things settled by our victory, all just and patriotic minds instinctively turn to Mr. Lincoln. To him, more than to any other man, the cause of Union and liberty is indebted for its final triumph. Besides, with all his wonderful sagacity, and wisdom, and logical faculty, dwelling intently, and anxiously, and prayerfully, during four years of awful trial and responsibility, on the questions which were continually arising to perplex and almost confound him, he at last became the very embodiment of the principles by which the country and its liberties were saved. All good citizens may now well listen to and heed his words. None have more reason to do it with respect and confidence, and a genuine regard, than those whom he addressed in his first inaugural speech as "my dissatisfied fellow-countrymen." The leader of the Union cause was so just and moderate, and patient and humane, that many supporters of the Union thought that he did not go far enough or fast enough, and assailed his opinions and his conduct; but now all men begin to see that the plain people, who at last came to love him, and to lean upon his wisdom and firmness with absolute trust, were altogether right, and that in deed and purpose he was earnestly devoted to the welfare of the whole country, and of all its inhabitants.

Believing that Mr. Lincoln's opinions are of higher authority on the questions of the war than those of any other public man on either side of the controversy, I desire to present them quite fully and in his own language.

In the third year of the war, and while its result was still undecided, Mr. Lincoln made his memorable address at the consecration of the Gettysburg National Cemetery, on the 19th of November, 1863. He was standing on the field of the greatest battle of the war. He was, no doubt, deeply impressed with the heavy responsibilities which he had borne so long. He spoke not as a partisan, embittered and narrow and sectional, but in the broad and generous spirit of a patriot, solicitous to say that which would be worthy to be pondered by all of his countrymen throughout all time. In his short speech of only two or three paragraphs he twice spoke of the objects of the war, once in its opening and again in its closing sentence. The words have been often quoted, but they cannot be too familiar. They bear clearly and forcibly on the question we are considering.

"Four score and seven years ago," said Mr. Lincoln, "our fathers brought forth on this continent a new Nation, conceived in liberty and dedicated to the proposition that all men are created equal. Now we are engaged in a great civil war, testing whether that Nation, or any Nation so conceived and so dedicated, can long endure."

And again, in closing, he said: "It is rather for us * * * that we here highly resolve that the dead shall not have died in vain; that the Nation shall, under God, have a new birth of freedom; and that Government of the people, by the people, and for the people, shall not perish from the earth."

No statement of the true objects of the war more complete than this has ever been made. It includes them all—Nationality, Liberty, Equal Rights, and Self-Government. These are the principles for which the Union soldier fought, and which it was his aim to maintain and to perpetuate.

If any one supposes that that construction of our National Constitution, which is known as the State-rights doctrine, is consistent with sound principles, let him consider a few paragraphs from Mr. Lincoln's first message to Congress, at the extra session of 1861.

Speaking of what was called the right of peaceful secession—that is, secession in accordance with the National Constitution—he said:

"This sophism derives much, perhaps the whole, of its currency from the assumption that there is some omnipotent and sacred supremacy pertaining to a *State*—to each State of our Federal Union. Our States have neither more nor less power than that reserved to them in the Union by the Constitution, no one of them ever having been a State *out* of the Union. The original ones passed into the Union even *before* they cast off their British colonial dependence, and the new ones each came into the Union directly from a condition of dependence, excepting Texas. And even Texas, in its temporary independence, was never designated a State. The new ones only took the designation of States on coming into the Union, while that name was first adopted for the old ones in and by the Declaration of Independence. Therein the 'United Colonies' were declared to be 'free and independent States;' but, even then, the object plainly was not to declare their independence of *one another*, or of the *Union*, but, directly the contrary, as their mutual pledge, and their mutual action, before, at the time, and afterwards, abundantly show. The express plighting of faith by each and all of the original thirteen, in the articles of Confederation, two years later, that the Union shall be perpetual, is most conclusive. Having never been States, either in substance or in name, *outside* of the Union, whence this magical omnipotence of 'State-rights,' asserting a claim of power to lawfully destroy the Union itself? Much is said about the 'sovereignty' of the States; but the word, even, is not in the National Constitution, nor, as is believed, in any of the State constitutions. What is a 'sovereignty,' in the political sense of the term? Would it be far wrong to define it 'A political community, without a political superior?' Tested by this, no one of our States, except Texas, ever was a sovereignty; and even Texas gave up the character on coming into the Union; by which act she acknowledged the Constitution of the United States, and the laws and treaties of the United States made in pursuance of the Constitution, to be, for her, the supreme law of the land. The States have their *status* IN the Union, and they have no other legal *status*. If they break from this, they can only do so against law, and by revolution. The Union, and not themselves separately, procured their independence and their liberty. By conquest, or purchase, the Union gave each of them whatever of independence and liberty it has. The Union is older than any of the States, and, in fact, it created them as States. Originally, some dependent colonies made the Union, and, in turn, the Union threw off their old dependence for them, and made them States, such as they are. Not one of them ever had a State constitution independent of the Union. Of course, it is not forgotten that all the new States framed their constitutions before they entered the Union; nevertheless, dependent upon, and preparatory to, coming into the Union."

Unquestionably the States have the powers and rights reserved to them in and by the National Constitution; and upon this point, in another part of this great message, Mr. Lincoln says:

"This relative matter of National power and State-rights, as a principle, is no other than the principle of *generality* and *locality*. Whatever concerns the whole should be confided to the whole—to the General Government; while whatever concerns *only* the State should be left exclusively to the State. This is all there is of original principle about it."

Mr. Lincoln held that the United States is a Nation, and that its Government possesses ample power under the Constitution to maintain its authority and enforce its laws in every part of its territory. The denial of this principle by those who asserted the doctrine of State-rights, and who rightly claimed that it was inconsistent with State sovereignty, made up an issue over which arose one of the leading controversies which led to the civil war. The result of the war decided that controversy in favor of nationality and in favor of the supremacy of the National Government.

On the question of human rights, Mr. Lincoln was equally explicit, and often declared that it was involved in the conflict, and to be decided by the result. In his matchless message, already quoted, he says:

"Our adversaries have adopted some declarations of independence, in which, unlike the good old one, penned by Jefferson, they omit the words, 'all men are created equal.' Why? They have adopted a temporary national constitution, in the preamble of which, unlike our good old one, signed by Washington, they omit, 'We, the people,' and substitute, 'We, the deputies of the sovereign and independent States.' Why? Why this deliberate pressing out of view the rights of men, and the authority of the people? This is essentially a People's contest. On the side of the Union it is a struggle for maintaining in the world that form and substance of government whose leading object is to elevate the condition of men; to lift artificial weights from all shoulders; to clear the paths of laudable pursuit to all; to afford all an unfettered start, and a fair chance in the race of life. Yielding to partial and temporary departures, from necessity, this is the leading object of the Government for whose existence we contend. I am most happy to believe that the plain people understand and appreciate this."

On the subject of suffrage, Mr. Lincoln's guiding principle was that "no man is good enough to govern another man without that other man's consent."

Thus we have from the lips and pen of Mr. Lincoln—the great leader and representative of the Union cause—in the most solemn and authentic form, a complete statement of the issues of the war. He held that the Union is perpetual; that its Government is national and supreme; and that all of its inhabitants should be free, and be accorded equal civil and political rights.

These are the great fundamental principles, affirmed on the one side, and denied on the other, upon which the appeal was made to the God of battles. I do not undertake to review the debate as to the nature and powers of the Government of the Union, and as to the doctrine of State-rights, which began with the foundation of our institutions, and which was continued until it was hushed by the clash of arms. It is enough for my present purpose to say that, as a matter of history, all of the political parties of the past, when charged with the responsibility of directing the affairs of the Government, have maintained, in their practical administration of it, precisely the same principles which were held by President Lincoln. The principles as to the powers of the National Government which were acted upon by Washington and Jackson, and which are sustained by the decisions of Chief Justice Marshall, and by which Lincoln and the Union armies crushed the rebellion and rescued the Republic, are among the legitimate and irreversible results of the war which ought not to be questioned.

Touching the remaining important controversy settled by the war, the public avowals of opinion are almost all in favor of the faithful acceptance of the new constitutional amendments. On this subject the speeches of public men and the creeds and platforms of the leading political parties have for some years past been explicit. In 1872, all parties in their respective National Conventions adopted resolutions recognizing the equality of all men before the law, and pledging themselves, in the words of the Democratic National Convention, "to maintain emancipation and enfranchisement, and to oppose the reopening of the questions settled by the recent amendments to the Constitution." In 1876, the great political parties again, in the language of the St. Louis National Convention, affirmed their "devotion to the Constitution of the United States, with its amendments *universally* accepted as a final settlement of the controversies that engendered the civil war." Notwithstanding these declarations, we are compelled to take notice that, while very few citizens anywhere would wish to re-establish slavery if they could, and no one would again attempt to break up the Union by secession, there still remains in some communities a dangerous practical denial to the colored citizens of the political rights which are guaranteed to them by the Constitution as it now is. In the crisis of the war, Mr. Lincoln appealed to the colored people to take up arms. About two hundred thousand responded to the call, enlisted in the Union armies, and fought for the Union cause under the Union flag. Equality of rights for the colored people, from that time, thus became one of the essential issues of the war. General Sherman said, "when the fight is over, the hand that drops the musket cannot be denied the ballot." Jefferson said long before, "the man who fights for the country is entitled to vote." When, with the help of the colored men, the victory was gained, the Fifteenth Amendment followed naturally as one of its legitimate results. No man can truthfully claim that he faithfully accepts the true settlements of the war, who sees with indifference the Fifteenth Amendment practically nullified.

No one can overstate the evils which the country must suffer if lawless and violent opposition to the enjoyment of constitutional rights is allowed to be permanently successful. The lawlessness which to-day assails the rights of the colored people will find other victims to-morrow. This question belongs to no race, to no party, and to no section. It is a question in which the whole country is deeply interested. Patriotism, justice, humanity, and our material interests, all plead on the right side of this question. The colored people are the laborers who produce the cotton which, going abroad to the markets of the world, gives us that favorable balance of trade which is now doing so much for the revival of all business. The whole fabric of society rests upon labor. If free laborers suffer from oppression and injustice, they will either become discontented and turbulent, destroyers of property, and not producers of property, or they will abandon the communities which deprive them of their inalienable rights. In either case, social order and the peaceful industries upon which prosperity depends are imperilled and perhaps sacrificed. It will not do to say that this is an affair which belongs solely to the distant States of the South. The whole country must suffer if this question is not speedily settled, and settled rightly. Where the two races are numerous, prosperity can only exist by the united and harmonious efforts of both the white people and the colored people. The only solid foundations for peace and progress in such communities are equal and exact justice to both races. Consider the present situation? Whatever complaints may have been heard during the progress of reconstruction, candid men must admit that all sections and all States are now equally regarded, and share alike the rights, the privileges, and the benefits of the common Government. All that is needed for the permanent pacification of the country is, the cordial co-operation of all well-disposed citizens to secure the faithful observance of the equal-rights amendments of the Constitution.

Happily, in the very communities where lawlessness has been most general and most successful, there are editors of newspapers and other influential citizens who speak out and denounce these crimes against free government. It is plain that a sound public opinion is forming where it is most needed. No community can afford to allow any of its citizens to be oppressed—to lose their rights. To be indifferent on the subject is to disregard interest and duty. The Union citizens and soldiers can do much to remove the evils we are considering. Let it be understood that no public man in any party will be sustained unless he will undertake to carry out in good faith the pledges made in all our platforms in regard to the rights of colored citizens; unless he will support laws providing the means required to punish crimes against them; and unless he will oppose the admission of any man to either House of Congress whose seat has been obtained by the violation of the Fifteenth Amendment. The right of suffrage is the right of self-protection. Its free exercise is the vital air of Republican institutions.

To establish now the State-rights doctrine of the supremacy of the States, and an oligarchy of race, is deliberately to throw away an essential part of the fruits of the Union victory. The settlements of the war in favor of equal rights and the supremacy of the laws of the Nation are just and wise, and necessary. Let them not be surrendered. Let them be faithfully accepted and firmly enforced. Let them stand, and, with the advancing tide of business prosperity, we may confidently hope, by the blessing of Divine Providence, that we shall soon enter upon an era of harmony and progress such as has been rarely enjoyed by any people.

ADDRESS

AT

THE MICHIGAN STATE FAIR, AT DETROIT,

SEPTEMBER 18, 1879.

ADDRESS.

FELLOW-CITIZENS OF MICHIGAN:

Reaching Detroit only a few hours ago, I cannot, from personal observation, speak of the condition of your agriculture, or of your mining, manufacturing, and other large business interests. The information which I get, however, from the newspapers and from conversations with intelligent citizens, leads me to suppose that the outlook for the laborer, the capitalist, and the people generally, is, in this State, at least as favorable as that of the people of the country at large. This is what one would expect from its well-known advantages. Your State is almost surrounded by the navigable waters of inland seas, which communicate with many markets in different States, and in countries beyond the ocean. It is midway, by the best of railway-routes of travel and trade, between the old and the new States. It has mines of copper and iron. It has manufactures, salt, and lumber, and raises in abundance the most valuable crops and animals which are produced in the north temperate zone. It possesses a climate which is healthful and friendly to labor, and which gives vigor and character to men and women. Satisfactory as the material resources of Michigan unquestionably are, they do not constitute that excellence which perhaps chiefly attracts the admiration, and possibly excites the envy, of your less fortunate neighbors. All the world knows that when the list is made up of the most favored States of this country, and of the most favored countries of the Old World, with respect to education—either general education or the higher education—an honored and very conspicuous place on that list must be given to the State of Michigan.

A year ago, making a visit of two or three weeks to the West and Northwest, I thought it might be useful to speak of the financial condition of the country, and to present a hopeful view of the situation and prospects. The business depression which followed the panic of 1873 had then lasted five years; but there were indications of improvement, and it seemed to me that what was most needed was confidence, and that a presentation of encouraging facts and figures would tend to inspire confidence. It was my opinion, also, that there could be no permanent revival of business prosperity until the currency was placed upon a sound basis, and was exchangeable at its par value in the universally-recognized money of the world. The friends of the constitutional currency generally believed that this end could only be reached by the faithful execution of the Resumption Act; that there was no need of further legislation; and that the true policy was to stop tinkering with the currency. Accordingly, the pith of what I wished to say last year to audiences like this was, that we ought to "let well enough alone." Now the resumption of specie payments has come, and with it have come also better times.

The evidences of good times are numerous, palpable, and cheering. One bright day in June last, more steamers—more shipping of all sorts—gathered in New York harbor than was ever before seen in that great mart of commerce, and their tonnage was in greater excess comparatively than the number of vessels. The lines of the Pennsylvania Railroad east of Pittsburgh and Erie, for the first seven months of this year, as compared with the same period in 1878, show an increase of gross earnings of $1,208,294, an increase of expenses of $759,985, and an increase in net earnings of $448,309; the lines of the Philadelphia and Reading Railroad (the great anthracite-coal road) a net increase of $1,340,000 for the same period. The latest published statement of the Erie Railway Company shows a net increase of $561,000. The Baltimore and Ohio Railroad Company shows a net increase of $532,000 for the first ten months of its current fiscal year, beginning in October last. It is estimated that more than a thousand miles of railroad track have already been laid this year in the United States—a greater mileage than in the same period in any year since 1873. Workers in iron and steel find their business recovering so rapidly from its great depression that they are unable to fill their orders, and their annual production is likely soon to surpass the highest figures ever reached. The building of iron steamships in successful competition with Europe is fully established on the Delaware. Our cotton factories are again all at work, and running on full time. Our mines of precious metals are increasing their product, and it mainly stays at home. Our manufactures go abroad more than ever before; our currency is exchangeable at par in the markets of the world with the money of the world; and, finally, and most important, the demand for labor has increased and is increasing. It extends to cotton-mills, iron and glass-works, machine-shops, brick-making, building, the clothing trade, and nearly all branches of industry. The "Philadelphia Record," on the authority of a well-known statistician, states that there are twenty thousand more laborers employed in that city than

LETTERS AND MESSAGES. 239

there were a year ago. Our exports for the year 1878 amounted to $710,439,441, and the excess of exports over imports was $264,661,661, both sums being greater than in any previous year.

The following tables show the rapid advance our farmers and manufacturers are making in supplying both the foreign and the home markets. They were prepared by Mr. Joseph Nimmo, jr., the able chief of the Bureau of Statistics of the Treasury Department:

DOMESTIC EXPORTS.

Values of the principal commodities of domestic production the exportation of which greatly increased from June 30, 1868, to June 30, 1879.

Commodities.	Value exported during the year ended June 30—		Increase in 1879 over 1868.
	1868.	1879.	
Agricultural implements	$673,381	$2,933,388	$2,260,007
Animals, living	733,395	11,487,754	10,754,359
Bread and breadstuffs	69,024,059	210,355,528	141,331,469
Coal	1,516,220	2,319,398	803,178
Copper and brass, and manufactures of, not including copper ore	496,329	3,031,924	2,535,595
Cotton, manufactures of	4,871,054	10,853,950	5,982,896
Fruit	406,512	1,916,382	1,509,870
Iron and steel, and manufactures of, exclusive of firearms, but including scales and balances, sewing-machines and fire-engines	5,491,306	12,766,294	7,274,988
Leather of all kinds	607,105	6,800,070	6,192,965
Mineral oil, illuminating	19,752,143	35,999,862	16,247,719
Provisions	30,436,642	116,858,650	86,422,008
Sugar, refined	313,378	6,164,024	5,850,646
Tallow	2,540,227	6,934,940	4,394,713
Total	136,861,751	428,422,164	291,560,413

VALUES OF CERTAIN DOMESTIC EXPORTS.

Comparative statement of the values of certain articles of domestic production exported from the United States during the fiscal years ended June 30, 1873, 1876, and 1879.

Articles.	Fiscal year ended June 30—			Increase in 1879 over 1876.	Per cent. of increase.
	1873.	1876.	1879.		
Indian-corn	$23,794,694	$33,265,280	$40,655,120	$7,389,840	22.2
Wheat	51,452,254	68,382,899	130,701,079	62,318,180	91.1
Wheat-flour	19,381,664	24,433,470	29,567,713	5,134,243	21.0
Cotton manufactured, (colored and uncolored)	2,252,028	6,770,200	9,497,416	2,727,216	40.3
Railroad-bars	104,054	57,109	233,514	176,405	308.9
Locomotives	952,655	561,559	567,302	5,743	1.0
Mineral oil, illuminating	37,195,735	28,755,638	35,999,862	7,244,224	25.2
Bacon and hams	35,022,137	39,664,456	51,074,433	11,409,977	28.8
Beef, fresh and salted	2,417,481	3,186,304	7,219,458	4,033,154	126.6
Butter	952,919	1,109,496	5,421,205	4,311,709	388.6
Cheese	10,492,010	12,270,083	12,579,968	309,885	2.5
Lard	21,245,815	22,499,485	22,866,673	427,188	1.9
Sugar, refined	1,142,824	5,552,587	6,164,024	611,437	11.0
Tobacco, leaf	22,680,135	22,737,383	25,157,364	2,419,981	10.6

LETTERS AND MESSAGES.

QUANTITIES OF CERTAIN DOMESTIC EXPORTS.

Comparative statement of the quantities of certain articles of domestic production exported from the United States during the fiscal years ended June 30, 1873, 1876, and 1879.

Articles.	Fiscal year ended June 30—			Increase in 1879 over 1876.	Per cent. of increase.
	1873.	1876.	1879.		
Indian-corn............bushels	38, 541, 930	49, 493, 572	86, 296, 252	36, 802, 680	74.4
Wheat................bushels	39, 204, 285	55, 073, 122	122, 353, 936	67, 280, 814	122.2
Wheat-flour............barrels	2, 562, 086	3, 935, 512	5, 629, 714	1, 694, 202	43.0
Cotton, manufactured, colored and uncolored......yds	13, 772, 774	75, 807, 481	129, 197, 377	53, 389, 896	70.4
Locomotives............No	58	44	73	29	65.9
Railroad-bars............pounds	2, 832, 592	2, 244, 704	14, 097, 583	11, 852, 879	528.0
Mineral oil, illuminating....galls	158, 102, 414	204, 814, 673	331, 586, 442	126, 771, 769	61.9
Bacon and hams.........pounds	395, 381, 737	327, 730, 172	732, 249, 576	404, 519, 404	123.4
Beef, fresh and salted....pounds	31, 605, 186	36, 506, 150	90, 976, 395	54, 380, 245	148.6
Butter....................pounds	4, 518, 844	4, 644, 894	38, 248, 016	33, 603, 122	723.4
Cheese..................pounds	80, 366, 540	97, 676, 264	141, 654, 474	43, 978, 210	45.0
Lard.....................pounds	230, 534, 207	168, 405, 839	326, 658, 686	158, 252, 847	94.0
Sugar, refined...........pounds	9, 870, 738	51, 840, 977	72, 309, 009	20, 468, 032	39.5
Tobacco, leaf............pounds	213, 995, 176	218, 310, 265	322, 279, 540	103, 969, 275	47.6

IMPORTS.

Values of the principal commodities of foreign production the importation of which greatly decreased from June 30, 1873, to June 30, 1879.

Commodities.	Value imported during the year ended June 30—			Decrease of 1879 as compared with 1873.
	1873.	1878.	1879.	
Watches and watch-movements and materials.	$3, 274, 825	$812, 582	$920, 599	$2, 354, 226
Textiles:				
Cotton, manufactures of, (not including hosiery, shirts, and drawers)............	$29, 752, 116	$14, 398, 791	$14, 930, 975	$14, 821, 141
Flax, manufactures of.....................	20, 428, 391	14, 413, 600	14, 693, 842	5, 734, 549
Silk, manufactures of.....................	29, 890, 035	19, 837, 972	24, 013, 398	5, 876, 637
Clothing, (including hosiery, shirts, and drawers of cotton and wool).............	8, 496, 993	6, 540, 587	6, 560, 456	1, 936, 537
Wool, and manufactures of:				
Unmanufactured.........................	20, 433, 938	8, 363, 015	5, 034, 555	15, 399, 383
Carpets.................................	4, 388, 257	398, 389	367, 105	4, 021, 152
Dress-goods.............................	19, 447, 797	12, 055, 806	12, 436, 861	7, 010, 936
Other manufactures of, (not including hosiery, shirts, and drawers)..........	26, 626, 721	12, 193, 037	11, 158, 030	15, 468, 691
Total textiles....................	159, 464, 248	88, 201, 197	89, 195, 222	70, 269, 026
Iron and steel, and manufactures of:				
Pig-iron...............................	$7, 283, 769	$1, 250, 057	$1, 924, 128	$5, 279, 641
Bar, boiler, band, hoop, scroll, and sheet-iron.	7, 477, 556	1, 627, 052	1, 378, 976	6, 098, 580
Anchors, cables, chains, castings, hardware, machinery, old and scrap iron...........	9, 416, 293	920, 790	845, 366	8, 570, 927
Railroad-bars or rails.....................	19, 740, 702	530	78, 257	19, 662, 445
Steel ingots, bars, sheets, and wire.........	4, 155, 234	1, 220, 037	1, 281, 942	2, 873, 292
Fire-arms, files, cutlery, saws, and tools.....	4, 093, 097	1, 629, 061	1, 846, 626	2, 246, 471
All other manufactures of..................	7, 221, 861	2, 410, 165	2, 091, 853	5, 129, 948
Total iron and steel...............	59, 308, 452	9, 057, 692	9, 447, 148	49, 861, 304
Copper, and manufactures of, (not including copper ore)............................	$3, 687, 096	$311, 518	$294, 707	$3, 392, 389
Lead, and manufactures of..................	3, 247, 153	361, 894	64, 340	3, 182, 813
Leather of all kinds........................	6, 766, 202	3, 784, 729	3, 667, 564	3, 098, 638
India-rubber and gutta-percha, manufactures of......................................	900, 187	242, 564	174, 137	726, 050
Tea......................................	24, 466, 170	15, 660, 168	14, 577, 618	9, 888, 552
Grand total.....................	261, 114, 333	118, 492, 284	118, 341, 335	142, 772, 998

With these authentic and significant facts and figures before us, we may reasonably assume that the country has entered again upon a period of business prosperity. The interesting questions now are, have the good times come to stay? What can we do in private and in public affairs to prolong the period of prosperity, and to mitigate the severity of hard times when they again return? The prospects are now bright, but all experience teaches that the wheel of human affairs, always turning, brings around those tremendous events called financial panics, if not with regularity, at any rate with certainty. The writer of an intelligent article in one of the monthlies says: "Panics, it has been observed, recur about every twenty years in this country, and almost every ten years in England." The explanation of this is not difficult to discover. In good times the tendency is to extravagance to speculation, and to running in debt. Many spend more than they earn, and the balance of trade soon begins to run against communities and individuals. When this has continued until the business of the country is loaded down with debts, a financial crisis is inevitable, and only waits for "the last straw." If this view is correct, the way to meet the dangerous tendencies of flush times is plain. Let two of Doctor Franklin's homely proverbs be strictly observed by individuals and by communities. One is: "Never live beyond your means;" and the other is like unto it, namely—"Pay as you go."

It is easy to see that, if these old maxims of the philosophy of common sense could have general practical acceptance, the period of good times would be greatly prolonged, and the calamities of hard times would be vastly diminished. There can be no great financial crisis without large indebtedness, and the distress which it brings is in proportion to the extent of the extravagance, speculation, and consequent indebtedness which have caused it. Those who are out of debt suffer least. Where the debts are heaviest the calamity is heaviest. But it is of public indebtedness, and especially of the debts of towns and cities, that I wish to say a few words.

The practice of creating public debts, as it prevails in this country, especially in municipal government, has long attracted very serious attention. It is a great and growing evil. States, whose good name and credit have been hitherto untarnished, are threatened with repudiation. Many towns and cities have reached a point where they must soon face the same peril. I do not now wish to discuss the mischiefs of repudiation. My purpose is merely to make a few suggestions as to the best way to avoid repudiation. But, in passing, let me observe: Experience in this country has shown that no State or community can, under any circumstances, gain by repudiation. The repudiators themselves cannot afford it. The community that deliberately refuses to provide for its honest debts loses its good name and shuts the door to all hope of future prosperity. It demoralizes and degrades all classes of its citizens. Capital and labor and good people will not go to such communities, but will surely leave them. If I thought my words could influence any of my countrymen who are so unfortunate as to be compelled to consider this question, I would say, let no good citizen be induced by any prospect of advantage to himself or to his party to take a single step towards repudiation. Let him set his face like flint against the first dawning of an attempt to enter upon that downward pathway. It has been well said that the most expensive way for a community to get rid of its honest debts is repudiation.

Returning to the subject of municipal debts, it is not alone those that live in towns and cities who are interested in their wise and economical government. All who trade with their citizens, all who buy of them, all who sell to them—in a word, the whole of the laboring and producing classes—must bear a share of their burdens. The taxes collected in the city find their way into the price-lists of what is bought of and sold to the farmers and laborers in the country. On the questions of debt and taxation the dwellers of the city and those who habitually deal with them form together one community and have a common interest.

The usual argument in favor of creating a city debt is, that the proposed building or improvement is not for this generation alone, but is also for the benefit of posterity, and, therefore, posterity ought to help to pay for it. This reasoning will not bear examination. Each generation has its own demands upon its purse. It should not be called on to pay for the cast-off garments of its ancestors.

The appliances and structures which our ancestors provided for water, light, streets, parks, cemeteries, for putting-out fires, for police, for locomotion, for education, and for the thousand other necessities of city life, would not be well suited to the tastes, habits, and wants of our day. This generation must have steam fire-engines and water-works, and its tax-payers do not want to be called upon to pay for the cisterns, the fire-buckets, and the pumps of thirty years ago.

Municipal borrowing is the parent of waste, profligacy, and corruption. Money that comes easily goes easily. In this career of reckless extravagance, cities build and buy what they do not need, and pay for what they get far more than it is worth. I adopt the words of the valuable report of the Pennsylvania Commission appointed to devise a plan for the government of cities. To sum it up, it too often happens that "the men who authorize the contracts are substantially the men who profess to perform them; the men who fix the prices are substantially the men who receive the pay for performing the labor; and the men who issue the bonds are the men who receive the money."

The magnitude and the growth of this evil are shown by statistics with which the public is familiar. I do not choose to detain you by repeating them in detail.

A few weeks ago the "New York Tribune" called attention to an excellent article on this subject in the "Princeton Review," by Mr. Robert P. Porter, in which it is shown that local debts have, since the war, increased out of all proportion to the increase of property and population. Mr. Porter shows that in one hundred and thirty cities the debt increased from $221,312,009, in 1866, to $644,378,663 in 1876. The percentage of increase is about 200 per cent. in ten years, while the property of these cities increased but 75 per cent., and their population only 33 per cent. The total local indebtedness of all of the States, omitting the Territories, it is estimated in the article referred to, at the close of 1878, was $1,051,106,112. In many instances it is shown that the annual amount of interest paid by cities on their debts is almost equal to the total annual expenses for carrying on their local governments. The volume of the local indebtedness of the country already exceeds one-half the great war debt of the Nation, and the interest upon them, from the high rates usually paid, will soon equal the total interest upon the National debt.

The urgent question that is now pressing for consideration is, how to deal with these large and increasing local debts. The best answer, it seems to me, is simple, ready at hand, and sufficient: Do not have any local debts. Let it be embodied in the constitution and laws of every State that local authorities shall create no debts; that they shall make no appropriations of money until it is collected and on hand; that all appropriations shall be for specific objects, and that as to existing debts, suitable provision shall be made for their extinguishment.

To pay off the old debts, to create no new debts, will be difficult and embarrassing. Valuable reforms always are difficult, and thorough work often is embarrassing. If we would be rid of the peril of approaching bankruptcy and repudiation which now threaten so many towns and cities, there must be a halt to this dangerous downward march. If the remedies I have suggested are too radical, let others be proposed and acted on, and that promptly.

The policy of preventing the creation of local debts by positive constitutional prohibition is fully sustained by the experience of the States with respect to State debts. Constitutions in many of the old, and in all of the new, States have been adopted within the last thirty or forty years, and almost all of them contain provisions denying to State legislatures the authority to create debts except in case of war, insurrection, or other extraordinary emergency. Under the operation of these prohibitory provisions, the debts existing at the time of their adoption have been greatly reduced, and the only States now embarrassed by debt are those whose constitutions do not contain this wise prohibition.

The general policy of the National Government on the subject of debt has always been sound. It may be summed up in a few words: No debts to be created in time of peace, and war debts to be paid off as rapidly as possible when the war ends.

The Revolutionary-War debt, at the inauguration of the present form of Government, March 4, 1789, amounted to $76,000,000, and after successive refundings, in long-time bonds, was paid off by their redemption, finally, in 1835.

The debt created by the War of 1812, after refunding in 4½ per cent. bonds, was also paid in 1835, and at the close of that year the Nation was practically free from debt.

The debt incurred on account of the Mexican War amounted to $83,552,698, the bonded debt bearing six per cent. interest, running from five to twenty years, and Treasury notes at various rates of interest, from one mill to five and two-fifths per cent. All of this debt was redeemed prior to 1870, excepting a very small amount not yet presented for redemption.

As a marked evidence of the fidelity with which our National obligations of this description have heretofore been met, it is worthy of note that, during the War of 1812, the interest on the portion of the debt held by British subjects was regularly paid, the agents of the holders in this country, owing to the interruption of direct commercial intercourse, being sometimes obliged to resort to circuitous and extremely difficult routes for the transmission of payment. I find the fact remarked upon by Mr. Alexander Trotter, the British author of a standard work published in 1839, upon our National financial position and credit at that time. The author also notes the fact that the act of Congress passed by the first Congress that assembled after the adoption of the Constitution, to make provision for the payment of all the outstanding engagements of the Government, "with a degree of integrity which is rare in the history of the financial embarrassments of States," postponed the claims of creditors at home until those of the foreign creditor were provided for.

Our war debt resulting from the War for the Union amounted to about $3,000,000,000, and has been reduced to about $2,000,000,000. During the last year there has been no reduction of the aggregate amount, but there has been a reduction of the amount of the interest-bearing debt of $13,760,900, and the rates of interest have been so reduced by refunding within the past year that there is an annual saving of $13,760,900 in interest. The annual interest on the National debt reached its highest point about fourteen years ago, when it was $150,977,697.87. It is now reduced to $83,744,710.50, a yearly saving of $67,232,987.37, or about forty-five per cent. of what was payable in 1865. The policy of paying off the National debt, which, at the close of the war, was urged upon the country with so much force by the Secretary of the Treasury, Mr. Hugh McCulloch, has borne good fruit. Young men of this audience can remember when the Government of the United States found great difficulty in borrowing so small a sum as $25,000,000, and for a considerable part of it was compelled to pay as high as twelve per cent. Last spring, by reason of improved and strengthened credit, the Government had no trouble in borrowing, in the single month of April, $225,000,000 at four per cent. interest. The amount offered in that month exceeded five hundred millions of dollars, and there was one day when the amount offered was $159,000,000.

Let the policy of extinguishing the National debt be adhered to. Let it be the fixed purpose of the people and all who administer the Government to pay off the debt within thirty-three years. It can be done by economy and prudence without a material increase of the burdens of the people. The payment of thirty-three millions a year upon the principal of the debt, or into a sinking-fund for that purpose, will, within thirty-three years, leave us free from debt as a Nation.

That which is sound policy in National and State affairs, in regard to public debts, is, I believe, also wise policy in local affairs and in private affairs. Let it be everywhere adopted, in public and private, and we may welcome the advancing tide of better times, confident that we have found the secret that will prolong their stay, and which will go far to make us independent in that, I trust, distant day when a financial panic may again strike down the general prosperity.

EXECUTIVE ORDER.

DEATH OF SENATOR ZACHARIAH CHANDLER.

NOVEMBER 1, 1879.

EXECUTIVE ORDER.

EXECUTIVE MANSION,
Washington, November 1, 1879.

The sad intelligence of the death of Zachariah Chandler, late Secretary of the Interior, and during so many years a Senator from the State of Michigan, has been communicated to the Government and to the country; and in proper respect to his memory I hereby order that the several Executive Departments be closed to public business, and their flags and those of their dependencies throughout the country be displayed at half-mast on the day of his funeral.

R. B. HAYES.

THANKSGIVING PROCLAMATION.

NOVEMBER 3, 1879.

PROCLAMATION.

BY THE PRESIDENT OF THE UNITED STATES OF AMERICA.

A PROCLAMATION.

At no recurrence of the season which the devout habit of a religious people has made the occasion for giving thanks to Almighty God and humbly invoking His continued favor, has the material prosperity enjoyed by our whole country been more conspicuous, more manifold, or more universal.

During the past year, also, unbroken peace with all foreign nations, the general prevalence of domestic tranquillity, the supremacy and security of the great institutions of civil and religious freedom, have gladdened the hearts of our people, and confirmed their attachment to their government, which the wisdom and courage of our ancestors so fitly framed, and the wisdom and courage of their descendants have so firmly maintained, to be the habitation of liberty and justice to successive generations:

Now, therefore, I, RUTHERFORD B. HAYES, President of the United States, do appoint Thursday, the 27th day of November, instant, as a Day of National Thanksgiving and Prayer; and I earnestly recommend that, withdrawing themselves from secular cares and labors, the people of the United States do meet together on that day in their respective places of worship, there to give thanks and praise to Almighty God for His mercies, and to devoutly beseech their continuance.

In witness whereof I have hereunto set my hand, and caused the seal of the United States to be affixed.

Done at the city of Washington this third day of November, in the year of our Lord one thousand eight hundred and seventy-
[SEAL.] nine, and of the Independence of the United States the one hundred and fourth.

RUTHERFORD B. HAYES.

By the President:
   WM. M. EVARTS,
      Secretary of State.

MESSAGE

TO THE

TWO HOUSES OF CONGRESS AT THE COMMENCEMENT OF THE SECOND
SESSION OF THE FORTY-SIXTH CONGRESS.

DECEMBER 1, 1879.

MESSAGE.

FELLOW-CITIZENS OF THE SENATE
AND HOUSE OF REPRESENTATIVES:

The members of the Forty-sixth Congress have assembled in their first regular session under circumstances calling for mutual congratulation and grateful acknowledgment to the Giver of all good for the large and unusual measure of national prosperity which we now enjoy.

The most interesting events which have occurred in our public affairs since my last annual message to Congress are connected with the financial operations of the Government, directly affecting the business interests of the country. I congratulate Congress on the successful execution of the Resumption Act. At the time fixed and in the manner contemplated by law, United States notes began to be redeemed in coin. Since the first of January last they have been promptly redeemed on presentation, and in all business transactions, public and private, in all parts of the country, they are received and paid out as the equivalent of coin. The demand upon the Treasury for gold and silver in exchange for United States notes has been comparatively small, and the voluntary deposit of coin and bullion in exchange for notes has been very large. The excess of the precious metals deposited or exchanged for United States notes over the amount of United States notes redeemed is about $40,000,000.

The resumption of specie payments has been followed by a very great revival of business. With a currency equivalent in value to the money of the commercial world, we are enabled to enter upon an equal competition with other Nations in trade and production. The increasing foreign demand for our manufactures and agricultural products has caused a large balance of trade in our favor, which has been paid in gold, from the 1st of July last to November 15, to the amount of about $59,000,000. Since the resumption of specie payments there has also been a marked and gratifying improvement of the public credit. The bonds of the Government bearing only four per cent. interest have been sold at or above par, sufficient in amount to pay off all of the National debt which was redeemable under present laws. The amount of interest saved annually by the process of refunding the debt, since March

1, 1877, is $14,297,177. The bonds sold were largely in small sums, and the number of our citizens now holding the public securities is much greater than ever before. The amount of the National debt which matures within less than two years is $792,121,700, of which $500,000,000 bear interest at the rate of five per cent., and the balance is in bonds bearing six per cent. interest. It is believed that this part of the public debt can be refunded by the issue of four per cent. bonds, and, by the reduction of interest which will thus be effected, about eleven millions of dollars can be annually saved to the Treasury. To secure this important reduction of interest to be paid by the United States, farther legislation is required, which, it is hoped, will be provided by Congress during its present session.

The coinage of gold by the mints of the United States during the last fiscal year was $40,986,912. The coinage of silver dollars, since the passage of the act for that purpose up to November 1, 1879, was $45,000,850, of which $12,700,344 have been issued from the Treasury, and are now in circulation, and $32,300,506 are still in the possession of the Government.

The pendency of the proposition for unity of action between the United States and the principal commercial nations of Europe, to effect a permanent system for the equality of gold and silver in the recognized money of the world, leads me to recommend that Congress refrain from new legislation on the general subject. The great revival of trade, internal and foreign, will supply during the coming year its own instructions, which may well be awaited before attempting further experimental measures with the coinage. I would, however, strongly urge upon Congress the importance of authorizing the Secretary of the Treasury to suspend the coinage of silver dollars upon the present legal ratio. The market value of the silver dollar being uniformly and largely less than the market value of the gold dollar, it is obviously impracticable to maintain them at par with each other if both are coined without limit. If the cheaper coin is forced into circulation, it will, if coined without limit, soon become the sole standard of value, and thus defeat the desired object, which is a currency of both gold and silver, which shall be of equivalent value, dollar for dollar, with the universally recognized money of the world.

The retirement from circulation of United States notes, with the capacity of legal-tender in private contracts, is a step to be taken in our progress towards a safe and stable currency, which should be accepted as the policy and duty of the Government, and the interest and security of the people. It is my firm conviction that the issue of legal-tender paper money based wholly upon the authority and credit of the Government, except in extreme emergency, is without warrant in the Constitution, and a violation of sound financial principles. The issue of United States notes during the late civil war with the capacity of legal-tender between private individuals was not authorized except as a means of rescuing the country from imminent peril. The circulation of these notes as paper money, for any protracted period of time after the accomplishment of this purpose, was not contemplated by the framers of the law under which they were issued. They anticipated the redemption and withdrawal of these notes at the earliest practicable period consistent with the attainment of the object for which they were provided.

The policy of the United States, steadily adhered to from the adoption of the Constitution, has been to avoid the creation of a National debt, and when, from necessity in time of war, debts have been created, they have been paid off on the return of peace as rapidly as possible. With this view, and for this purpose, it is recommended that the existing laws for the accumulation of a sinking-fund sufficient to extinguish the public debt within a limited period be maintained. If any change of the objects or rates of taxation is deemed necessary by Congress, it is suggested that experience has shown that a duty can be placed on tea and coffee, which will not enhance the price of those articles to the consumer, and which will add several millions of dollars annually to the Treasury.

The continued deliberate violation by a large number of the prominent and influential citizens of the Territory of Utah of the laws of the United States for the prosecution and punishment of polygamy demands the attention of every department of the Government. This Territory has a population sufficient to entitle it to admission as a State, and the general interests of the Nation, as well as the welfare of the citizens of the Territory, require its advance from the territorial form of government to the responsibilities and privileges of a State. This important change will not, however, be approved by the country while the citizens of Utah in very considerable number uphold a practice which is condemned as a crime by the laws of all civilized communities throughout the world.

The law for the suppression of this offence was enacted with great unanimity by Congress more than seventeen years ago, but has remained until recently a dead-letter in the Territory of Utah, because of the peculiar difficulties attending its enforcement. The opinion widely prevailed among the citizens of Utah that the law was in contravention of the constitutional guarantee of religious freedom. This objection is now removed. The Supreme Court of the United States has decided the law to be within the legislative power of Congress, and binding as a rule of action for all who reside within the Territories. There is no longer any reason for delay or hesitation in its enforcement. It should be firmly and effectively executed. If not sufficiently stringent in its provisions it should be amended, and, in aid of the purpose in view, I recommend that more comprehensive and more searching methods for preventing as well as punishing this crime be provided. If necessary to secure obedience to the law, the enjoyment and exercise of the rights and privileges of citizenship in the Territories of the United States may be withheld or withdrawn from those who violate or oppose the enforcement of the law on this subject.

The elections of the past year, though occupied only with State offices, have not failed to elicit, in the political discussions which attended them all over the country, new and decisive evidence of the deep interest which the great body of citizens take in the progress of the country towards a more general and complete establishment, at whatever cost, of universal security and freedom in the exercise of the elective franchise. While many topics of political concern demand great attention from our people, both in the sphere of National and State authority, I find no reason to qualify the opinion I expressed in my last annual message, that no temporary or administrative interests of government, however urgent or weighty, will ever displace the zeal of our people in defence of the primary rights of citizenship, and that the power of public opinion will override all political prejudices, and all sectional and State attachments, in demanding that all over our wide territory the name and character of citizen of the United States shall mean one and the same thing, and carry with them unchallenged security and respect. I earnestly appeal to the intelligence and patriotism of all good citizens of every part of the country, however much they may be divided in opinions on other political subjects, to unite in compelling obedience to existing laws aimed at the protection of the right of suffrage. I respectfully urge upon Congress to supply any defects in these laws which experience has shown, and which it is within its power to remedy. I again invoke the co-operation of the executive and legislative authorities of the States in this great purpose. I am fully convinced that if the public mind can be set at rest on this paramount question of popular rights, no serious obstacle will thwart or delay the complete pacification of the country, or retard the general diffusion of prosperity.

In a former message I invited the attention of Congress to the subject of the reformation of the civil service of the Government, and expressed the intention of transmitting to Congress, as early as practicable, a report upon this subject by the chairman of the Civil Service Commission.

In view of the facts that, during a considerable period, the Government of Great Britain has been dealing with administrative problems and abuses, in various particulars analogous to those presented in this country, and that in recent years the measures adopted were understood to have been effective and in every respect highly satisfactory, I thought it desirable to have fuller information upon the subject, and accordingly requested the chairman of the Civil-Service Commission to make a thorough investigation for this purpose. The result has been an elaborate and comprehensive report.

The report sets forth the history of the partisan-spoils system in Great Britain, and of the rise and fall of the parliamentary patronage, and of official interference with the freedom of elections. It shows that after long trials of various kinds of examinations, those which are competitive and open on equal terms to all, and which are carried on under the superintendence of a single commission, have, with great advantage, been established as conditions of admission to almost every official place in the subordinate administration of that country and of British India. The completion of the report, owing to the extent of the labor involved in its preparation, and the omission of Congress to make any provision either for the compensation or the expenses of the Commission, has been postponed until the present time. It is herewith transmitted to Congress.

While the reform measures of another Government are of no authority for us, they are entitled to influence, to the extent to which their intrinsic wisdom, and their adaptation to our institutions and social life, may commend them to our consideration.

The views I have heretofore expressed concerning the defects and abuses in our civil administration remain unchanged, except in so far as an enlarged experience has deepened my sense of the duty both of officers and of the people themselves to co-operate for their removal. The grave evils and perils of a partisan-spoils system of appointment to office and of office tenure, are now generally recognized. In the resolutions of the great parties, in the reports of Departments, in the debates and proceedings of Congress, in the messages of Executives, the gravity of these evils has been pointed out and the need of their reform has been admitted.

To command the necessary support, every measure of reform must be based on common right and justice, and must be compatible with the healthy existence of great parties, which are inevitable and essential in a free State.

When the people have approved a policy at a National election, confidence on the part of the officers they have selected, and of the advisers who, in accordance with our political institutions, should be consulted, in the policy which it is their duty to carry into effect, is indispensable. It is eminently proper that they should explain it before the people, as well as illustrate its spirit in the performance of their official duties.

Very different considerations apply to the greater number of those who fill the subordinate places in the civil service. Their responsibility is to their superiors in official position. It is their duty to obey the legal instructions of those upon whom that authority is devolved, and their best public service consists in the discharge of their functions irrespective of partisan politics. Their duties are the same, whatever party is in power and whatever policy prevails. As a consequence, it follows that their tenure of office should not depend on the prevalence of any policy or the supremacy of any party, but should be determined by their capacity to serve the people most usefully, quite irrespective of partisan interests. The same considerations that should govern the tenure should also prevail in the appointment, discipline, and removal of these subordinates. The authority of appointment and removal is not a perquisite which may be used to aid a friend or reward a partisan, but is a trust to be exercised in the public interest, under all the sanctions which attend the obligation to apply the public funds only for public purposes.

Every citizen has an equal right to the honor and profit of entering the public service of his country. The only just ground of discrimination is the measure of character and capacity he has to make that service most useful to the people. Except in cases where, upon just and recognized principles, as upon the theory of pensions, offices and promotions are bestowed as rewards for past services, their bestowal upon any theory which disregards personal merit is an act of injustice to the citizen, as well as a breach of that trust subject to which the appointing power is held.

In the light of these principles, it becomes of great importance to provide just and adequate means, especially for every department, and large administrative office, where personal discrimination on the part of its head it not practicable, for ascertaining those qualifications to which appointments and removals should have reference. To fail to provide such means is not only to deny the opportunity of ascertaining the facts upon which the most righteous claim to office depends, but, of necessity, to discourage all worthy aspirants by handing over appointments and removals to mere influence and favoritism. If it is the right of the worthiest claimant to gain the appointment, and the interest of the people to bestow it upon him, it would seem clear that a wise and just method of ascertaining personal fitness for office must be an important and permanent function of every just and wise government. It has long since become impossible, in the great offices, for those having the duty of nomination and appointment to personally examine into the individual qualifications of more than a small proportion of those seeking office, and, with the enlargement of the civil service, that proportion must continue to become less.

In the earlier years of the Government, the subordinate offices were so few in number that it was quite easy for those making appointment and promotions to personally ascertain the merits of candidates. Party managers and methods had not then become powerful agencies of coercion, hostile to the free and just exercise of the appointing power.

A large and responsible part of the duty of restoring the civil service to the desired purity and efficiency rests upon the President, and it is my purpose to do what is within my power to advance such prudent and gradual measures of reform as will most surely and rapidly bring about that radical change of system essential to make our administrative methods satisfactory to a free and intelligent people. By a proper exercise of authority, it is in the power of the Executive to do much to promote such a reform. But it cannot be too clearly understood that nothing adequate can be accomplished without co-operation on the part of Congress and considerate and intelligent support among the people. Reforms which challenge the generally accepted theories of parties, and demand changes in the methods of departments, are not the work of a day. Their permanent foundations must be laid in sound principles, and in an experience which demonstrates their wisdom and exposes the errors of their adversaries. Every worthy officer desires to make his official action a gain and an honor to his country, but the people themselves, far more than their officers in public station, are interested in a pure, economical, and vigorous administration.

By laws enacted in 1853 and 1855, and now in substance incorporated in the Revised Statutes, the practice of arbitrary appointments to the several subordinate grades in the great Departments was condemned, and examinations, as to capacity, to be conducted by departmental boards of examiners, were provided for and made conditions of admission to the public service. These statutes are a decision by Congress that examinations of some sort, as to attainments and capacity, are essential to the well-being of the public service. The important questions since the enactment of these laws have been as to the character of these examinations, and whether official favor and partisan influence, or common right and merit, were to control the access to the examinations. In practice, these examinations have not always been open to worthy persons generally, who might wish to be examined. Official favoritism and partisan influence, as a rule, appear to have designated those who alone were permitted to go before the examining-boards, subjecting even the examiners to a pressure from the friends of the candidates very difficult to resist. As a consequence, the standard of admission fell below that which the public interest demanded. It was also almost inevitable that a system which provided for various separate boards of examiners, with no common supervision or uniform method of procedure, should result in confusion, inconsistency, and inadequate tests of capacity highly detrimental to the public interests. A further and more radical change was obviously required.

In the annual message of December, 1870, my predecessor declared that "there is no duty which so much embarrasses the Executive and heads of Departments as that of appointments; nor is there any such arduous and thankless labor imposed on Senators and Representatives as that of finding places for constituents. The present system does not secure the best men, and often not even fit men for the public places. The elevation and purification of the civil service of the Government will be hailed with approval by the whole people of the United States." Congress accordingly passed the act, approved March 3, 1871, "to regulate the civil service of the United States and promote the efficiency thereof," giving the necessary authority to the Executive to inaugurate a civil-service reform.

Acting under this statute, which was interpreted as intended to secure a system of just and effectual examinations under uniform supervision, a number of eminently competent persons were selected for the purpose, who entered with zeal upon the discharge of their duties, prepared, with an intelligent appreciation of the requirements of the service, the regulations contemplated, and took charge of the examinations, and who, in their capacity as a board, have been known as the "Civil-Service Commission." Congress for two years appropriated the money needed for the compensation and for the expense of carrying on the work of the Commission.

It appears from the report of the Commission, submitted to the President in April, 1874, that examinations had been held in various sections of the country, and that an appropriation of about $25,000 would be required to meet the annual expenses, including salaries, involved in discharging the duties of the Commission. The report was transmitted to Congress by special message of April 18, 1874, with the following favorable comment upon the labors of the Commission: "If sustained by Congress, I have no doubt the rules can, after the experience gained, be so improved and enforced as to still more materially benefit the public service and relieve the Executive, Members of Congress, and the heads of Departments, from influences prejudicial to good administration. The rules, as they have hitherto been enforced, have resulted beneficially, as is shown by the opinions of the members of the Cabinet and their subordinates in the Departments, and in that opinion I concur." And in the annual message of December of the same year similar views are expressed, and an appropriation for continuing the work of the Commission again advised.

The appropriation was not made, and, as a consequence, the active work of the Commission was suspended, leaving the Commission itself still in existence. Without the means, therefore, of causing qualifications to be tested in any systematic manner, or of securing for the public service the advantages of competition upon any extensive plan, I recommended in my annual message of December, 1877, the making of an appropriation for the resumption of the work of the Commission.

In the meantime, however, competitive examinations under many embarrassments have been conducted within limited spheres in the Executive Departments in Washington, and in a number of the custom-houses and post offices of the principal cities of the country, with a view to further test their effects, and, in every instance, they have been found to be as salutary as they are stated to have been under the administration of my predecessor. I think the economy, purity, and efficiency of the public service would be greatly promoted by their systematic introduction, wherever practicable, throughout the entire civil service of the Government, together with ample provision for their general supervision, in order to secure consistency and uniform justice.

Reports from the Secretary of the Interior, from the Postmaster-General, from the postmaster in the city of New York, where such examinations have been sometime on trial, and also from the collector of the port, the naval officer, and the surveyor in that city, and from the postmasters and collectors in several of the other large cities, show that the competitive system, where applied, has, in various ways, contributed to improve the public service.

The reports show that the results have been salutary in a marked degree, and that the general application of similar rules cannot fail to be of decided benefit to the service.

The reports of the Government officers in the city of New York especially, bear decided testimony to the utility of open competitive examinations in their respective offices, showing that "these examinations, and the excellent qualifications of those admitted to the service through them, have had a marked incidental effect upon the persons previously in the service, and particularly upon those aspiring to promotion. There has been, on the part of these latter, an increased interest in the work, and a desire to extend acquaintance with it beyond the particular desk occupied, and thus the *morale* of the entire force has been raised. * * * The examinations have been attended by many citizens who have had an opportunity to thoroughly investigate the scope and character of the tests and the method of determining the results, and those visitors have, without exception, approved the methods employed, and several of them have publicly attested their favorable opinion."

Upon such considerations, I deem it my duty to renew the recommendation contained in my annual message of December, 1877, requesting Congress to make the necessary appropriation for the resumption of the work of the Civil-Service Commission. Economy will be promoted by authorizing a moderate compensation to persons in the public service who may perform extra labor upon or under the Commission, as the Executive may direct.

I am convinced that if a just and adequate test of merit is enforced for admission to the public service and in making promotions, such abuses as removals without good cause and partisan and official interference with the proper exercise of the appointing power, will in large measure disappear.

There are other administrative abuses to which the attention of Congress should be asked in this connection. Mere partisan appointments, and the constant peril of removal without cause, very naturally lead to an absorbing and mischievous political activity, on the part of those thus appointed, which not only interferes with the due discharge of official duty, but is incompatible with the freedom of elections. Not without warrant, in the views of several of my predecessors in the Presidential office, and directly within the law of 1871, already cited, I endeavored by regulation, made on the 22d day of June, 1877, to put some reasonable limits to such abuses. It may not be easy, and it may never perhaps be necessary, to define with precision the proper limit of political action on the part of Federal officers. But while their right to hold and freely express their opinions cannot be questioned, it is very plain that they should neither be allowed to devote to other subjects the time needed for the proper discharge of their official duties, nor to use the authority of their office to enforce their own opinions, or to coerce the political action of those who hold different opinions.

Reasons of justice and public policy, quite analogous to those which forbid the use of official power for the oppression of the private citizen, impose upon the Government the duty of protecting its officers and agents from arbitrary exactions. In whatever aspect considered, the practice of making levies, for party purposes, upon the salaries of officers is highly demoralizing to the public service and discreditable to the country. Though an officer should be as free as any other citizen to give his own money in aid of his opinions or his party, he should also be as free as any other citizen to refuse to make such gifts. If salaries are but a fair compensation for the time and labor of the officer, it is gross injustice to levy a tax upon them. If they are made excessive in order that they may bear the tax, the excess is an indirect robbery of the public funds.

I recommend, therefore, such a revision and extension of present statutes as shall secure to those in every grade of official life or public employment the protection with which a great and enlightened Nation should guard those who are faithful in its service.

Our relations with foreign countries have continued peaceful.

With Great Britain there are still unsettled questions, growing out of the local laws of the maritime provinces and the action of provincial authorities, deemed to be in derogation of rights secured by treaty to American fishermen. The United States Minister in London has been instructed to present a demand for $105,305.02, in view of the damages received by American citizens at Fortune Bay on the 6th day of January, 1878. The subject has been taken into consideration by the British Government, and an early reply is anticipated.

Upon the completion of the necessary preliminary examinations, the subject of our participation in the provincial fisheries, as regulated by treaty, will at once be brought to the attention of the British Government with a view to an early and permanent settlement of the whole question, which was only temporarily adjusted by the Treaty of Washington.

Efforts have been made to obtain the removal of restrictions found injurious to the exportation of cattle to the United Kingdom.

Some correspondence has also occurred with regard to the rescue and saving of life and property upon the lakes, which has resulted in important modifications of the previous regulations of the Dominion Government on the subject, in the interest of humanity and commerce.

In accordance with the joint resolution of the last session of Congress, commissioners were appointed to represent the United States at the two International Exhibitions in Australia, one of which is now in progress at Sydney, and the other to be held next year at Melbourne. A desire has been expressed by our merchants and manufacturers interested in the important and growing trade with Australia, that an increased provision should be made by Congress for the representation of our industries at the Melbourne Exhibition of next year, and the subject is respectfully submitted to your favorable consideration.

The assent of the Government has been given to the landing, on the coast of Massachusetts, of a new and independent transatlantic cable between France, by way of the French island of St. Pierre, and this country, subject to any future legislation of Congress on the subject. The conditions imposed, before allowing this connection with our shores to be established, are such as to secure its competition with any existing or future lines of marine cable, and preclude amalgamation therewith, to provide for entire equality of rights to our Government and people with those of France in the use of the cable, and prevent any exclusive possession of the privilege as accorded by France to the disadvantage of any future cable communication between France and the United States which may be projected and accomplished by our citizens. An important reduction of the present rates of cable communication with Europe, felt to be too burdensome to the interests of our commerce, must necessarily flow from the establishment of this competing line.

The attention of Congress was drawn to the propriety of some general regulation by Congress of the whole subject of transmarine cables by my predecessor in his message of December 7, 1875, and I respectfully submit to your consideration the importance of Congressional action in this matter.

The questions of grave importance with Spain, growing out of the incidents of the Cuban insurrection, have been, for the most part, happily and honorably settled. It may reasonably be anticipated that the Commission now sitting in Washington, for the decision of private cases in this connection, will soon be able to bring its labors to a conclusion.

The long-standing question of East Florida claims has lately been renewed as a subject of correspondence, and may possibly require Congressional action for its final disposition.

A treaty with the Netherlands, with respect to consular rights and privileges, similar to those with other Powers, has been signed and ratified, and the ratifications were exchanged on the 31st of July last. Negotiations for extradition treaties with the Netherlands and with Denmark are now in progress.

Some questions with Switzerland, in regard to pauper and convict emigrants, have arisen, but it is not doubted that they will be arranged upon a just and satisfactory basis. A question has also occurred with respect to an asserted claim by Swiss municipal authorities to exercise tutelage over persons and property of Swiss citizens naturalized in this country. It is possible this may require adjustment by treaty.

With the German Empire frequent questions arise in connection with the subjects of naturalization and expatriation, but the Imperial Government has constantly manifested a desire to strictly maintain and comply with all treaty stipulations in regard to them.

In consequence of the omission of Congress to provide for a diplomatic representative at Athens, the legation to Greece has been withdrawn. There is now no channel of diplomatic communication between the two countries, and the expediency of providing for one, in some form, is submitted to Congress.

Relations with Austria, Russia, Italy, Portugal, Turkey, and Belgium continue amicable, and marked by no incident of especial importance.

A change of the personal head of the Government of Egypt has taken place. No change, however, has occurred in the relations between Egypt and the United States. The action of the Egyptian Government in presenting to the city of New York one of the ancient obelisks, which possess such historic interest, is highly appreciated as a generous mark of international regard. If prosperity should attend the enterprise of its transportation across the Atlantic, its erection in a conspicuous position in the chief commercial city of the Nation will soon be accomplished.

The treaty recently made between Japan and the United States in regard to the revision of former commercial treaties, it is now believed, will be followed by similar action on the part of other treaty Powers. The attention of Congress is again invited to the subject of the indemnity funds received some years since from Japan and China, which, with their accumulated interest, now amount to considerable sums. If any part of these funds is justly due to American citizens, they should receive it promptly, and whatever may have been received by this Government in excess of strictly just demands should, in some form, be returned to the Nations to whom it equitably belongs.

The Government of China has signified its willingness to consider the question of the emigration of its subjects to the United States with a dispassionate fairness, and to co-operate in such measures as may tend to prevent injurious consequences to the United States. The negotiations are still proceeding, and will be pressed with diligence.

A question having arisen between China and Japan about the Lew Chew Islands, the United States Government has taken measures to inform those Powers of its readiness to extend its good offices for the maintenance of peace, if they shall mutually deem it desirable, and find it practicable to avail themselves of the proffer.

It is a gratification to be able to announce that, through the judicious and energetic action of the military commanders of the two Nations on each side of the Rio Grande, under the instructions of their respective Governments, raids and depredations have greatly decreased, and, in the localities where formerly most destructive, have now almost wholly ceased. In view of this result, I entertain a confident expectation that the prevalence of quiet on the border will soon become so assured as to justify a modification of the present orders to our military commanders as to crossing the border, without encouraging such disturbances as would endanger the peace of the two countries.

The third instalment of the award against Mexico under the Claims Commission of July 4, 1868, was duly paid, and has been put in course of distribution in pursuance of the act of Congress providing for the same. This satisfactory situation between the two countries leads me to anticipate an expansion of our trade with Mexico, and an increased contribution of capital and industry by our people to the development of the great resources of that country. I earnestly commend to the wisdom of Congress the provision of suitable legislation looking to this result.

Diplomatic intercourse with Colombia is again fully restored by the arrival of a minister from that country to the United States. This is especially fortunate in view of the fact that the question of an interoceanic canal has recently assumed a new and important aspect, and is now under discussion with the Central American countries through whose territory the canal, by the Nicaragua route, would have to pass. It is trusted that enlightened statesmanship on their part will see that the early prosecution of such a work will largely enure to the benefit, not only of their own citizens and those of the United States, but of the commerce of the civilized world. It is not doubted that should the work be undertaken under the protective auspices of the United States, and upon satisfactory concessions for the right of way, and its security, by the Central American governments, the capital for its completion would be readily furnished from this country and Europe, which might, failing such guarantees, prove inaccessible.

Diplomatic relations with Chili have also been strengthened by the reception of a minister from that country.

The war between Peru, Bolivia, and Chili still continues. The United States have not deemed it proper to interpose in the matter further than to convey to all the Governments concerned the assurance that the friendly offices of the Government of the United States for the restoration of peace upon an honorable basis will be extended, in case the belligerents shall exhibit a readiness to accept them.

Cordial relations continue with Brazil and the Argentine Republic, and trade with those countries is improving. A provision for regular and more frequent mail communication, in our own ships, between the ports of this country and the Nations of South America seems to me to deserve the attention of Congress, as an essential precursor of an enlargement of our commerce with them, and an extension of our carrying trade.

A recent revolution in Venezuela has been followed by the establishment of a provisional government. The Government has not yet been formally recognized, and it is deemed desirable to await the proposed action of the people, which is expected to give it the sanction of constitutional forms.

A naval vessel has been sent to the Samoan Islands to make surveys and take possession of the privileges ceded to the United States by Samoa in the harbor of Pago Pago. A coaling-station is to be established there, which will be convenient and useful to United States vessels.

The subject of opening diplomatic relations with Roumania and Servia, now become independent sovereignties, is at present under consideration, and is the subject of diplomatic correspondence.

There is a gratifying increase of trade with nearly all European and American countries, and it is believed that with judicious action in regard to its development it can and will be still more enhanced, and that American products and manufactures will find new and expanding markets. The reports of diplomatic and consular officers upon this subject, under the system now adopted, have resulted in obtaining much valuable information, which has been and will continue to be laid before Congress and the public from time to time.

The third article of the treaty with Russia, of March 30, 1867, by which Alaska was ceded to the United States, provides that the inhabitants of the ceded territory, with the exception of the uncivilized native tribes, shall be admitted to the enjoyment of all the rights of citizens of the United States, and shall be maintained and protected in the free enjoyment of their liberty, property, and religion. The uncivilized tribes are subject to such laws and regulations as the United States may from time to time adopt in regard to the aboriginal tribes of that country.

Both the obligations of this treaty and the necessities of the people require that some organized form of government over the Territory of Alaska be adopted.

There appears to be no law for the arrest of persons charged with common-law offences, such as assault, robbery, and murder, and no magistrate authorized to issue or execute process in such cases. Serious difficulties have already arisen from offences of this character, not only among the original inhabitants, but among citizens of the United States and other countries, who have engaged in mining, fishing, and other business operations within the Territory. A bill authorizing the appointment of justices of the peace and constables, and the arrest and detention of persons charged with criminal offences, and providing for an appeal to United States courts for the district of Oregon, in suitable cases, will, at a proper time, be submitted to Congress.

The attention of Congress is called to the annual report of the Secretary of the Treasury on the condition of the public finances.

The ordinary revenues from all sources for the fiscal year ended June 30, 1879, were $273,827,184.46; the ordinary expenditures for the same period were $266,947,883.53; leaving a surplus revenue for the year of $6,879,300.93.

The receipts for the present fiscal year, ended June 30, 1880, actual and estimated, are as follows: Actual receipts for the first quarter commencing July 1, 1879, $79,843,663.61; estimated receipts for the remaining three-quarters of the year, $208,156,336.39; total receipts for the current fiscal year, actual and estimated, $288,000,000.

The expenditures for the same period will be, actual and estimated, as follows: For the quarter commencing July 1, 1879, actual expenditures, $91,683,385.10; and for the remaining three-quarters of the year the expenditures are estimated at $172,315,614.90—making the total expenditures $264,000,000, and leaving an estimated surplus revenue for the year ending June 30, 1880, of $24,000,000. The total receipts during the next fiscal year ending June 30, 1881, estimated according to existing laws, will be $288,000,000; and the estimated ordinary expenditures for the same period will be $278,097,364.39; leaving a surplus of $9,902,635.61 for that year.

The large amount expended for arrears of pensions during the last and the present fiscal year, amounting to $21,747,249.60, has prevented the application of the full amount required by law to the sinking-fund for the current year; but these arrears having been substantially paid, it is believed that the sinking-fund can hereafter be maintained without any change of existing law.

The Secretary of War reports that the War-Department estimates for the fiscal year ending June 30, 1881, are $40,380,428.93, the same being for a less sum of money than any annual estimate rendered to Congress from that Department during a period of at least twelve years.

He concurs with the General of the Army in recommending such legislation as will authorize the enlistment of the full number of twenty-five thousand men for the line of the Army, exclusive of the three thousand four hundred and sixty-three men required for detached duty, and therefore not available for service in the field.

He also recommends that Congress be asked to provide by law for the disposition of a large number of abandoned military posts and reservations, which, though very valuable in themselves, have been rendered useless for military purposes by the advance of civilization and settlement.

He unites with the Quartermaster-General in recommending that an appropriation be made for the construction of a cheap and perfectly fire-proof building for the safe storage of a vast amount of money accounts, vouchers, claims, and other valuable records now in the Quartermaster-General's office, and exposed to great risk of total destruction by fire.

He also recommends, in conformity with the views of the Judge-Advocate General, some declaratory legislation in reference to the military statute of limitations as applied to the crime of desertion.

In these several recommendations I concur.

The Secretary of War further reports, that the work for the improvement of the South Pass of the Mississippi river, under contract with Mr. James B. Eads, made in pursuance of an act of Congress, has been prosecuted during the past year, with a greater measure of success in the attainment of results than during any previous year. The channel through the South Pass, which, at the beginning of operations in June, 1875, had a depth of only seven and one-half feet of water, had, on the 8th of July, 1879, a minimum depth of twenty-six feet, having a width of not less than two hundred feet, and a central depth of thirty feet. Payments have been made in accordance with the statute, as the work progressed, amounting in the aggregate to $4,250,000; and further payments will become due, as provided by the statute, in the event of success in maintaining the channel now secured.

The reports of the General of the Army and of his subordinates, present a full and detailed account of the military operations for the suppression of hostilities among the Indians of the Ute and Apache tribes, and praise is justly awarded to the officers and troops engaged, for promptness, skill, and courage displayed.

The past year has been one of almost unbroken peace and quiet on the Mexican frontier, and there is reason to believe that the efforts of this Government and of Mexico, to maintain order in that region, will prove permanently successful.

This Department was enabled during the past year to find temporary though crowded accommodations, and a safe depository for a portion of its records, in the completed east wing of the building, designed for the State, War, and Navy Departments. The construction of the north wing of the building, a part of the structure intended for the use of the War Department, is being carried forward with all possible dispatch, and the work should receive from Congress such liberal appropriations as will secure its speedy completion.

The report of the Secretary of the Navy shows continued improvement in that branch of the service during the last fiscal year. Extensive repairs have been made upon vessels, and two new ships have been completed and made ready for sea.

The total expenditures of the year ending June 30, 1879, including specific appropriations not estimated for by the Department, were $13,555,710.09. The expenses chargeable to the year, after deducting the amount of these specific appropriations, were $13,343,317.79; but this is subject to a reduction of $283,725.99, that amount having been drawn upon warrants, but not paid out during the year. The amount of appropriations applicable to the last fiscal year was $14,538,646.17. There was, therefore, a balance of $1,479,054.37 remaining unexpended, and to the credit of the Department, on June 30, 1879. The estimates for the fiscal year ending June 30, 1881, are $14,864,147.95, which exceeds the appropriations for the present fiscal year $361,897.28. The reason for this increase is explained in the Secretary's report. The appropriations available for the present fiscal year are $14,502,250.67, which will, in the opinion of the Secretary, answer all the ordinary demands of the service. The amount drawn from the Treasury from July 1 to November 1, 1879, was $5,770,404.12, of which $1,095,440.33 has been refunded, leaving as the expenditure for that period $4,674,963.79. If the expenditures of the remaining two-thirds of the year do not exceed the proportion for these four months, there will remain unexpended, at the end of the year, $477,359.30 of the current appropriations. The report of the Secretary shows the gratifying fact that among all the disbursing officers of the pay corps of the Navy there is not one who is a defaulter to the extent of a single dollar. I unite with him in recommending the removal of the Observatory to a more healthful location. That institution reflects credit upon the Nation, and has obtained the approbation of scientific men in all parts of the world. Its removal from its present location would not only be conducive to the health of its officers and professors, but would greatly increase its usefulness.

The appropriation for judicial expenses, which has heretofore been made for the Department of Justice, in gross, was subdivided at the last session of Congress, and no appropriation whatever was made for the payment of the fees of marshals and their deputies, either in the service of process or for the discharge of other duties; and, since June 30, these officers have continued the performance of their duties without compensation from the Government, taking upon themselves the necessary incidental outlays, as well as rendering their own services. In only a few unavoidable instances has the proper execution of the process of the United States failed by reason of the absence of the requisite appropriation. This course of official conduct on the part of these officers, highly creditable to their fidelity, was advised by the Attorney-General, who informed them, however, that they would necessarily have to rely for their compensation upon the prospect of future legislation by Congress. I therefore especially recommend that immediate appropriation be made by Congress for this purpose.

The act making the principal appropriation for the Department of Justice at previous sessions has uniformly contained the following clause: "And for defraying the expenses which may be incurred in the enforcement of the act approved February 28, 1870, entitled 'An act to amend an act approved May 30, 1870, entitled 'An act to enforce the right of citizens of the United States to vote in the several States of the United States, and for other purposes,' or any acts amendatory thereof or supplementary thereto.' "

No appropriation was made for this purpose for the current year. As no general election for members of Congress occurred, the omission was a matter of little practical importance. Such election will, however, take place during the ensuing year, and the appropriation made for the pay of marshals and deputies should be sufficient to embrace compensation for the services they may be required to perform at such elections.

The business of the Supreme Court is, at present, largely in arrears. It cannot be expected that more causes can be decided than are now disposed of in its annual session, or that by any assiduity the distinguished magistrates who compose the Court can accomplish more than is now done. In the courts of many of the circuits, also, the business has increased to such an extent that the delay of justice will call the attention of Congress to an appropriate remedy. It is believed that all is done in each circuit which can fairly be expected from its judicial force. The evils arising from delay are less heavily felt by the United States than by private suitors, as its causes are advanced by the courts when it is seen that they involve the discussion of questions of a public character.

The remedy suggested by the Attorney-General is the appointment of additional circuit judges, and the creation of an intermediate court of errors and appeals, which shall relieve the Supreme Court of a part of its jurisdiction, while a larger force is also obtained for the performance of circuit duties.

I commend this suggestion to the consideration of Congress. It would seem to afford a complete remedy, and would involve, if ten additional circuit judges are appointed, an expenditure, at the present rate of salaries, of not more than sixty thousand dollars a year, which would certainly be small in comparison with the objects to be attained.

The report of the Postmaster-General bears testimony to the general revival of business throughout the country. The receipts of the Post-Office Department for the fiscal year ended June 30, 1879, were $30,041,982.86, being $764,465.91 more than the revenues of the preceding year. The amount realized from the sale of postage-stamps, stamped envelopes, and postal-cards was $764,465.91 more than in the preceding year, and $2,387,559.23 more than in 1877. The expenditures of the Department were $33,449,899.45, of which the sum of $376,461.63 was paid on liabilities incurred in preceding years.

The expenditures during the year were $801,209.77 less than in the preceding year. This reduction is to be attributed mainly to the operation of the law passed June 17, 1878, changing the compensation of postmasters from a commission on the value of stamps sold to a commission on stamps cancelled.

The amount drawn from the Treasury on appropriations, in addition to the revenues of the Department, was $3,031,454.96, being $2,276,197.86 less than in the preceding year.

The expenditures for the fiscal year ending June 30, 1881, are estimated at $39,920,900, and the receipts from all sources at $32,210,000, leaving a deficiency to be appropriated for, out of the Treasury, of $7,710,900.

The relations of the Department with railroad companies have been harmonized, notwithstanding the general reduction by Congress of their compensation, by the appropriation for special facilities, and the railway post-office lines have been greatly extended, especially in the Southern States. The interests of the railway-mail service and of the public would be greatly promoted, and the expenditures could be more readily controlled by the classification of the employés of the railway-mail service as recommended by the Postmaster-General, the appropriation for salaries, with respect to which the maximum limit is already fixed by law, to be made in gross.

The Postmaster-General recommends an amendment of the law regulating the increase of compensation for increased service and increased speed on star routes, so as to enable him to advertise for proposals for such increased service and speed. He also suggests the advantages to accrue to the commerce of the country from the enactment of a general law authorizing contracts with American-built steamers, carrying the American flag, for transporting the mail between ports of the United States and ports of the West Indies and South America, at a fixed maximum price per mile, the amount to be expended being regulated by annual appropriations, in like manner with the amount paid for the domestic star service.

The arrangement made by the Postmaster-General and the Secretary of the Treasury for the collection of duty upon books received in the mail from foreign countries has proved so satisfactory in its practical operation that the recommendation is now made that Congress shall extend the provisions of the act of March 3, 1879, under which this arrangement was made, so as to apply to all other dutiable articles received in the mails from foreign countries.

The reports of the Secretary of the Interior and of the Commissioner of Indian Affairs, setting forth the present state of our relations with the Indian tribes on our territory, the measures taken to advance their civilization and prosperity, and the progress already achieved by them, will be found of more than ordinary interest. The general conduct of our Indian population has been so satisfactory that the occurrence of two disturbances, which resulted in bloodshed and destruction of property, is all the more to be lamented.

The history of the outbreak on the White River Ute reservation, in Western Colorado, has become so familiar by elaborate reports in the public press that its remarkable incidents need not be stated here in detail. It is expected that the settlement of this difficulty will lead to such arrangements as will prevent further hostile contact between the Indians and the border settlements in Western Colorado.

The other disturbance occurred at the Mescalero agency, in New Mexico, where Victoria, the head of a small band of marauders, after committing many atrocities, being vigorously chased by a military force, made his way across the Mexican border and is now on foreign soil.

While these occurrences, in which a comparatively small number of Indians were engaged, are most deplorable, a vast majority of our Indian population have fully justified the expectations of those who believe that by humane and peaceful influences the Indians can be led to abandon the habits of savage life and to develop a capacity for useful and civilized occupations. What they have already accomplished in the pursuit of agricultural and mechanical work, the remarkable success which has attended the experiment of employing as freighters a class of Indians hitherto counted among the wildest and most intractable, and the general and urgent desire expressed by them for the education of their children, may be taken as sufficient proof that they will be found capable of accomplishing much more if they continue to be wisely and fairly guided. The "Indian policy" sketched in the report of the Secretary of the Interior, the object of which is to make liberal provision for the education of Indian youth, to settle the Indians upon farm-lots in severalty, to give them title in fee to their farms, inalienable for a certain number of years, and when their wants are thus provided for, to dispose by sale of the lands on their reservations not occupied and used by them, a fund to be formed out of the proceeds for the benefit of the Indians, which will gradually relieve the Government of the expenses now provided for by annual appropriations, must commend itself as just and beneficial to the Indians, and as also calculated to remove those obstructions which the existence of large reservations presents to the settlement and development of the country. I, therefore, earnestly recommend the enactment of a law enabling the Government to give Indians a title in fee, inalienable for twenty-five years, to the farm-lands assigned to them by allotment. I also repeat the recommendation made in my first annual message, that a law be passed admitting Indians who can give satisfactory proof of having by their own labor, supported their families for a number of years, and who are willing to detach themselves from their tribal relations, to the benefit of the homestead act, and to grant them patents containing the same provision of inalienability for a certain period.

The experiment of sending a number of Indian children, of both sexes, to the Hampton Normal and Agricultural Institute, in Virginia, to receive an elementary English education and practical instruction in farming and other useful industries, has led to results so promising, that it was thought expedient to turn over the cavalry barracks at Carlisle, in Pennsylvania, to the Interior Department for the establishment of an Indian school on a larger scale. This school has now one hundred and fifty-eight pupils, selected from various tribes, and is in full operation. Arrangements are also made for the education of a number of Indian boys and girls belonging to tribes on the Pacific slope, in a similar manner, at Forest Grove, in Oregon. These institutions will commend themselves to the liberality of Congress and to the philanthropic munificence of the American people.

Last spring, information was received of the organization of an extensive movement in the Western States, the object of which was the occupation by unauthorized persons of certain lands in the Indian Territory ceded by the Cherokees to the Government for the purpose of settlement by other Indian tribes.

On the 29th of April, I issued a proclamation warning all persons against participation in such an attempt, and, by the co-operation of a military force, the invasion was promptly checked. It is my purpose to protect the rights of the Indian inhabitants of that Territory to the full extent of the Executive power. But it would be unwise to ignore the fact that a Territory so large and so fertile, with a population so sparse and with so great a wealth of unused resources, will be found more exposed to the repetition of such attempts as happened this year when the surrounding States are more densely settled and the westward movement of our population looks still more eagerly for fresh lands to occupy. Under such circumstances, the difficulty of maintaining the Indian Territory in its present state will greatly increase, and the Indian tribes inhabiting it would do well to prepare for such a contingency. I, therefore, fully approve of the advice given to them by the Secretary of the Interior on a recent occasion, to divide among themselves in severalty as large a quantity of their lands as they can cultivate, to acquire individual title in fee, instead of their present tribal ownership in common, and to consider in what manner the balance of their lands may be disposed of by the Government for their benefit. By adopting such a policy they would more certainly secure for themselves the value of their possessions, and at the same time promote their progress in civilization and prosperity, than by endeavoring to perpetuate the present state of things in the Territory.

The question whether a change in the control of the Indian service should be made was, in the Forty-fifth Congress, referred to a joint committee of both Houses for inquiry and report. In my last annual message I expressed the hope that the decision of that question, then in prospect, "would arrest further agitation of this subject, such agitation being apt to produce a disturbing effect upon the service as well as the Indians themselves." Since then, the committee having reported, the question has been decided in the negative by a vote in the House of Representatives.

For the reasons here stated, and in view of the fact that further uncertainty on this point will be calculated to obstruct other much-needed legislation, to weaken the discipline of the service, and to unsettle salutary measures now in progress for the government and improvement of the Indians, I respectfully recommend that the decision arrived at by Congress at its last session be permittted to stand.

The efforts made by the Department of the Interior to arrest the depredations on the timber-lands of the United States have been continued, and have met with considerable success. A large number of cases of trespass have been prosecuted in the courts of the United States; others have been settled, the trespassers offering to make payment to the Government for the value of the timber taken by them. The proceeds of these prosecutions and settlements turned into the Treasury far exceed in amount the sums appropriated by Congress for this purpose. A more important result, however, consists in the fact that the destruction of our public forests by depredation, although such cases still occur, has been greatly reduced in extent, and it is probable that if the present policy is vigorously pursued, and sufficient provision to that end is made by Congress, such trespasses, at least those on a large scale, can be entirely suppressed, except in the Territories where timber for the daily requirements of the population cannot, under the present state of the law, be otherwise obtained. I, therefore, earnestly invite the attention of Congress to the recommendation made by the Secretary of the Interior, that a law be enacted enabling the Government to sell timber from the public lands without conveying the fee, where such lands are principally valuable for the timber thereon, such sales to be so regulated as to conform to domestic wants and business requirements, while at the same time guarding against a sweeping destruction of the forests. The enactment of such a law appears to become a more pressing necessity every day.

My recommendations in former messages are renewed in favor of enlarging the facilities of the Department of Agriculture. Agriculture is the leading interest and the permanent industry of our people. It is to the abundance of agricultural production, as compared with our home consumption, and the largely-increased and highly-profitable market abroad which we have enjoyed in recent years, that we are mainly indebted for our present prosperity as a people. We must look for its continued maintenance to the same substantial resource. There is no branch of industry in which labor, directed by scientific knowledge, yields such increased production in comparison with unskilled labor, and no branch of the public service to which the encouragement of liberal appropriations can be more appropriately extended. The omission to render such aid is not a wise economy; but, on the contrary, undoubtedly results in losses of immense sums annually that might be saved through well-directed efforts by the Government to promote this vital interest.

The results already accomplished with the very limited means heretofore placed at the command of the Department of Agriculture are an earnest of what may be expected with increased appropriations for the several purposes indicated in the report of the Commissioner, with a view to placing the Department upon a footing which will enable it to prosecute more effectively the objects for which it is established.

Appropriations are needed for a more complete laboratory, for the establishment of a veterinary division, and a division of forestry, and for an increase of force.

The requirements for these and other purposes, indicated in the report of the Commissioner under the head of the immediate necessities of the Department, will not involve any expenditure of money that the country cannot with propriety now undertake in the interests of agriculture.

It is gratifying to learn from the Bureau of Education the extent to which educational privileges throughout the United States have been advanced during the year. No more fundamental responsibility rests upon Congress than that of devising appropriate measures of financial aid to education, supplemental to local action in the States and Territories and in the District of Columbia. The wise forethought of the founders of our Government has not only furnished the basis for the support of the common-school systems of the newer States, but laid the foundations for the maintenance of their universities and colleges of agriculture and the mechanic arts. Measures in accordance with this traditional policy for the further benefit of all these interests, and the extension of the same advantages to every portion of the country, it is hoped, will receive your favorable consideration.

To preserve and perpetuate the National literature should be among the foremost cares of the National legislature. The library gathered at the Capitol still remains unprovided with any suitable accommodations for its rapidly-increasing stores. The magnitude and importance of the collection, increased as it is by the deposits made under the law of copyright, by domestic and foreign exchanges, and by the scientific library of the Smithsonian Institution, call for building accommodations which shall be at once adequate and fire-proof. The location of such a public building, which should provide for the pressing necessities of the present, and for the vast increase of the Nation's books in the future, is a matter which addresses itself to the discretion of Congress. It is earnestly recommended as a measure which should unite all suffrages, and which should no longer be delayed.

The Joint Commission created by the act of Congress of August 2, 1876, for the purpose of supervising and directing the completion of the Washington National Monument, of which Commission the President is a member, has given careful attention to this subject, and already the strengthening of the foundation has so far progressed as to insure the entire success of this part of the work. A massive layer of masonry has been introduced below the original foundation, widening the base, increasing the stability of the structure, and rendering it possible to carry the shaft to completion. It is earnestly recommended that such further appropriations be made for the continued prosecution of the work as may be necessary for the completion of this National Monument at an early day.

In former messages, impressed with the importance of the subject, I have taken occasion to commend to Congress the adoption of a generous policy towards the District of Columbia. The report of the Commissioners of the District, herewith transmitted, contains suggestions and recommendations, to all of which I earnestly invite your careful attention. I ask your early and favorable consideration of the views which they express as to the urgent need of legislation for the reclamation of the marshes of the Potomac and its Eastern Branch, within the limits of the city, and for the repair of the streets of the Capital, heretofore laid with wooden blocks, and now, by decay, rendered almost impassable, and a source of imminent danger to the health of its citizens. The means at the disposal of the Commissioners are wholly inadequate for the accomplishment of these important works, and should be supplemented by timely appropriations from the Federal treasury.

The filling of the flats in front of the city will add to the adjacent lands and parks now owned by the United States a large and valuable domain, sufficient, it is thought, to reimburse its entire cost, and will also, as an incidental result, secure the permanent improvement of the river for the purposes of navigation.

The Constitution having invested Congress with supreme and exclusive jurisdiction over the District of Columbia, its citizens must, of necessity, look to Congress alone for all needful legislation affecting their interests; and, as the territory of this District is the common property of the people of the United States, who, equally with its resident citizens, are interested in the prosperity of their Capital, I cannot doubt that you will be amply sustained by the general voice of the country in any measures you may adopt for this purpose.

I also invite the favorable consideration of Congress to the wants of the public schools of this District, as exhibited in the report of the Commissioners. While the number of pupils is rapidly increasing, no adequate provision exists for a corresponding increase of school accommodation, and the Commissioners are without the means to meet this urgent need. A number of the buildings now used for school purposes are rented, and are, in important particulars, unsuited for the purpose. The cause of popular education in the District of Columbia is surely entitled to the same consideration at the hands of the National Government as in the several States and Territories, to which munificent grants of the public lands have been made for the endowment of schools and universities.

RUTHERFORD B. HAYES.

EXECUTIVE MANSION, *December* 1, 1879.

PROCLAMATION.

INVASION OF INDIAN TERRITORY.

FEBRUARY 12, 1880.

PROCLAMATION.

BY THE PRESIDENT OF THE UNITED STATES OF AMERICA.

A PROCLAMATION.

Whereas it has become known to me that certain evil-disposed persons have, within the territory and jurisdiction of the United States, begun and set on foot preparations for an organized and forcible possession of and settlement upon the lands of what is known as the Indian Territory, west of the State of Arkansas, which Territory is designated, recognized, and described by the treaties and laws of the United States, and by the executive authorities, as Indian Country, and as such is only subject to occupation by Indian tribes, officers of the Indian Department, military posts, and such persons as may be privileged to reside and trade therein under the intercourse laws of the United States;

And whereas those laws provide for the removal of all persons residing and trading therein, without express permission of the Indian Department and agents, and also of all persons whom such agents may deem to be improper persons to reside in the Indian Country;

And whereas, in aid and support of such organized movement, it has been represented that no further action will be taken by the Government to prevent persons from going into said Territory and settling therein, but such representations are wholly without authority:

Now, therefore, for the purpose of properly protecting the interests of the Indian nations and tribes, as well as of the United States, in said Indian Territory, and of duly enforcing the laws governing the same, I, RUTHERFORD B. HAYES, President of the United States, do admonish and warn all such persons so intending or preparing to remove upon said lands, or into said Territory, without permission of the proper agent of the Indian Department, against any attempt to so remove or settle upon any of the lands of said Territory; and I do further warn and notify any and all such persons who may so offend that they will be speedily and immediately removed therefrom by the agent, according to the laws made and provided, and that no efforts will be spared to prevent the invasion of said Territory, rumors spread by evil-disposed persons to the contrary notwithstanding; and if necessary the aid and assistance of the military forces of the United States will be invoked to carry into proper execution the laws of the United States herein referred to.

In testimony whereof I have hereunto set my hand, and caused the seal of the United States to be affixed.

Done at the city of Washington, this twelfth day of February, in the year of our Lord one thousand eight hundred and eighty, and [SEAL.] of the Independence of the United States the one hundred and fourth.

R. B. HAYES.

By the President:
  WM. M. EVARTS,
    Secretary of State.

MESSAGE

TO

THE HOUSE OF REPRESENTATIVES.

MARCH 8, 1880.

MESSAGE.

To the House of Representatives:

I transmit herewith the report of the Secretary of State, and the accompanying papers, in response to the resolution adopted by the House of Representatives on the 10th of February last, requesting "copies of all correspondence in relation to the interoceanic canal which may have passed between this Government and foreign Governments; also between this Government and its own representatives in other countries; and between this Government and individuals interested in, or proposing to be interested in, negotiations for the construction of such a canal; and that he communicate to this House what, if any, treaty obligations with other Governments rest upon this Government."

In further compliance with the resolution of the House, I deem it proper to state briefly my opinion as to the policy of the United States with respect to the construction of an interoceanic canal by any route across the American Isthmus.

The policy of this country is a canal under American control. The United States cannot consent to the surrender of this control to any European Power or to any combination of European Powers. If existing treaties between the United States and other Nations, or if the rights of sovereignty or property of other Nations, stand in the way of this policy—a contingency which is not apprehended—suitable steps should be taken by just and liberal negotiations to promote and establish the American policy on this subject, consistently with the rights of the Nations to be affected by it.

The capital invested by corporations or citizens of other countries in such an enterprise must in a great degree look for protection to one or more of the great Powers of the world. No European Power can intervene for such protection without adopting measures on this continent which the United States would deem wholly inadmissible. If the protection of the United States is relied upon, the United States must exercise such control as will enable this country to protect its national interests and maintain the rights of those whose private capital is embarked in the work.

An interoceanic canal across the American Isthmus will essentially change the geographical relations between the Atlantic and Pacific coasts of the United States, and between the United States and the rest of the world. It will be the great ocean thoroughfare between our Atlantic and our Pacific shores, and virtually a part of the coast line of the United States. Our merely commercial interest in it is greater than that of all other countries, while its relations to our power and prosperity as a Nation, to our means of defence, our unity, peace, and safety, are matters of paramount concern to the people of the United States. No other great Power would, under similar circumstances, fail to assert a rightful control over a work so closely and vitally affecting its interest and welfare.

Without urging further the grounds of my opinion, I repeat, in conclusion, that it is the right and the duty of the United States to assert and maintain such supervision and authority over any interoceanic canal across the Isthmus that connects North and South America, as will protect our national interests. This I am quite sure will be found not only compatible with, but promotive of the widest and most permanent advantage to commerce and civilization.

RUTHERFORD B. HAYES.

EXECUTIVE MANSION, *March* 8, 1880.

MESSAGE

TO

THE TWO HOUSES OF CONGRESS.

APRIL 22, 1880.

MESSAGE.

To the Senate and House of Representatives:

I have the honor to inform Congress that Mr. J. Randolph Coolidge, Dr. Algernon Coolidge, Mr. Thomas Jefferson Coolidge, and Mrs. Ellen Dwight, of Massachusetts, the heirs of the late Joseph Coolidge, jr., desire to present to the United States the desk on which the Declaration of Independence was written. It bears the following inscription in the handwriting of Thomas Jefferson:

"Thomas Jefferson gives this writing-desk to Joseph Coolidge, jr., as a memorial of his affection. It was made from a drawing of his own, by Ben. Randall, cabinet-maker of Philadelphia, with whom he first lodged on his arrival in that city in May, 1776, and is the identical one on which he wrote the Declaration of Independence.

"Politics as well as religion has its superstitions. These, gaining strength, with time, may one day give imaginary value to this relic for its association with the birth of the great charter of our Independence.

"MONTICELLO, *November* 18, 1825."

The desk was placed in my possession by Hon. Robert C. Winthrop, and is herewith transmitted to Congress, with the letter of Mr. Winthrop, expressing the wish of the donors "to offer it to the United States, that it may hereafter have a place in the Department of State in connection with the immortal instrument which was written upon it in 1776."

I respectfully recommend that such action may be taken by Congress as may be deemed appropriate with reference to a gift to the Nation so precious in its history and for the memorable associations which belong to it.

RUTHERFORD B. HAYES.

EXECUTIVE MANSION, *April* 22, 1880.

"WASHINGTON, D. C., *April* 14, 1880.

"MY DEAR SIR: I have been privileged to bring with me from Boston, as a present to the United States, a very precious historical relic. It is the little desk on which Mr. Jefferson wrote the original draught of the Declaration of Independence.

"This desk was given by Mr. Jefferson himself to my friend the late Joseph Coolidge, of Boston, at the time of his marriage to Jefferson's granddaughter, Miss Randolph; and it bears an autograph inscription, of singular interest, written by the illustrious author of the Declaration in the very last year of his life.

"On the recent death of Mr. Coolidge, whose wife had died a year or two previously, the desk became the property of their children—Mr. J. Randolph Coolidge, Dr. Algernon Coolidge, Mr. Thomas Jefferson Coolidge, and Mrs. Ellen Dwight—who now desire to offer it to the United States, so that it may henceforth have a place in the Department of State, in connection with the immortal instrument which was written upon it in 1776.

"They have done me the honor to make me the medium of this distinguished gift, and I ask permission to place it in the hands of the Chief Magistrate of the Nation in their name and at their request.

"Believe me, dear Mr. President, with the highest respect, very faithfully, your obedient servant,

"ROBERT C. WINTHROP.

"His Excellency RUTHERFORD B. HAYES,
"*President of the United States.*"

MESSAGE

RETURNING TO THE

HOUSE OF REPRESENTATIVES THE BILL ENTITLED "AN ACT MAKING APPROPRIATIONS TO SUPPLY CERTAIN DEFICIENCIES IN THE APPROPRIATIONS FOR THE SERVICE OF THE GOVERNMENT FOR THE FISCAL YEAR ENDING JUNE 30, 1880, AND FOR OTHER PURPOSES."

MAY 4, 1880.

MESSAGE.

To the House of Representatives:

After mature consideration of the bill entitled "An act making appropriations to supply certain deficiencies in the appropriations for the service of the Government for the fiscal year ending June 30, 1880, and for other purposes," I return it to the House of Representatives, in which it originated, with my objections to its passage.

The bill appropriates about $8,000,000, of which over $600,000 is for the payment of the fees of United States marshals, and of the general and special deputy marshals, earned during the current fiscal year, and their incidental expenses. The appropriations made in the bill are needed to carry on the operations of the Government and to fulfil its obligations for the payment of money long since due to its officers for services and expenses essential to the execution of their duties under the laws of the United States. The necessity for these appropriations is so urgent, and they have been already so long delayed, that if the bill before me contained no permanent or general legislation unconnected with these appropriations it would receive my prompt approval. It contains, however, provisions which materially change, and by implication repeal, important parts of the laws for the regulation of the United States elections. These laws have for several years past been the subject of vehement political controversy, and have been denounced as unnecessary, oppressive, and unconstitutional. On the other hand, it has been maintained with equal zeal and earnestness, that the election laws are indispensable to fair and lawful elections, and are clearly warranted by the Constitution. Under these circumstances, to attempt in an appropriation bill the modification or repeal of these laws is to annex a condition to the passage of needed and proper appropriations which tends to deprive the Executive of that equal and independent exercise of discretion and judgment which the Constitution contemplates.

The objection to the bill, therefore, to which I respectfully ask your attention, is that it gives a marked and deliberate sanction, attended by no circumstances of pressing necessity, to the questionable and, as I am clearly of opinion, the dangerous practice of tacking upon appropriation bills general and permanent legislation. This practice opens a wide door to hasty, inconsiderate, and sinister legislation. It invites attacks upon the independence and constitutional powers of the Executive by providing an easy and effective way of constraining Executive discretion. Although of late this practice has been resorted to by all political parties, when clothed with power, it did not prevail until forty years after the adoption of the Constitution, and it is confidently believed that it is condemned by the enlightened judgment of the country. The States which have adopted new constitutions during the last quarter of a century have generally provided remedies for the evil. Many of them have enacted that no law shall contain more than one subject, which shall be plainly expressed in its title. The constitutions of more than half of the States contain substantially this provision, or some other of like intent and meaning. The public welfare will be promoted in many ways by a return to the early practice of the Government and to the true rule of legislation, which is that every measure should stand upon its own merits.

I am firmly convinced that appropriation bills ought not to contain any legislation not relevant to the application or expenditure of the money thereby appropriated, and that by a strict adherence to this principle an important and much-needed reform will be accomplished.

Placing my objection to the bill on this feature of its frame, I forbear any comment upon the important general and permanent legislation which it contains, as matter for specific and independent consideration.

RUTHERFORD B. HAYES.

Executive Mansion, *May* 4, 1880.

ADDRESS

AT THE

OHIO SOLDIERS' REUNION, COLUMBUS, OHIO.

AUGUST 11, 1880.

ADDRESS.

Mr. President:

The citizens of Ohio who were soldiers in the Union Army, and who have assembled here in such large numbers, have many reasons for mutual congratulations as they exchange greetings and renew old friendships at this State Reunion. We rejoice that we had the glorious privilege of enlisting and serving on the right side in the great conflict for the Union and for equal rights.

The time that has passed since the contest ended is not so great but that we can without effort recall freshly and vividly the events and scenes and feelings and associations of that most interesting period of our lives. We rejoice, also, that we have been permitted to live long enough to see and to enjoy the results of the victory we gained, and to measure the vast benefits which it conferred on our country and on the world. I shall not attempt to make a catalogue of those benefits, or to estimate their value. A single fact, to which I call your attention, will sufficiently illustrate, for my present purpose, the immeasurable blessings conferred upon the United States by the success of the Union arms.

The statistics of emigration showing the movements of population which are going on in the world, afford a very good test of the comparative advantages and prosperity of the various civilized Nations. People leave their own country and seek new homes in foreign lands to better their condition. Immigration into a country, therefore, is an evidence of that country's prosperity. It is also a most efficient cause of the progress of the country which receives it. During our civil war, and during the disturbed and troubled years which immediately preceded and followed it, immigration fell off and became of comparatively small importance. But now, our country's prosperity, the stability of our Government, and the permanent prevalence of peace at home and with foreign Nations, blessings which could not have been enjoyed by this country if the Union arms had failed, have given to the world a confidence in the future welfare and greatness of the United States which is pouring upon our shores such streams of immigration as were never known before.

This is a fact of the most pregnant significance in our present condition. If we take a survey of the globe we shall find everywhere, among civilized Nations especially, many people who are eagerly looking forward to the time when they can emigrate to some more favored land. Only one of the great Nations is in no danger of losing its capital and labor and skill by emigration. We find only one which, by immigration, is gaining rapidly in numbers, wealth, and power. All are losing by this cause except the United States. The United States alone is gaining. Other Nations see their people going, going. We see, from every quarter, the people of other countries coming, coming, coming.

There is one flag, and in all the world only one, whose protection, good men and women born under it will never willingly leave. There is one flag, and only one in the world, whose protecting folds, good men and women born under every other flag that floats under the whole heavens, are eagerly and gladly seeking. That flag, so loved at home, so longed for by millions abroad, is the old flag under which we marched, to save, what in our soldier days we were fond of calling "God's country."

It is easily seen what it is that chiefly attracts this immigration. It goes where good land is cheap; where labor and capital find profitable employment; where peace and social order prevail; and where civil and religious liberty are secure. If we draw nearer to the subject, and ask where in our own country does this immigration mainly go, the recent census, whose results we are now getting, gives us the answer. That census shows us parts of our country, where land is cheap and where capital and labor are needed, that are not rapidly increasing in population. In these States it will be found that two things are wanting: the means for popular education are not sufficiently provided, and the good order of society is disturbed by a practical popular refusal to accept the results of the war for the Union. These two defects, wherever they prevail in our American society, are hostile to the increase of population and to prosperity. They are found generally to exist together. Where popular education prevails, the equal-rights "amendments to the Constitution of the United States, embodying the results of the war, are inviolable."

It must, perhaps, be conceded that there was one great error in the measures by which it was sought to secure the results—to harvest the fruits of our Union victory. The system of slavery in the South of necessity kept in ignorance four millions of slaves. It also left unprovided with education, a large number of non-slaveholding white people. With the end of the war the slaves inevitably became citizens. The uneducated whites remained as they had been, also citizens. Thus the grave duties and responsibilities of citizenship were devolved largely in the States lately in rebellion, upon uneducated people, white and colored. And with what result? Liberty and the exercise of the rights of citizenship are excellent educators. In many respects, we are glad to believe, that encouraging progress has been made at the South. The labor system has been reorganized, material prosperity is increasing, race prejudices and antagonisms have diminished, the passions and animosities of the war are subsiding, and the ancient harmony and concord, and patriotic national sentiments are returning. But, after all, we cannot fail to observe that immigration, which so infallibly and instinctively finds out the true condition of all countries, does not largely go into the late slaveholding region of the United States. A great deal of cheap and productive land can there be found where population is not rapidly increasing. When our Revolutionary Fathers adopted the ordinance of 1787, for the government of the Northwest Territory, out of which Ohio and four other great States have been carved, they were not content with merely putting into that organic law a firm prohibition against slavery, and providing effectual guarantees of civil and religious liberty, but they established, as the corner-stone of the free institutions they wished to build, this Article: "*Religion, morality, and knowledge being necessary to good government and the happiness of mankind*, SCHOOLS AND THE MEANS OF EDUCATION SHALL FOREVER BE ENCOURAGED." Unfortunately for the complete success of reconstruction in the South, this stone was rejected by its builders. Slavery had been destroyed by the war; but its evils live after it, and deprive many parts of the South of that intelligent self-government without which, in America at least, great and permanent prosperity is impossible.

To perpetuate the Union and to abolish slavery were the work of the war. To educate the uneducated is the appropriate work of peace. As long as any considerable numbers of our countrymen are uneducated, the citizenship of every American in every State is impaired in value and is constantly imperilled. It is plain that at the end of the war the tremendous change in the labor and social systems of the Southern States, and the ravages and impoverishment of the conflict, added to the burden of their debts, and the loss of their whole circulating medium, which died in their hands, left the people of those States in no condition to provide for universal popular education. In a recent memorial to Congress on this subject, in behalf of the trustees of the

Peabody Educational Fund, Hon. A. H. H. Stuart, of Virginia, shows that "two millions of children in the Southern States are without the means of instruction;" and adds, with great force, "Where millions of citizens are growing up in the grossest ignorance, it is obvious that neither individual charity nor the resources of impoverished States will be sufficient to meet the emergency. Nothing short of the wealth and power of the Federal Government will suffice to overcome the evil."

The principle applied by general consent to works of public improvement is in point. That principle is, that wherever a public improvement is of national importance, and local and private enterprise are inadequate to its prosecution, the General Government should undertake it. On this principle I would deal with the question of education by the aid of the National Government. Wherever in the United States the local systems of popular education are inadequate, they should be supplemented by the General Government, by devoting to the purpose, by suitable legislation and with proper safeguards, the public lands, or if necessary, appropriations from the Treasury of the United States.

The soldier of the Union has done his work, and has done it well. The work of the schoolmaster is now in order. Wherever his work shall be well done, in all our borders, it will be found that there, also, the principles of the Declaration of Independence will be cherished, the sentiment of Nationality will prevail, the equal-rights amendments will be cheerfully obeyed, and there will be "the home of freedom and the refuge of the oppressed of every race and of every clime."

THANKSGIVING PROCLAMATION.

NOVEMBER 1, 1880.

PROCLAMATION.

BY THE PRESIDENT OF THE UNITED STATES OF AMERICA.

A PROCLAMATION.

At no period in their history since the United States became a Nation has this people had so abundant and so universal reasons for joy and gratitude at the favor of Almighty God, or been subject to so profound an obligation to give thanks for His loving kindness and humbly to implore His continued care and protection.

Health, wealth, and prosperity throughout all our borders; peace, honor, and friendship with all the world; firm and faithful adherence by the great body of our population to the principles of liberty and justice which have made our greatness as a Nation; and to the wise institutions and strong frame of government and society which will perpetuate it. For all these let the thanks of a happy and united people, as with one voice, ascend in devout homage to the Giver of all good.

I, therefore, recommend that on Thursday, the twenty-fifth day of November next, the people meet in their respective places of worship to make their acknowledgments to Almighty God for His bounties and His protection, and to offer to Him prayers for their continuance.

In witness whereof I have hereunto set my hand, and caused the seal of the United States to be affixed.

Done at the city of Washington this first day of November, in the
       year of our Lord one thousand eight hundred and eighty, and
[SEAL.] of the Independence of the United States the one hundred and
       fifth.

                                       R. B. HAYES.

By the President:
  WM. M. EVARTS,
    Secretary of State.

MESSAGE

TO THE

TWO HOUSES OF CONGRESS AT THE COMMENCEMENT OF THE THIRD SESSION OF THE FORTY-SIXTH CONGRESS.

DECEMBER 6, 1880.

MESSAGE.

Fellow-Citizens of the Senate
    and House of Representatives:

I congratulate you on the continued and increasing prosperity of our country. By the favor of Divine Providence we have been blessed, during the past year, with health, with abundant harvests, with profitable employment for all our people, and with contentment at home, and with peace and friendship with other Nations.

The occurrence of the twenty-fourth election of Chief Magistrate has afforded another opportunity to the people of the United States to exhibit to the world a significant example of the peaceful and safe transmission of the power and authority of government from the public servants whose terms of office are about to expire, to their newly-chosen successors. This example cannot fail to impress profoundly, thoughtful people of other countries with the advantages which republican institutions afford. The immediate, general, and cheerful acquiescence of all good citizens, in the result of the election, gives gratifying assurance to our country, and to its friends throughout the world, that a Government based on the free consent of an intelligent and patriotic people possesses elements of strength, stability, and permanency not found in any other form of government.

Continued opposition to the full and free enjoyment of the rights of citizenship, conferred upon the colored people by the recent amendments to the Constitution, still prevails in several of the late slaveholding States. It has, perhaps, not been manifested in the recent election to any large extent in acts of violence or intimidation. It has, however, by fraudulent practices in connection with the ballots, with the regulations as to the places and manner of voting, and with counting, returning, and canvassing the votes cast, been successful in defeating the exercise of the right preservative of all rights, the right of suffrage, which the Constitution expressly confers upon our enfranchised citizens.

It is the desire of the good people of the whole country that sectionalism as a factor in our politics should disappear. They prefer that no section of the country should be united in solid opposition to any other section. The disposition to refuse a prompt and hearty obedience to the equal-rights amendments to the Constitution, is all that now stands in the way of a complete obliteration of sectional lines in our political contests. As long as either of these amendments is flagrantly violated or disregarded, it is safe to assume that the people who placed them in the Constitution, as embodying the legitimate results of the war for the Union, and who believe them to be wise and necessary, will continue to act together, and to insist that they shall be obeyed. The paramount question still is, as to the enjoyment of the right by every American citizen who has the requisite qualifications, to freely cast his vote and to have it honestly counted. With this question rightly settled, the country will be relieved of the contentions of the past; bygones will indeed be bygones; and political and party issues with respect to economy and efficiency of administration, internal improvements, the tariff, domestic taxation, education, finance, and other important subjects, will then receive their full share of attention; but resistance to and nullification of the results of the war, will unite together in resolute purpose for their support all who maintain the authority of the Government and the perpetuity of the Union, and who adequately appreciate the value of the victory achieved. This determination proceeds from no hostile sentiment or feeling to any part of the people of our country, or to any of their interests. The inviolability of the amendments rests upon the fundamental principle of our Government. They are the solemn expression of the will of the people of the United States.

The sentiment that the constitutional rights of all our citizens must be maintained does not grow weaker. It will continue to control the Government of the country. Happily, the history of the late election shows that in many parts of the country where opposition to the fifteenth amendment has heretofore prevailed, it is diminishing, and is likely to cease altogether, if firm and well-considered action is taken by Congress. I trust the House of Representatives and the Senate, which have the right to judge of the elections, returns, and qualifications of their own members, will see to it that every case of violation of the letter or spirit of the fifteenth amendment is thoroughly investigated, and that no benefit from such violation shall accrue to any person or party. It will be the duty of the Executive, with sufficient appropriations for the purpose, to prosecute unsparingly all who have been engaged in depriving citizens of the rights guaranteed to them by the Constitution.

It is not, however, to be forgotten that the best and surest guarantee of the primary rights of citizenship is to be found in that capacity for self-protection which can belong only to a people whose right to universal suffrage is supported by universal education. The means at the command of the local and State authorities are, in many cases, wholly inadequate to furnish free instruction to all who need it. This is especially true where, before emancipation, the education of the people was neglected or prevented, in the interest of slavery. Firmly convinced that the subject of popular education deserves the earnest attention of the people of the whole country, with a view to wise and comprehensive action by the Government of the United States, I respectfully recommend that Congress, by suitable legislation and with proper safeguards, supplement the local educational funds in the several States where the grave duties and responsibilities of citizenship have been devolved on uneducated people, by devoting to the purpose grants of the public lands, and, if necessary, by appropriations from the Treasury of the United States. Whatever Government can fairly do to promote free popular education ought to be done. Wherever general education is found, peace, virtue, and social order prevail, and civil and religious liberty are secure.

In my former annual messages I have asked the attention of Congress to the urgent necessity of a reformation of the civil-service system of the Government. My views concerning the dangers of patronage, or appointments for personal or partisan considerations, have been strengthened by my observation and experience in the Executive office, and I believe these dangers threaten the stability of the Government. Abuses so serious in their nature cannot be permanently tolerated. They tend to become more alarming with the enlargement of administrative service, as the growth of the country in population increases the number of officers and placemen employed.

The reasons are imperative for the adoption of fixed rules for the regulation of appointments, promotions, and removals, establishing a uniform method, having exclusively in view, in every instance, the attainment of the best qualifications for the position in question. Such a method alone is consistent with the equal rights of all citizens, and the most economical and efficient administration of the public business.

Competitive examinations, in aid of impartial appointments and promotions, have been conducted for some years past in several of the Executive Departments, and by my direction this system has been adopted in the custom-houses and post offices of the larger cities of the country. In the city of New York over two thousand positions in the civil service have been subject, in their appointments and tenure of place, to the operation of published rules for this purpose, during the past two years. The results of these practical trials have been very satisfactory, and have confirmed my opinion in favor of this system of selection. All are subjected to the same tests, and the result is free from prejudice by personal favor or partisan influence. It secures for the position applied for the best qualifications attainable among the competing applicants. It is an effectual protection from the pressure of importunity which, under any other course pursued, largely exacts the time and attention of appointing officers, to their great detriment in the discharge of other official duties, preventing the abuse of the service for the mere furtherance of private or party purposes, and leaving the employé of the Government, freed from the obligations imposed by patronage, to depend solely upon merit for retention and advancement, and with this constant incentive to exertion and improvement.

These invaluable results have been attained in a high degree in the offices where the rules for appointment by competitive examination have been applied.

A method which has so approved itself by experimental tests at points where such tests may be fairly considered conclusive, should be extended to all subordinate positions under the Government. I believe that a strong and growing public sentiment demands immediate measures for securing and enforcing the highest possible efficiency in the civil service, and its protection from recognized abuses, and that the experience referred to has demonstrated the feasibility of such measures.

The examinations in the custom-houses and post offices have been held under many embarrassments and without provision for compensation for the extra labor performed by the officers who have conducted them, and whose commendable interest in the improvement of the public service has induced this devotion of time and labor without pecuniary reward. A continuance of these labors gratuitously ought not to be expected, and without an appropriation by Congress for compensation, it is not practicable to extend the system of examinations generally throughout the civil service. It is also highly important that all such examinations should be conducted upon a uniform system and under general supervision. Section 1753 of the Revised Statutes authorizes the President to prescribe the regulations for admission to the civil service of the United States, and for this purpose to employ suitable persons to conduct the requisite inquiries with reference to "the fitness of each candidate, in respect to age, health, character, knowledge, and ability, for the branch of service into which he seeks to enter;" but the law is practically inoperative for want of the requisite appropriation.

I therefore recommend an appropriation of $25,000 per annum to meet the expenses of a commission, to be appointed by the President in accordance with the terms of this section, whose duty it shall be to devise a just, uniform, and efficient system of competitive examinations, and to supervise the application of the same throughout the entire civil service of the Government. I am persuaded that the facilities which such a commission will afford for testing the fitness of those who apply for office will not only be as welcome a relief to members of Congress as it will be to the President and heads of Departments, but that it will also greatly tend to remove the causes of embarrassment which now inevitably and constantly attend the conflicting claims of patronage between the Legislative and Executive Departments. The most effectual check upon the pernicious competition of influence and official favoritism, in the bestowal of office, will be the substitution of an open competition of merit between the applicants, in which every one can make his own record with the assurance that his success will depend upon this alone.

I also recommend such legislation as, while leaving every officer as free as any other citizen to express his political opinions and to use his means for their advancement, shall also enable him to feel as safe as any private citizen in refusing all demands upon his salary for political purposes. A law which should thus guarantee true liberty and justice to all who are engaged in the public service, and likewise contain stringent provisions against the use of official authority to coerce the political action of private citizens or of official subordinates, is greatly to be desired.

The most serious obstacle, however, to an improvement of the civil service, and especially to a reform in the method of appointment and removal, has been found to be the practice, under what is known as the spoils system, by which the appointing power has been so largely encroached upon by members of Congress. The first step in the reform of the civil service must be a complete divorce between Congress and the Executive in the matter of appointments. The corrupting doctrine that " to the victors belong the spoils" is inseparable from Congressional patronage as the established rule and practice of parties in power. It comes to be understood by applicants for office, and by the people generally, that Representatives and Senators are entitled to disburse the patronage of their respective districts and States. It is not necessary to recite at length the evils resulting from this invasion of the Executive functions. The true principles of government on the subject of appointments to office, as stated in the National Conventions of the leading parties of the country, have again and again been approved by the American people, and have not been called in question in any quarter. These authentic expressions of public opinion upon this all-important subject are the statement of principles that belong to the constitutional structure of the Government.

"Under the Constitution, the President and heads of Departments are to make nominations for office. The Senate is to advise and consent to appointments, and the House of Representatives is to accuse and prosecute faithless officers. The best interests of the public service demand that these distinctions be respected; that Senators and Representatives, who may be judges and accusers, should not dictate appointments to office." To this end the co-operation of the Legislative Department of the Government is required alike by the necessities of the case and by public opinion. Members of Congress will not be relieved from the demands made upon them with reference to appointments to office until, by legislative enactment, the pernicious practice is condemned and forbidden.

It is, therefore, recommended that an act be passed defining the relations of members of Congress with respect to appointments to office by the President, and I also recommend that the provisions of section 1767, and of the sections following, of the Revised Statutes, comprising the Tenure-of-Office Act, of March 2, 1867, be repealed.

Believing that to reform the system and methods of the civil service in our country is one of the highest and most imperative duties of statesmanship, and that it can be permanently done only by the co-operation of the Legislative and Executive Departments of the Government, I again commend the whole subject to your considerate attention.

It is the recognized duty and purpose of the people of the United States to suppress polygamy where it now exists in our Territories, and to prevent its extension. Faithful and zealous efforts have been made by the United States authorities in Utah to enforce the laws against it. Experience has shown that the legislation upon this subject, to be effective, requires extensive modification and amendment. The longer action is delayed the more difficult it will be to accomplish what is desired. Prompt and decided measures are necessary. The Mormon sectarian organization which upholds polygamy has the whole power of making and executing the local legislation of the Territory. By its control of the grand and petit juries, it possesses large influence over the administration of justice. Exercising, as the heads of this sect do, the local political power of the Territory, they are able to make effective their hostility to the law of Congress on the subject of polygamy, and, in fact, do prevent its enforcement. Polygamy will not be abolished if the enforcement of the law depends on those who practice and uphold the crime. It can only be suppressed by taking away the political power of the sect which encourages and sustains it. The power of Congress to enact suitable laws to protect the Territories is ample. It is not a case for half-way measures. The political power of the Mormon sect is increasing; it controls now one of our wealthiest and most populous Territories. It is extending steadily into other Territories. Wherever it goes it establishes polygamy and sectarian political power. The sanctity of marriage and the family relation are the corner-stone of our American society and civilization. Religious liberty and the separation of Church and State are among the elementary ideas of free institutions. To re-establish the interests and principles which polygamy and Mormonism have imperilled, and to fully reopen to intelligent and virtuous immigrants of all creeds that part of our domain which has been, in a great degree, closed to general immigration by intolerant and immoral institutions, it is recommended that the government of the Territory of Utah be reorganized.

I recommend that Congress provide for the government of Utah by a governor and judges, or commissioners, appointed by the President and confirmed by the Senate—a government analogous to the provisional government established for the Territory northwest of the Ohio, by the ordinance of 1787. If, however, it is deemed best to continue the existing form of local government, I recommend that the right to vote, hold office, and sit on juries in the Territory of Utah, be confined to those who neither practice nor uphold polygamy. If thorough measures are adopted, it is believed that within a few years the evils which now afflict Utah will be eradicated, and that this Territory will in good time become one of the most prosperous and attractive of the new States of the Union.

Our relations with all foreign countries have been those of undisturbed peace, and have presented no occasion for concern as to their continued maintenance.

My anticipation of an early reply from the British Government to the demand of indemnity to our fishermen for the injuries suffered by that industry at Fortune Bay, in January, 1878, which I expressed in my last annual message, was disappointed. This answer was received only in the latter part of April in the present year, and, when received, exhibited a failure of accord between the two Governments, as to the measure of the inshore-fishing privilege secured to our fishermen by the Treaty of Washington, of so serious a character that I made it the subject of a communication to Congress, in which I recommended the adoption of the measures which seemed to me proper to be taken by this Government in maintenance of the rights accorded to our fishermen under the treaty, and towards securing an indemnity for the injury these interests had suffered. A bill to carry out these recommendations was under consideration by the House of Representatives at the time of the adjournment of Congress in June last.

Within a few weeks I have received a communication from Her Majesty's Government, renewing the consideration of the subject, both of the indemnity for the injuries at Fortune Bay, and of the interpretation of the treaty in which the previous correspondence had shown the two Governments to be at variance. Upon both these topics the disposition towards a friendly agreement is manifested by a recognition of our right to an indemnity for the transaction at Fortune Bay, leaving the measure of such indemnity to further conference, and by an assent to the view of this Government, presented in the previous correspondence, that the regulation of conflicting interests of the shore fishery of the Provincial sea-coasts, and the vessel fishery of our fishermen, should be made the subject of conference and concurrent arrangement between the two Governments.

I sincerely hope that the basis may be found for a speedy adjustment of the very serious divergence of views of the interpretation of the fishery clauses of the Treaty of Washington, which, as the correspondence between the two Governments stood at the close of the last session of Congress, seemed to be irreconcilable.

In the important exhibition of arts and industries, which was held last year at Sydney, New South Wales, as well as in that now in progress at Melbourne, the United States have been efficiently and honorably represented. The exhibitors from this country at the former place received a large number of awards in some of the most considerable departments, and the participation of the United States was recognized by a special mark of distinction. In the exhibition at Melbourne, the share taken by our country is no less notable, and an equal degree of success is confidently expected.

The state of peace and tranquillity now enjoyed by all the Nations of the continent of Europe has its favorable influence upon our diplomatic and commercial relations with them. We have concluded and ratified a convention with the French Republic for the settlement of claims of the citizens of either country against the other. Under this convention a commission, presided over by a distinguished publicist, appointed, in pursuance of the request of both Nations, by His Majesty the Emperor of Brazil, has been organized and has begun its sessions in this city. A congress to consider means for the protection of industrial property has recently been in session in Paris, to which I have appointed the Ministers of the United States in France and in Belgium as delegates. The International Commission upon Weights and Measures also continues its work in Paris. I invite your attention to the necessity of an appropriation to be made in time to enable this Government to comply with its obligations under the Metrical Convention.

Our friendly relations with the German Empire continue without interruption. At the recent International Exhibition of Fish and Fisheries at Berlin, the participation of the United States, notwithstanding the haste with which the commission was forced to make its preparations, was extremely successful and meritorious, winning for private exhibitors numerous awards of a high class, and for the country at large the principal prize of honor offered by His Majesty the Emperor. The results of this great success cannot but be advantageous to this important and growing industry. There have been some questions raised between the two Governments as to the proper effect and interpretation of our treaties of naturalization, but recent despatches from our Minister at Berlin show that favorable progress is making toward an understanding, in accordance with the views of this Government, which makes and admits no distinction whatever between the rights of a native and a naturalized citizen of the United States. In practice, the complaints of molestation suffered by naturalized citizens abroad have never been fewer than at present.

There is nothing of importance to note in our unbroken friendly relations with the Governments of Austria-Hungary, Russia, Portugal, Sweden and Norway, Switzerland, Turkey, and Greece.

During the last summer several vessels belonging to the merchant marine of this country, sailing in neutral waters of the West Indies, were fired at, boarded, and searched by an armed cruiser of the Spanish Government. The circumstances, as reported, involve not only a private injury to the persons concerned, but also seemed too little observant of the friendly relations existing for a century between this country and Spain. The wrong was brought to the attention of the Spanish Government in a serious protest and remonstrance, and the matter is undergoing investigation by the royal authorities, with a view to such explanation or reparation as may be called for by the facts.

The commission sitting in this city for the adjudication of claims of our citizens against the Government of Spain, is, I hope, approaching the termination of its labors.

The claims against the United States under the Florida Treaty with Spain were submitted to Congress for its action at the late session, and I again invite your attention to this long-standing question, with a view to a final disposition of the matter.

At the invitation of the Spanish Government, a conference has recently been held at the city of Madrid to consider the subject of protection by foreign Powers of native Moors in the Empire of Morocco. The Minister of the United States, in Spain, was directed to take part in the deliberations of this conference, the result of which is a convention signed on behalf of all the Powers represented. The instrument will be laid before the Senate for its consideration. The Government of the United States has also lost no opportunity to urge upon that of the Emperor of Morocco the necessity, in accordance with the humane and enlightened spirit of the age, of putting an end to the persecutions, which have been so prevalent in that country, of persons of a faith other than the Moslem, and especially of the Hebrew residents of Morocco.

The consular treaty concluded with Belgium has not yet been officially promulgated, owing to the alteration of a word in the text by the Senate of the United States, which occasioned a delay, during which the time allowed for ratification expired. The Senate will be asked to extend the period for ratification.

The attempt to negotiate a treaty of extradition with Denmark failed on account of the objection of the Danish Government to the usual clause providing that each Nation should pay the expense of the arrest of the persons whose extradition it asks.

The provision made by Congress, at its last session, for the expense of the commission which had been appointed to enter upon negotiations with the Imperial Government of China, on subjects of great interest to the relations of the two countries, enabled the commissioners to proceed at once upon their mission. The Imperial Government was prepared to give prompt and respectful attention to the matters brought under negotiation, and the conferences proceeded with such rapidity and success that, on the 17th of November last, two treaties were signed at Pekin, one relating to the introduction of Chinese into this country and one relating to commerce. Mr. Trescot, one of the commissioners, is now on his way home bringing the treaties, and it is expected that they will be received in season to be laid before the Senate early in January.

Our Minister in Japan has negotiated a convention for the reciprocal relief of shipwrecked seamen. I take occasion to urge once more upon Congress the propriety of making provision for the erection of suitable fire-proof buildings at the Japanese capital for the use of the American legation, and the court-house and jail connected with it. The Japanese Government, with great generosity and courtesy, has offered for this purpose an eligible piece of land.

In my last annual message I invited the attention of Congress to the subject of the indemnity funds received some years ago from China and Japan. I renew the recommendation then made, that whatever portions of these funds are due to American citizens should be promptly paid, and the residue returned to the Nations, respectively, to which they justly and equitably belong.

The extradition treaty with the Kingdom of the Netherlands, which has been for sometime in course of negotiation, has, during the past year, been concluded and duly ratified.

Relations of friendship and amity have been established between the Government of the United States and that of Roumania. We have sent a diplomatic representative to Bucharest, and have received at this capital the special envoy, who has been charged by his Royal Highness, Prince Charles, to announce the independent sovereignty of Roumania. We hope for a speedy development of commercial relations between the two countries.

In my last annual message I expressed the hope that the prevalence of quiet on the border between this country and Mexico would soon become so assured as to justify the modification of the orders, then in force, to our military commanders, in regard to crossing the frontier, without encouraging such disturbances as would endanger the peace of the two countries. Events moved in accordance with these expectations, and the orders were accordingly withdrawn, to the entire satisfaction of our own citizens and the Mexican Government. Subsequently the peace of the border was again disturbed by a savage foray, under the command of the Chief Victorio, but, by the combined and harmonious action of the military forces of both countries, his band has been broken up and substantially destroyed.

There is reason to believe that the obstacles which have so long prevented rapid and convenient communication between the United States and Mexico by railways, are on the point of disappearing, and that several important enterprises of this character will soon be set on foot which cannot fail to contribute largely to the prosperity of both countries.

New envoys from Guatemala, Colombia, Bolivia, Venezuela, and Nicaragua have recently arrived at this capital, whose distinction and enlightenment afford the best guarantee of the continuance of friendly relations between ourselves and these sister Republics.

The relation between this Government and that of the United States of Colombia have engaged public attention during the past year, mainly by reason of the project of an interoceanic canal across the Isthmus of Panama, to be built by private capital under a concession from the Colombian Government for that purpose. The treaty obligations subsisting between the United States and Colombia, by which we guarantee the neutrality of the transit and the sovereignty and property of Colombia in the Isthmus, make it necessary that the conditions under which so stupendous a change in the region embraced in this guarantee should be effected—transforming, as it would, this Isthmus, from a barrier between the Atlantic and Pacific Oceans, into a gateway and thoroughfare between them, for the navies and the merchant-ships of the world—should receive the approval of this Government, as being compatible with the discharge of these obligations on our part, and consistent with our interests as the principal commercial power of the Western Hemisphere. The views which I expressed in a special message to Congress in March last, in relation to this project, I deem it my duty again to press upon your attention. Subsequent consideration has but confirmed the opinion "that it is the right and duty of the United States to assert and maintain such supervision and authority over any interoceanic canal across the isthmus that connects North and South America as will protect our national interest."

The war between the Republic of Chili on the one hand, and the allied Republics of Peru and Bolivia on the other, still continues. This Government has not felt called upon to interfere in a contest that is within the belligerent rights of the parties as independent States. We have, however, always held ourselves in readiness to aid in accommodating their difference, and have at different times reminded both belligerents of our willingness to render such service.

Our good offices, in this direction, were recently accepted by all the belligerents, and it was hoped they would prove efficacious; but I regret to announce that the measures, which the Ministers of the United States at Santiago and Lima were authorized to take, with the view to bring about a peace, were not successful. In the course of the war some questions have arisen affecting neutral rights; in all of these the Ministers of the United States have, under their instructions, acted with promptness and energy in protection of American interests.

The relations of the United States with the Empire of Brazil continue to be most cordial, and their commercial intercourse steadily increases to their mutual advantage.

The internal disorders with which the Argentine Republic has for sometime past been afflicted, and which have more or less influenced its external trade, are understood to have been brought to a close. This happy result may be expected to redound to the benefit of the foreign commerce of that Republic as well as to the development of its vast interior resources.

In Samoa, the Government of King Malietoa, under the support and recognition of the consular representatives of the United States, Great Britain, and Germany, seems to have given peace and tranquillity to the Islands. While it does not appear desirable to adopt as a whole the scheme of tripartite local government, which has been proposed, the common interests of the three great treaty Powers require harmony in their relations to the native frame of government, and this may be best secured by a simple diplomatic agreement between them. It would be well if the consular jurisdiction of our representative at Apia were increased in extent and importance, so as to guard American interests in the surrounding and outlying Islands of Oceanica.

The obelisk, generously presented by the Khedive of Egypt to the city of New York, has safely arrived in this country, and will soon be erected in that metropolis. A commission for the liquidation of the Egyptian debt has lately concluded its work, and this Government, at the earnest solicitation of the Khedive, has acceded to the provisions adopted by it, which will be laid before Congress for its information. A commission for the revision of the judicial code of the Reform Tribunal of Egypt is now in session in Cairo. Mr. Farman, consul-general, and J. M. Batchelder, Esq., have been appointed as commissioners to participate in this work. The organization of the reform tribunals will probably be continued for another period of five years.

In pursuance of the act passed at the last session of Congress, invitations have been extended to foreign maritime States to join in a sanitary conference in Washington, beginning the first of January. The acceptance of this invitation by many prominent Powers gives promise of success in this important measure, designed to establish a system of international notification by which the spread of infectious or epidemic diseases may be more effectively checked or prevented. The attention of Congress is invited to the necessary appropriations for carrying into effect the provisions of the act referred to.

The efforts of the Department of State to enlarge the trade and commerce of the United States, through the active agency of consular officers and through the dissemination of information obtained from them, have been unrelaxed. The interest in these efforts, as developed in our commercial communities, and the value of the information secured by this means to the trade and manufactures of the country, were recognized by Congress at its last session, and provision was made for the more frequent publication of consular and other reports by the Department of State. The first issue of this publication has now been prepared, and subsequent issues may regularly be expected. The importance and interest attached to the reports of consular officers are witnessed by the general demand for them by all classes of merchants and manufacturers engaged in our foreign trade. It is believed that the system of such publications is deserving of the approval of Congress, and that the necessary appropriations for its continuance and enlargement will commend itself to your consideration.

The prosperous energies of our domestic industries, and their immense production of the subjects of foreign commerce, invite, and even require, an active development of the wishes and interests of our people in that direction. Especially important is it that our commercial relations with the Atlantic and Pacific coasts of South America, with the West Indies and the Gulf of Mexico, should be direct, and not through the circuit of European systems, and should be carried on in our own bottoms. The full appreciation of the opportunities which our front on the Pacific ocean gives to commerce with Japan, China, and the East Indies, with Australia and the Island groups which lie along these routes of navigation, should inspire equal efforts to appropriate to our own shipping, and to administer, by our own capital, a due proportion of this trade. Whatever modifications of our regulations of trade and navigation may be necessary or useful to meet and direct these impulses to the enlargement of our exchanges and of our carrying trade, I am sure the wisdom of Congress will be ready to supply. One initial measure, however, seems to me so clearly useful and efficient that I venture to press it upon your earnest attention. It seems to be very evident that the provision of regular steam-postal communication, by aid from Government, has been the forerunner of the commercial predominance of Great Britain on all these coasts and seas, a greater share in whose trade is now the desire and the intent of our people. It is also manifest that the efforts of other European Nations to contend with Great Britain for a share of this commerce have been successful in proportion with their adoption of regular steam-postal communication with the markets whose trade they sought. Mexico and the States of South America are anxious to receive such postal communications with this country, and to aid in their development. Similar co-operation may be looked for, in due time, from the Eastern Nations and from Australia. It is difficult to see how the lead in this movement can be expected from private interests. In respect of foreign commerce, quite as much as in internal trade, postal communication seems necessarily a matter of common and public administration, and thus pertaining to Government. I respectfully recommend to your prompt attention such just and efficient measures as may conduce to the development of our foreign commercial exchanges and the building up of our carrying trade.

In this connection I desire also to suggest the very great service which might be expected in enlarging and facilitating our commerce on the Pacific Ocean were a transmarine cable laid from San Francisco to the Sandwich Islands, and thence to Japan at the North and Australia at the South. The great influence of such means of communication on those routes of navigation, in developing and securing the due share of our Pacific coast in the commerce of the world, needs no illustration or enforcement. It may be that such an enterprise, useful and in the end profitable as it would prove to private investment, may need to be accelerated by prudent legislation by Congress in its aid, and I submit the matter to your careful consideration.

An additional, and not unimportant, although secondary, reason for fostering and enlarging the Navy may be found in the unquestionable service to the expansion of our commerce, which would be rendered by the frequent circulation of naval ships in the seas and ports of all quarters of the globe. Ships of the proper construction and equipment, to be of the greatest efficiency in case of maritime war, might be made constant and active agents in time of peace in the advancement and protection of our foreign trade, and in the nurture and discipline of young seamen, who would naturally, in some numbers, mix with and improve the crews of our merchant-ships. Our merchants at home and abroad recognize the value to foreign commerce of an active movement of our naval vessels, and the intelligence and patriotic zeal of our naval officers in promoting every interest of their countrymen is a just subject of national pride.

The condition of the financial affairs of the Government, as shown by the report of the Secretary of the Treasury, is very satisfactory. It is believed that the present financial situation of the United States, whether considered with respect to trade, currency, credit, growing wealth, or the extent and variety of our resources, is more favorable than that of any other country of our time, and has never been surpassed by that of any country at any period of its history. All our industries are thriving; the rate of interest is low; new railroads are being constructed; a vast immigration is increasing our population, capital, and labor; new enterprises in great number are in progress; and our commercial relations with other countries are improving.

The ordinary revenues, from all sources, for the fiscal year ended June 30, 1880, were—

From customs	$186,522,064 60
From internal revenue	124,009,373 92
From sales of public lands	1,016,506 60
From tax on circulation and deposits of national banks	7,014,971 44
From repayment of interest by Pacific Railway Companies	1,707,367 18
From sinking-fund for Pacific Railway Companies	786,621 22
From customs, fees, fines, penalties, &c	1,148,800 16
From fees—consular, letters-patent, and lands	2,337,029 00
From proceeds of sales of Government property	282,616 50
From profits on coinage, &c	2,792,186 78
From revenues of the District of Columbia	1,809,469 70
From miscellaneous sources	4,099,603 88
Total ordinary receipts	333,526,610 98

The ordinary expenditures for the same period were—

For civil expenses	$15,693,963 55
For foreign intercourse	1,211,490 58
For Indians	5,945,457 09
For pensions, including $19,341,025.20 arrears of pensions	56,777,174 44
For the military establishment, including river and harbor improvements and arsenals	38,116,916 22
For the naval establishment, including vessels, machinery, and improvements at navy-yards	13,536,984 74
For miscellaneous expenditures, including public buildings, light-houses, and collecting the revenue	34,535,691 00
For expenditures on account of District of Columbia	3,272,384 63
For interest on the public debt	95,757,575 11
For premium on bonds purchased	2,795,320 42
Total ordinary expenditures	267,642,957 78
Leaving a surplus revenue of	865,883,653 20
Which, with an amount drawn from the cash balance in Treasury, of	8,084,434 21
Making	73,968,087 41

Was applied to the redemption—

Of bonds for the sinking-fund	$73,652,900 00
Of fractional currency	251,717 41
Of the loan of 1858	40,000 00
Of temporary loan	100 00
Of bounty-land scrip	25 00
Of compound-interest notes	16,500 00
Of 7.30 notes of 1864–'5	2,650 00
Of one and two-year notes	3,700 00
Of old demand notes	495 00
	73,968,087 41

The amount due the sinking-fund for this year was $37,931,643.55. There was applied thereto the sum of $73,904,617.41, being $35,972,973.86 in excess of the actual requirements for the year.

The aggregate of the revenues from all sources during the fiscal year ended June 30, 1880, was $333,526,610.98, an increase over the preceding year of $59,699,426.52. The receipts thus far, of the current year, together with the estimated receipts for the remainder of the year, amount to $350,000,000, which will be sufficient to meet the estimated expenditures of the year, and leave a surplus of $90,000,000.

It is fortunate that this large surplus revenue occurs at a period when it may be directly applied to the payment of the public debt soon to be redeemable. No public duty has been more constantly cherished in the United States than the policy of paying the Nation's debt as rapidly as possible.

The debt of the United States, less cash in the Treasury and exclusive of accruing interest, attained its maximum of 2,756,431,571.43 in August, 1865, and has since that time been reduced to $1,886,019,504.65. Of the principal of the debt, $108,758,100 has been paid since March 1, 1877, effecting an annual saving of interest of $6,107,593. The burden of interest has also been diminished by the sale of bonds bearing a low rate of interest, and the application of the proceeds to the redemption of bonds bearing a higher rate. The annual saving thus secured since March 1, 1877, is $14,290,453.50.

Within a short period over six hundred millions of five and six per cent. bonds will become redeemable. This presents a very favorable opportunity not only to further reduce the principal of the debt, but also to reduce the rate of interest on that which will remain unpaid. I call the attention of Congress to the views expressed on this subject by the Secretary of the Treasury in his annual report, and recommend prompt legislation, to enable the Treasury Department to complete the refunding of the debt which is about to mature.

The continuance of specie payments has not been interrupted or endangered since the date of resumption. It has contributed greatly to the revival of business and to our remarkable prosperity. The fears that preceded and accompanied resumption have proved groundless.

No considerable amount of United States notes have been presented for redemption, while very large sums of gold bullion, both domestic and imported, are taken to the mints and exchanged for coin or notes. The increase of coin and bullion in the United States since January 1, 1879, is estimated at $227,399,128.

There are still in existence, uncancelled, $346,681,016 of United States legal-tender notes. These notes were authorized as a war measure, made necessary by the exigencies of the conflict in which the United States was then engaged. The preservation of the Nation's existence required, in the judgment of Congress, an issue of legal-tender paper money. That it served well the purpose for which it was created is not questioned, but the employment of the notes as paper money indefinitely, after the accomplishment of the object for which they were provided, was not contemplated by the framers of the law under which they were issued. These notes long since became like any other pecuniary obligation of the Government—a debt to be paid, and, when paid, to be cancelled as a mere evidence of an indebtedness no longer existing. I therefore repeat what was said in the annual message of last year, that the retirement from circulation of United States notes, with the capacity of legal-tender in private contracts, is a step to be taken in our progress towards a safe and stable currency, which should be accepted as the policy and duty of the Government and the interest and security of the people.

At the time of the passage of the act now in force requiring the coinage of silver dollars, fixing their value and giving them legal-tender character, it was believed by many of the supporters of the measure that the silver dollar, which it authorized, would speedily become, under the operations of the law, of equivalent value to the gold dollar. There were other supporters of the bill, who, while they doubted as to the probability of this result, nevertheless were willing to give the proposed experiment a fair trial, with a view to stop the coinage, if experience should prove that the silver dollar authorized by the bill continued to be of less commercial value than the standard gold dollar.

The coinage of silver dollars, under the act referred to, began in March, 1878, and has been continued as required by the act. The average rate per month to the present time has been $2,276,492. The total amount coined prior to the first of November last was $72,847,750. Of this amount $47,084,450 remain in the Treasury, and only $25,763,291 are in the hands of the people. A constant effort has been made to keep this currency in circulation, and considerable expense has been necessarily incurred for this purpose, but its return to the Treasury is prompt and sure. Contrary to the confident anticipation of the friends of the measure at the time of its adoption, the value of the silver dollar, containing 412½ grains of silver, has not increased. During the year prior to the passage of the bill authorizing its coinage, the market value of the silver which it contained was from ninety to ninety-two cents, as compared with the standard gold dollar. During the last year the average market value of the silver dollar has been eighty-eight and a half cents.

It is obvious, that the legislation of the last Congress in regard to silver, so far as it was based on an anticipated rise in the value of silver as a result of that legislation, has failed to produce the effect then predicted. The longer the law remains in force, requiring as it does the coinage of a nominal dollar, which in reality is not a dollar, the greater becomes the danger that this country will be forced to accept a single metal as the sole legal standard of value, in circulation, and this a standard of less value than it purports to be worth in the recognized money of the world.

The Constitution of the United States, sound financial principles, and our best interests, all require that the country should have as its legal-tender money both gold and silver coin, of an intrinsic value, as bullion, equivalent to that which, upon its face, it purports to possess. The Constitution in express terms recognizes both gold and silver as the only true legal-tender money. To banish either of these metals from our currency is to narrow and limit the circulating medium of exchange to the disparagement of important interests. The United States produces more silver than any other country, and is directly interested in maintaining it as one of the two precious metals which furnish the coinage of the world. It will, in my judgment, contribute to this result if Congress will repeal so much of existing legislation as requires the coinage of silver dollars containing only 412½ grains of silver, and in its stead will authorize the Secretary of the Treasury to coin silver dollars of equivalent value as bullion, with gold dollars. This will defraud no man, and will be in accordance with familiar precedents. Congress, on several occasions, has altered the ratio of value between gold and silver, in order to establish it more nearly in accordance with the actual ratio of value between the two metals.

In financial legislation every measure in the direction of greater fidelity in the discharge of pecuniary obligations, has been found by experience to diminish the rates of interest which debtors are required to pay, and to increase the facility with which money can be obtained for every legitimate purpose. Our own recent financial history shows how surely money becomes abundant whenever confidence in the exact performance of moneyed obligations is established.

The Secretary of War reports that the expenditures of the War Department for the fiscal year ended June 30, 1880, were $39,924,773.03. The appropriations for this Department, for the current fiscal year, amount to $41,993,630.40.

With respect to the Army, the Secretary invites attention to the fact that its strength is limited by statute (section 1115, Revised Statutes) to not more than 30,000 enlisted men, but that provisos contained in appropriation bills have limited expenditures to the enlistment of but 25,000. It is believed the full legal strength is the least possible force at which the present organization can be maintained, having in view efficiency, discipline, and economy. While the enlistment of this force would add somewhat to the appropriation for pay of the Army, the saving made in other respects would be more than an equivalent for this additional outlay, and the efficiency of the Army would be largely increased.

The rapid extension of the railroad system west of the Mississippi river, and the great tide of settlers which has flowed in upon new territory, impose on the military an entire change of policy. The maintenance of small posts along wagon and stage-routes of travel is no longer necessary. Permanent quarters at points selected, of a more substantial character than those heretofore constructed, will be required. Under existing laws, permanent buildings cannot be erected without the sanction of Congress, and when sales of military sites and buildings have been authorized, the moneys received have reverted to the Treasury, and could only become available through a new appropriation. It is recommended that provision be made, by general statute, for the sale of such abandoned military posts and buildings as are found to be unnecessary, and for the application of the proceeds to the construction of other posts. While many of the present posts are of but slight value for military purposes, owing to the changed condition of the country, their occupation is continued at great expense and inconvenience, because they afford the only available shelter for troops.

The absence of a large number of officers of the line, in active duty, from their regiments, is a serious detriment to the maintenance of the service. The constant demand for small detachments, each of which should be commanded by a commissioned officer, and the various details of officers for necessary service away from their commands, occasion a scarcity in the number required for company duties. With a view to lessening this drain to some extent, it is recommended that the law authorizing the detail of officers from the active list as professors of tactics and military science at certain colleges and universities, be so amended as to provide that all such details be made from the retired list of the Army.

Attention is asked to the necessity of providing by legislation for organizing, arming, and disciplining the *active* militia of the country, and liberal appropriations are recommended in this behalf. The reports of the Adjutant-General of the Army and the Chief of Ordnance touching this subject fully set forth its importance.

The report of the officer in charge of education in the Army shows that there are seventy-eight schools now in operation in the Army, with an aggregate attendance of 2,305 enlisted men and children. The Secretary recommends the enlistment of one hundred and fifty schoolmasters, with the rank and pay of commissary-sergeants. An appropriation is needed to supply the judge-advocates of the Army with suitable libraries, and the Secretary recommends that the corps of judge-advocates be placed upon the same footing, as to promotion, with the other staff corps of the Army. Under existing laws, the Bureau of Military Justice consists of one officer, the Judge-Advocate General, and the corps of judge-advocates, of eight officers of equal rank, (majors,) with a provision that the limit of the corps shall remain at four, when reduced by casualty or resignation to that number. The consolidation of the Bureau of Military Justice, and the corps of judge-advocates, upon the same basis with the other staff corps of the Army, would remove an unjust discrimination against deserving officers, and subserve the best interests of the service.

Especial attention is asked to the report of the Chief of Engineers upon the condition of our national defences. From a personal inspection of many of the fortifications referred to, the Secretary is able to emphasize the recommendations made, and to state that their incomplete and defenceless condition is discreditable to the country. While other Nations have been increasing their means for carrying on offensive warfare and attacking maritime cities, we have been dormant in preparation for defence; nothing of importance has been done towards strengthening and finishing our casemated works since our late civil war, during which the great guns of modern warfare and the heavy armor of modern fortifications and ships came into use among the Nations, and our earthworks left, by a sudden failure of appropriations some years since, in all stages of incompletion, are now being rapidly destroyed by the elements.

The two great rivers of the North American Continent, the Mississippi and the Columbia, have their navigable waters wholly within the limits of the United States, and are of vast importance to our internal and foreign commerce. The permanency of the important work on the South Pass of the Mississippi river seems now to be assured. There has been no failure whatever in the maintenance of the maximum channel during the six months ended August 9, last. This experiment has opened a broad deep highway to the ocean, and is an improvement, upon the permanent success of which, congratulations may be exchanged among people abroad and at home, and especially among the communities of the Mississippi valley, whose commercial exchanges float in an unobstructed channel safely to and from the sea.

A comprehensive improvement of the Mississippi and its tributaries is a matter of transcendent importance. These great water-ways comprise a system of inland transportation spread like net-work over a large portion of the United States, and navigable to the extent of many thousands of miles. Producers and consumers alike, have a common interest in such unequalled facilities for cheap transportation. Geographically, commercially, and politically, they are the strongest tie between the various sections of the country. These channels of communication and interchange are the property of the Nation. Its jurisdiction is paramount over their waters, and the plainest principles of public interest require their intelligent and careful supervision, with a view to their protection, improvement, and the enhancement of their usefulness.

The channel of the Columbia river, for a distance of about one hundred miles from its mouth, is obstructed by a succession of bars, which occasion serious delays in navigation, and heavy expense for lighterage and towage. A depth of at least twenty feet at low tide should be secured and maintained, to meet the requirements of the extensive and growing inland and ocean commerce it subserves. The most urgent need, however, for this great water-way is a permanent improvement of the channel at the mouth of the river.

From Columbia river to San Francisco, a distance of over six hundred miles, there is no harbor on our Pacific coast which can be approached during stormy weather. An appropriation of $150,000 was made by the Forty-fifth Congress for the commencement of a breakwater and harbor of refuge, to be located at some point between the Straits of Fuca and San Francisco, at which the necessities of commerce, local and general, will be best accommodated. The amount appropriated is thought to be quite inadequate for the purpose intended. The cost of the work, when finished, will be very great, owing to the want of natural advantages for a site at any point on the coast between the designated limits, and it has not been thought to be advisable to undertake the work without a larger appropriation. I commend the matter to the attention of Congress.

The completion of the new building for the War Department is urgently needed, and the estimates for continuing its construction are especially recommended.

The collections of books, specimens, and records constituting the Army Medical Museum and Library are of national importance. The library now contains about fifty-one thousand five hundred (51,500) volumes and fifty-seven thousand (57,000) pamphlets relating to medicine, surgery, and allied topics. The contents of the Army Medical Museum consist of twenty-two thousand (22,000) specimens, and are unique in the completeness with which both military surgery and the diseases of armies are illustrated. Their destruction would be an irreparable loss, not only to the United States, but to the world. There are filed in the record and pension division, over sixteen thousand (16,000) bound volumes of hospital records, together with a great quantity of papers, embracing the original records of the hospitals of our armies during the civil war. Aside from their historical value, these records are daily searched for evidence needed in the settlement of large numbers of pension and other claims, for the protection of the Government against attempted frauds as well as for the benefit of honest claimants. These valuable collections are now in a building which is peculiarly exposed to the danger of destruction by fire. It is therefore earnestly recommended that an appropriation be made for a new fire-proof building, adequate for the present needs and reasonable future expansion of these valuable collections. Such a building should be absolutely fire-proof; no expenditure for mere architectural display is required. It is believed that a suitable structure can be erected at a cost not to exceed two hundred and fifty thousand dollars, ($250,000.)

I commend to the attention of Congress the great services of the commander and chief of our armies during the war for the Union, whose wise, firm, and patriotic conduct did so much to bring that momentous conflict to a close. The legislation of the United States contains many precedents for the recognition of distinguished military merit, authorizing rank and emoluments to be conferred for eminent services to the country. An act of Congress authorizing the appointment of a Captain-General of the Army, with suitable provisions relating to compensation, retirement, and other details, would, in my judgment, be altogether fitting and proper, and would be warmly approved by the country.

The report of the Secretary of the Navy exhibits the successful and satisfactory management of that Department during the last fiscal year. The total expenditures for the year were $12,916,639.45, leaving unexpended at the close of the year $2,141,682.23 of the amount of available appropriations. The appropriations for the present fiscal year ending June 30, 1881, are $15,095,061.45; and the total estimates for the next fiscal year ending June 30, 1882, are $15,953,751.61. The amount drawn by warrant from July 1, 1880, to November 1, 1880, is $5,041,570.45.

The recommendation of the Secretary of the Navy, that provision be made for the establishment of some form of civil government for the people of Alaska, is approved. At present there is no protection of persons or property in that Territory, except such as is afforded by the officers of the United States ship Jamestown. This vessel was dispatched to Sitka, because of the fear that, without the immediate presence of the National authority, there was impending danger of anarchy. The steps taken to restore order have been accepted in good faith by both white and Indian inhabitants, and the necessity for this method of restraint does not, in my opinion, now exist. If however, the Jamestown should be withdrawn, leaving the people, as at present, without the ordinary, judicial, and administrative authority of organized local government, serious consequences might ensue.

The laws provide only for the collection of revenue, the protection of public property, and the transmission of the mails. The problem is to supply a local rule for a population so scattered and so peculiar in its origin and condition. The natives are reported to be teachable and self-supporting, and, if properly instructed, doubtless would advance rapidly in civilization, and a new factor of prosperity would be added to the national life. I therefore recommend the requisite legislation upon this subject.

The Secretary of the Navy has taken steps towards the establishment of naval coaling-stations at the Isthmus of Panama, to meet the requirements of our commercial relations with Central and South America, which are rapidly growing in importance. Locations eminently suitable, both as regards our naval purposes and the uses of commerce, have been selected, one on the east side of the Isthmus, at Chiriqui Lagoon, in the Caribbean Sea, and the other on the Pacific coast, at the Bay of Golfito. The only safe harbors, sufficiently commodious, on the Isthmus, are at these points, and the distance between them is less than one hundred miles. The report of the Secretary of the Navy concludes with valuable suggestions with respect to the building up of our merchant-marine service, which deserve the favorable consideration of Congress.

The report of the Postmaster-General exhibits the continual growth and the high state of efficiency of the postal service. The operations of no Department of the Government, perhaps, represent with greater exactness the increase in the population and the business of the country. In 1860, the postal receipts were $8,518,067.40; in 1880, the receipts were $33,315,479.34. All the inhabitants of the country are directly and personally interested in having proper mail facilities, and naturally watch the Post Office very closely. This careful oversight on the part of the people has proved a constant stimulus to improvement. During the past year there was an increase of 2,134 post offices, and the mail routes were extended 27,177 miles, making an additional annual transportation of 10,804,191 miles. The revenues of the postal service for the ensuing year are estimated at $38,845,174.10, and the expenditures at $42,475,932, leaving a deficiency to be appropriated out of the Treasury of $3,630,757.90.

The Universal Postal Union has received the accession of almost all the countries and colonies of the world maintaining organized postal services, and it is confidently expected that all the other countries and colonies now outside the Union will soon unite therewith, thus realizing the grand idea and aim of the founders of the Union, of forming, for purposes of international mail communication, a single postal territory embracing the world, with complete uniformity of postal charges, and conditions of international exchange, for all descriptions of correspondence. To enable the United States to do its full share of this great work, additional legislation is asked by the Postmaster-General, to whose recommendations especial attention is called.

The suggestion of the Postmaster-General, that it would be wise to encourage by appropriate legislation, the establishment of American lines of steamers by our own citizens, to carry the mails between our own ports and those of Mexico, Central America, South America, and of trans-Pacific countries, is commended to the serious consideration of Congress.

The attention of Congress is also invited to the suggestions of the Postmaster-General in regard to postal savings.

The necessity for additional provision, to aid in the transaction of the business of the Federal courts, becomes each year more apparent. The dockets of the Supreme Court, and of the circuit courts, in the greater number of the circuits, are encumbered with the constant accession of cases. In the former court, and in many instances in the circuit courts, years intervene before it is practicable to bring cases to hearing.

The Attorney-General recommends the establishment of an intermediate court of errors and appeals. It is recommended that the number of judges of the circuit court in each circuit, with the exception of the second circuit, should be increased by the addition of another judge; in the second circuit, that two should be added; and that an intermediate appellate court should be formed in each circuit, to consist of the circuit judges and the circuit justice, and that in the event of the absence of either of these judges the place of the absent judge should be supplied by the judge of one of the district courts in the circuit. Such an appellate court could be safely invested with large jurisdiction, and its decisions would satisfy suitors in many cases where appeals would still be allowed in the Supreme Court. The expense incurred for this intermediate court will require a very moderate increase of the appropriations for the expenses of the Department of Justice. This recommendation is commended to the careful consideration of Congress.

It is evident that a delay of justice, in many instances oppressive and disastrous to suitors, now neccessarily occurs in the Federal courts, which will in this way be remedied.

The report of the Secretary of the Interior presents an elaborate account of the operations of that Department during the past year. It gives me great pleasure to say that our Indian affairs appear to be in a more hopeful condition now than ever before. The Indians have made gratifying progress in agriculture, herding, and mechanical pursuits. Many who were a few years ago in hostile conflict with the Government are quietly settling down on farms where they hope to make their permanent homes, building houses and engaging in the occupations of civilized life. The introduction of the freighting business among them has been remarkably fruitful of good results, in giving many of them congenial and remunerative employment, and in stimulating their ambition to earn their own support. Their honesty, fidelity, and efficiency as carriers are highly praised. The organization of a police force of Indians has been equally successful in maintaining law and order upon the reservations, and in exercising a wholesome moral influence among the Indians themselves. I concur with the Secretary of the Interior in the recommendation that the pay of this force be increased, as an inducement to the best class of young men to enter it.

Much care and attention has been devoted to the enlargement of educational facilities for the Indians. The means available for this important object have been very inadequate. A few additional boarding-schools at Indian agencies have been established, and the erection of buildings has been begun for several more, but an increase of the appropriations for this interesting undertaking is greatly needed to accommodate the large number of Indian children of school-age. The number offered by their parents from all parts of the country for education in the Government schools is much larger than can be accommodated with the means at present available for that purpose. The number of Indian pupils at the Normal School at Hampton, Virginia, under the direction of General Armstrong, has been considerably increased, and their progress is highly encouraging. The Indian school established by the Interior Department in 1879, at Carlisle, Pennsylvania, under the direction of Captain Pratt, has been equally successful. It has now nearly two hundred pupils of both sexes, representing a great variety of the tribes east of the Rocky Mountains. The pupils in both these institutions receive not only an elementary English education, but are also instructed in house-work, agriculture, and useful mechanical pursuits. A similar school was established this year at Forest Grove, Oregon, for the education of Indian youth on the Pacific coast. In addition to this, thirty-six Indian boys and girls were selected from the Eastern Cherokees and placed in boarding-schools in North Carolina, where they are to receive an elementary English education and training in industrial pursuits. The interest shown by Indian parents, even among the so-called wild tribes, in the education of their children, is very gratifying, and gives promise that the results accomplished by the efforts now making will be of lasting benefit.

The expenses of Indian education have so far been drawn from the permanent civilization-fund at the disposal of the Department of the Interior; but the fund is now so much reduced, that the continuance of this beneficial work will in the future depend on specific appropriations by Congress for the purpose, and I venture to express the hope that Congress will not permit institutions so fruitful of good results to perish for want of means for their support. On the contrary, an increase of the number of such schools appears to me highly advisable.

The past year has been unusually free from disturbances among the Indian tribes. An agreement has been made with the Utes, by which they surrender their large reservation in Colorado in consideration of an annuity, to be paid to them, and agree to settle in severalty on certain lands designated for that purpose, as farmers, holding individual title to their land in fee-simple, inalienable for a certain period. In this way a costly Indian war has been avoided, which, at one time, seemed imminent, and, for the first time in the history of the country, an Indian nation has given up its tribal existence to be settled in severalty, and to live as individuals under the common protection of the laws of the country. The conduct of the Indians throughout the country during the past year, with but few noteworthy exceptions, has been orderly and peaceful. The guerilla warfare carried on for two years by Victorio and his band of Southern Apaches has virtually come to an end by the death of that chief and most of his followers, on Mexican soil. The disturbances caused on our northern frontier by Sitting Bull and his men, who had taken refuge in the British dominions, are also likely to cease. A large majority of his followers have surrendered to our military forces, and the remainder are apparently in progress of disintegration.

I concur with the Secretary of the Interior in expressing the earnest hope that Congress will at this session take favorable action on the bill providing for the allotment of lands on the different reservations in severalty to the Indians, with patents conferring fee-simple title inalienable for a certain period, and the eventual disposition of the residue of the reservations, for general settlement, with the consent and for the benefit of the Indians, placing the latter under the equal protection of the laws of the country. This measure, together with a vigorous prosecution of our educational efforts, will work the most important and effective advance toward the solution of the Indian problem, in preparing for the gradual merging of our Indian population in the great body of American citizenship.

A large increase is reported in the disposal of public lands for settlement during the past year, which marks the prosperous growth of our agricultural industry, and a vigorous movement of population toward our unoccupied lands. As this movement proceeds, the codification of our land laws, as well as proper legislation to regulate the disposition of public lands, become of more pressing necessity, and I therefore invite the consideration of Congress to the report and the accompaning draft of a bill, made by the Public Lands Commission, which were communicated by me to Congress at the last session. Early action upon this important subject is highly desirable.

The attention of Congress is again asked to the wasteful depredations committed on our public timber-lands, and the rapid and indiscriminate destruction of our forests. The urgent necessity for legislation to this end is now generally recognized. In view of the lawless character of the depredations committed, and the disastrous consequences which will inevitably follow their continuance, legislation has again and again been recommended to arrest the evil, and to preserve for the people of our Western States and Territories the timber needed for domestic and other essential uses.

The report of the Director of the Geological Survey is a document of unusual interest. The consolidation of the various geological and geographical surveys and exploring enterprises, each of which has heretofore operated upon an independent plan, without concert, cannot fail to be of great benefit to all those industries of the country which depend upon the development of our mineral resources. The labors of the scientific men, of recognized merit, who compose the corps of the Geological Survey, during the first season of their field operations and inquiries, appear to have been very comprehensive, and will soon be communicated to Congress in a number of volumes. The Director of the Survey recommends that the investigations, carried on by his bureau, which, so far, have been confined to the so-called publicland States and Territories, be extended over the entire country, and that the necessary appropriation be made for this purpose. This would be particularly beneficial to the iron, coal, and other mining interests of the Mississippi valley, and of the Eastern and Southern States. The subject is commended to the careful consideration of Congress.

The Secretary of the Interior asks attention to the want of room in the public buildings of the capital, now existing and in progress of construction, for the accommodation of the clerical force employed, and of the public records. Necessity has compelled the renting of private buildings in different parts of the city for the location of public offices, for which a large amount of rent is annually paid, while the separation of offices belonging to the same Department impedes the transaction of current business. The Secretary suggests that the blocks surrounding Lafayette Square, on the east, north, and west, be purchased as the sites for new edifices, for the accommodation of the Government offices, leaving the square itself intact; and that, if such buildings were constructed upon a harmonious plan of architecture, they would add much to the beauty of the National capital, and would, together with the Treasury and the new State, Navy, and War-Department building, form one of the most imposing groups of public edifices in the world.

The Commissioner of Agriculture expresses the confident belief that his efforts in behalf of the production of our own sugar and tea have been encouragingly rewarded. The importance of the results attained have attracted marked attention at home, and have received the special consideration of foreign Nations. The successful cultivation of our own tea, and the manufacture of our own sugar, would make a difference of many millions of dollars annually in the wealth of the Nation.

The report of the Commissioner asks attention particularly to the continued prevalence of an infectious and contagious cattle-disease, known and dreaded in Europe and Asia as cattle-plague, or pleuro-pneumonia. A mild type of this disease, in certain sections of our country, is the occasion of great loss to our farmers, and of serious disturbance to our trade with Great Britain, which furnishes a market for most of our live-stock and dressed meats. The value of neat-cattle exported from the United States for the eight months ended August 31, 1880, was more than twelve million dollars, and nearly double the value for the same period in 1879, an unexampled increase of export trade. Your early attention is solicited to this important matter.

The Commissioner of Education reports a continued increase of public interest in educational affairs, and that the public schools generally throughout the country are well sustained. Industrial training is attracting deserved attention, and colleges for instruction, theoretical and practical, in agriculture and the mechanic arts, including the Government schools recently established for the instruction of Indian youth, are gaining steadily in public estimation. The Commissioner asks special attention to the depredations committed on the lands reserved for the future support of public instruction, and to the very great need of help from the Nation for schools in the Territories and in the Southern States. The recommendation heretofore made is repeated and urged, that an educational fund be set apart from the net proceeds of the sales of the public lands annually, the income of which, and the remainder of the net annual proceeds, to be distributed on some satisfactory plan to the States and Territories and the District of Columbia.

The success of the public schools of the District of Columbia, and the progress made, under the intelligent direction of the Board of Education and the superintendent, in supplying the educational requirements of the District with thoroughly-trained and efficient teachers, is very gratifying. The acts of Congress, from time to time, donating public lands to the several States and Territories, in aid of educational interests, have proved to be wise measures of public policy, resulting in great and lasting benefit. It would seem to be a matter of simple justice to extend the benefits of this legislation, the wisdom of which has been so fully vindicated by experience, to the District of Columbia.

I again commend the general interests of the District of Columbia to the favorable consideration of Congress. The affairs of the District, as shown by the report of the Commissioners, are in a very satisfactory condition.

In my annual messages heretofore, and in my special message of December 19, 1879, I have urged upon the attention of Congress the necessity of reclaiming the marshes of the Potomac adjacent to the capital, and I am constrained by its importance to advert again to the subject. These flats embrace an area of several hundred acres. They are an impediment to the drainage of the city, and seriously impair its health. It is believed that, with this substantial improvement of its river front, the capital would be, in all respects, one of the most attractive cities in the world. Aside from its permanent popularity, this city is necessarily the place of residence of persons from every section of the country, engaged in the public service. Many others reside here temporarily, for the transaction of business with the Government.

It should not be forgotten that the land acquired will probably be worth the cost of reclaiming it, and that the navigation of the river will be greatly improved. I therefore again invite the attention of Congress to the importance of prompt provision for this much-needed and too long delayed improvement.

The water supply of the city is inadequate. In addition to the ordinary use throughout the city, the consumption by Government is necessarily very great in the navy-yard, arsenal, and the various Departments, and a large quantity is required for the proper preservation of the numerous parks and the cleansing of sewers. I recommend that this subject receive the early attention of Congress, and that, in making provision for an increased supply, such means be adopted as will have in view the future growth of the city. Temporary expedients for such a purpose cannot but be wasteful of money, and therefore unwise. A more ample reservoir, with corresponding facilities for keeping it filled, should, in my judgment, be constructed. I commend again to the attention of Congress the subject of the removal, from their present location, of the depots of the several railroads entering the city; and I renew the recommendations of my former messages in behalf of the erection of a building for the Congressional Library; the completion of the Washington Monument; and of liberal appropriations in support of the benevolent, reformatory, and penal institutions of the District.

RUTHERFORD B. HAYES.

EXECUTIVE MANSION, *December* 6, 1880.

SPECIAL MESSAGE

TO

THE SENATE AND HOUSE OF REPRESENTATIVES, IN RELATION TO THE PONCA INDIANS.

FEBRUARY 1, 1881.

SPECIAL MESSAGE.

To the Senate and House of Representatives:

In compliance with the request of a large number of intelligent and benevolent citizens, and believing that it was warranted by the extraordinary circumstances of the case, on the 18th day of December, 1880, I appointed a commission consisting of George Crook and Nelson A. Miles, brigadier-generals in the Army, William Stickney, of the District of Columbia, and Walter Allen, of Massachusetts, and requested them to confer with the Ponca Indians in the Indian Territory, and if, in their judgment, it was advisable, also with that part of the tribe which remained in Dakota, and "to ascertain the facts in regard to their removal and present condition so far as was necessary to determine the question as to what justice and humanity require should be done by the Government of the United States, and to report their conclusions and recommendations in the premises."

The commission, in pursuance of these instructions, having visited the Ponca Indians at their homes in the Indian Territory and in Dakota, and made a careful investigation of the subject referred to them, have reported their conclusions and recommendations, and I now submit their report, together with the testimony taken, for the consideration of Congress. A minority report by Mr. Allen is also herewith submitted.

On the 27th of December, 1880, a delegation of Ponca chiefs from the Indian Territory presented to the Executive a declaration of their wishes, in which they stated that it was their desire "to remain on the lands now occupied by the Poncas in the Indian Territory," and "to relinquish all their right and interest in the lands formerly owned and occupied by the Ponca tribe in the State of Nebraska and the Territory of Dakota;" and the declaration sets forth the compensation which they will accept for the lands to be surrendered, and for the injuries done to the tribe by their removal to the Indian Territory. This declaration, agreeably to the request of the chiefs making it, is herewith transmitted to Congress.

The public attention has frequently been called to the injustice and wrong which the Ponca tribe of Indians has suffered at the hands of the Government of the United States. This subject was first brought before Congress and the country by the Secretary of the Interior in his annual report for the year 1877, in which he said:

The case of the Poncas seems entitled to especial consideration at the hands of Congress. They have always been friendly to the whites. It is said, and, as far as I have been able to learn, truthfully, that no Ponca ever killed a white man. The orders of the Government always met with obedient compliance at their hands. Their removal from their old homes on the Missouri river was to them a great hardship. They had been born and raised there. They had houses there in which they lived according to their ideas of comfort. Many of them had engaged in agriculture, and possessed cattle and agricultural implements. They were very reluctant to leave all this, but when Congress had resolved upon their removal they finally overcame that reluctance and obeyed. Considering their constant good conduct, their obedient spirit, and the sacrifices they have made, they are certainly entitled to more than ordinary care at the hands of the Government, and I urgently recommend that liberal provision be made to aid them in their new settlement.

In the same volume, the report of E. A. Howard, the agent of the Poncas, is published, which contains the following:

* * * * * *

I am of the opinion that the removal of the Poncas from the northern climate of Dakota to the southern climate of the Indian Territory, at the season of the year it was done, will prove a mistake, and that a great mortality will surely follow among the people when they shall have been here for a time and become poisoned with the malaria of the climate. Already the effects of the climate may be seen upon them in the *ennui* that seems to have settled upon each, and in the large number now sick.

It is a matter of astonishment to me that the Government should have ordered the removal of the Ponca Indians from Dakota to the Indian Territory without having first made some provision for their settlement and comfort. Before their removal was carried into effect, an appropriation should have been made by Congress sufficient to have located them in their new home, by building a comfortable house for the occupancy of every family of the tribe. As the case now is, no appropriation has been made by Congress, except for a sum but little more than sufficient to remove them; no houses have been built for their use, and the result is, that these people have been placed on an uncultivated reservation to live in their tents as best they may, and await further legislative action.

* * * * * *

These Indians claim that the Government had no right to move them from their reservation without first obtaining from them by purchase or treaty the title which they had acquired from the Government, and for which they rendered a valuable consideration. They claim that the date of the settlement of their tribe upon the land composing their old reservation is prehistoric; that they were all born there, and that their ancestors from generations back beyond their knowledge were born and lived upon its soil, and that they finally acquired a complete and perfect title from the Government by treaty made with the "Great

Father" at Washington, which they claimed made it as legitimately theirs as is the home of the white man acquired by gift or purchase.

* * * * * * *

The subject was again referred to in similar terms in the annual report of the Interior Department for 1878, in the reports of the Commissioner of Indian Affairs and of the agent for the Poncas; and in 1879 the Secretary of the Interior said:

That the Poncas were grievously wronged by their removal from their location on the Missouri river to the Indian Territory, their old reservation having, by a mistake in making the Sioux treaty, been transferred to the Sioux, has been at length and repeatedly set forth in my reports as well as those of the Commissioner of Indian Affairs. All that could be subsequently done by this Department in the absence of new legislation to repair that wrong and to indemnify them for their losses has been done with more than ordinary solicitude. They were permitted to select a new location for themselves in the Indian Territory, the Quapaw reserve, to which they had first been taken, being objectionable to them. They chose a tract of country on the Arkansas river and the Salt Fork northwest of the Pawnee reserve. I visited their new reservation personally to satisfy myself of their condition. The lands they now occupy are among the very best in the Indian Territory in point of fertility, well watered and well timbered, and admirably adapted for agriculture as well as stock-raising. In this respect their new reservation is unquestionably superior to that which they left behind them on the Missouri river. Seventy houses have been built by and for them of far better quality than the miserable huts they formerly occupied in Dakota, and the construction of a larger number is now in progress, so that, as the agent reports, every Ponca family will be comfortably housed before January. A very liberal allowance of agricultural implements and stock-cattle has been given them, and if they apply themselves to agricultural work there is no doubt that their condition will soon be far more prosperous than it has ever been before. During the first year after their removal to the Indian Territory they lost a comparatively large number of their people by death in consequence of the change of climate, which is greatly to be deplored; but their sanitary condition is now very much improved. The death rate among them during the present year has been very low, and the number of cases of sickness is constantly decreasing. It is thought that they are now sufficiently acclimated to be out of danger.

* * * * * * *

A committee of the Senate, after a very full investigation of the subject, on the 31st of May, 1880, reported their conclusions to the Senate, and both the majority and minority of the committee agreed that "a great wrong had been done to the Ponca Indians." The majority of the committee says:

* * * * * * *

Nothing can strengthen the Government in a just policy to the Indians so much as a demonstration of its willingness to do ample and complete justice whenever it can be shown that it has inflicted a wrong upon a weak and trusting tribe. It is impossible for the United States to hope for any confidence to be reposed in them by the Indian until there shall be shown on their part a readiness to do justice.

The minority report is equally explicit as to the duty of the Government to repair the wrong done the Poncas. It says:

* * * * * * *

We should be more prompt and anxious because they are weak and we are strong. In my judgment we should be liberal to the verge of lavishness in the expenditure of our money to improve their condition, so that they and all others may know that, although like all Nations and all men we may do wrong, we are willing to make ample reparation.

The report of the commission appointed by me, of which General Crook was chairman, and the testimony taken by them and their investigations, add very little to what was already contained in the official reports of the Secretary of the Interior and the report of the Senate committee touching the injustice done to the Poncas by their removal to the Indian Territory. Happily, however, the evidence reported by the commission and their recommendations point out conclusively the true measures of redress which the Government of the United States ought now to adopt.

The commission in its conclusions omit to state the important facts as to the present condition of the Poncas in the Indian Territory, but the evidence they have reported shows clearly and conclusively that the Poncas now residing in that Territory, five hundred and twenty-one in number, are satisfied with their new homes; that they are healthy, comfortable, and contented, and that they have freely and firmly decided to adhere to the choice announced in their letter of October 25, 1880, and in the declaration of December 27, 1880, to remain in the Indian Territory and not to return to Dakota.

The evidence reported also shows that the fragment of the Ponca tribe—perhaps one hundred and fifty in number—which is still in Dakota and Nebraska prefer to remain on their old reservation.

In view of these facts I am convinced that the recommendations of the commission, together with the declaration of the chiefs of December last, if substantially followed, will afford a solution of the Ponca question which is consistent with the wishes and interests of both branches of the tribe, with the settled Indian policy of the Government, and as nearly as is now practicable with the demands of justice.

Our general Indian policy for the future should embrace the following leading ideas:

1. The Indians should be prepared for citizenship by giving to their young of both sexes that industrial and general education which is required to enable them to be self-supporting and capable of self-protection in a civilized community.

2. Lands should be allotted to the Indians in severalty, inalienable for a certain period.

3. The Indians should have a fair compensation for their lands not required for individual allotment, the amount to be invested with suitable safeguards for their benefit.

4. With these prerequisites secured, the Indians should be made citizens, and invested with the rights and charged with the responsibilities of citizenship.

It is therefore recommended that legislation be adopted in relation to the Ponca Indians, authorizing the Secretary of the Interior to secure to the individual members of the Ponca tribe, in severalty, sufficient land for their support, inalienable for a term of years and until the restriction upon alienation may be removed by the President. Ample time and opportunity should be given to the members of the tribe freely to choose their allotments either on their old or their new reservation.

Full compensation should be made for the lands to be relinquished, for their losses by the Sioux depredations, and by reason of their removal to the Indian Territory, the amount not to be less than the sums named in the declaration of the chiefs, made December 27, 1880.

In short, nothing should be left undone to show to the Indians that the Government of the United States regards their rights as equally sacred with those of its citizens.

The time has come when the policy should be to place the Indians as rapidly as practicable on the same footing with the other permanent inhabitants of our country.

I do not undertake to apportion the blame for the injustice done to the Poncas. Whether the Executive or Congress or the public is chiefly in fault is not now a question of practical importance. As the Chief Executive at the time when the wrong was consummated, I am deeply sensible that enough of the responsibility for that wrong justly attaches to me to make it my particular duty and earnest desire to do all I can to give to these injured people that measure of redress which is required alike by justice and by humanity.

RUTHERFORD B. HAYES.

EXECUTIVE MANSION, *February* 1, 1881.

MESSAGE

TRANSMITTING

TO THE SENATE AND HOUSE OF REPRESENTATIVES A REPORT OF
THE RESULTS IN THE NEW YORK CITY POST OFFICE AND
CUSTOM-HOUSE OF THE APPLICATION OF THE CIVIL-
SERVICE REFORM RULES.

FEBRUARY 28, 1881.

MESSAGE.

To the Senate and House of Representatives:

I transmit herewith a copy of a letter addressed to the chairman of the civil service commission on the 3d of December last, requesting to be furnished with a report upon the results in the post office and custom-house in the city of New York of the application of the civil-service rules requiring open competitive examinations for appointments and promotions, together with the report of Hon. Dorman B. Eaton, the chairman of the commission, in response.

The report presents a very gratifying statement of the results of the application of the rules referred to, in the two largest and most important local offices in the civil service of the Government. The subject is one of great importance to the people of the whole country.

I commend the suggestions and recommendations of the chairman of the commission to the careful consideration of Congress.

R. B. HAYES.

Executive Mansion, *February* 28, 1881.

PROCLAMATION

CONVENING

THE SENATE OF THE UNITED STATES.

FEBRUARY 28, 1881.

PROCLAMATION.

BY THE PRESIDENT OF THE UNITED STATES OF AMERICA.

A PROCLAMATION.

Whereas objects of interest to the United States require that the Senate should be convened at twelve o'clock on the fourth of March next, to receive and act upon such communications as may be made to it on the part of the Executive:

Now, therefore, I, RUTHERFORD B. HAYES, President of the United States, have considered it to be my duty to issue this my proclamation, declaring that an extraordinary occasion requires the Senate of the United States to convene for the transaction of business at the Capitol, in the city of Washington, on the fourth day of March next, at twelve o'clock at noon on that day, of which all who shall at that time be entitled to act as members of that body are hereby required to take notice.

Given under my hand and the seal of the United States, at Washington, the twenty-eighth day of February, in the year of our [SEAL.] Lord one thousand eight hundred and eighty-one, and of the Independence of the United States of America the one hundred and fifth.

R. B. HAYES.

By the President:
WM. M. EVARTS,
    Secretary of State.

MESSAGE

RETURNING TO

THE HOUSE OF REPRESENTATIVES THE BILL ENTITLED "AN ACT TO FACILITATE THE REFUNDING OF THE NATIONAL DEBT."

MARCH 3, 1881.

MESSAGE.

To the House of Representatives:

Having considered the bill entitled "An act to facilitate the refunding of the National debt," I am constrained to return it to the House of Representatives, in which it originated, with the following statement of my objections to its passage.

The imperative necessity for prompt action, and the pressure of public duties in this closing week of my term of office, compel me to refrain from any attempt to make a full and satisfactory presentation of the objections to the bill.

The importance of the passage at the present session of Congress of a suitable measure for the refunding of the National debt, which is about to mature, is generally recognized. It has been urged upon the attention of Congress by the Secretary of the Treasury and in my last annual message. If successfully accomplished, it will secure a large decrease in the annual interest payment of the Nation; and I earnestly recommend, if the bill before me shall fail, that another measure for this purpose be adopted before the present Congress adjourns.

While in my opinion it would be wise to authorize the Secretary of the Treasury, in his discretion, to offer to the public bonds bearing 3½ per cent. interest in aid of refunding, I should not deem it my duty to interpose my constitutional objection to the passage of the present bill if it did not contain, in its fifth section, provisions which in my judgment seriously impair the value and tend to the destruction of the present National banking system of the country. This system has now been in operation almost twenty years. No safer or more beneficial banking system was ever established. Its advantages as a business are free to all who have the necessary capital. It furnishes a currency to the public which for convenience and the security of the bill-holder has probably never been equalled by that of any other banking system. Its notes are secured by the deposit with the Government of the interest-bearing bonds of the United States.

The section of the bill before me which relates to the National banking system, and to which objection is made, is not an essential part of a refunding measure. It is as follows:

SEC. 5. From and after the 1st day of July, 1881, the 3 per cent. bonds authorized by the first section of this act shall be the only bonds receivable as security for national-bank circulation, or as securitiy for the safe-keeping and prompt payment of the public money deposited with such banks; but when any such bonds deposited for the purposes aforesaid shall be designated for purchase or redemption by the Secretary of the Treasury, the banking association depositing the same shall have the right to substitute other issues of the bonds of the United States in lieu thereof: *Provided*, That no bond upon which interest has ceased shall be accepted or shall be continued on deposit as security for circulation or for the safe-keeping of the public money; and in case bonds so deposited shall not be withdrawn, as provided by law, within thirty days after interest has ceased thereon, the banking association depositing the same shall be subject to the liabilities and proceedings on the part of the Comptroller provided for in section 5234 of the Revised Statutes of the United States: *And provided further*, That section 4 of the act of June 20, 1874, entitled "An act fixing the amount of United States notes providing for a redistribution of the national-bank currency, and for other purposes," be and the same is hereby, repealed; and sections 5159 and 5160 of the Revised Statutes of the United States be, and the same are hereby, re-enacted.

Under this section it is obvious that no additional banks will hereafter be organized, except possibly in a few cities or localities where the prevailing rates of interest in ordinary business are extremely low. No new banks can be organized, and no increase of the capital of existing banks can be obtained except by the purchase and deposit of 3 per cent. bonds. No other bonds of the United States can be used for the purpose. The one thousand millions of other bonds recently issued by the United States, and bearing a higher rate of interest than 3 per cent., and therefore a better security for the bill-holder, cannot, after the 1st of July next, be received as security for bank circulation. This is a radical change in the banking law. It takes from the banks the right they have heretofore had under the law to purchase and deposit, as security for their circulation, any of the bonds issued by the United States, and deprives the bill-holder of the best security which the banks are able to give, by requiring them to deposit bonds having the least value of any bonds issued by the Government.

The average rate of taxation of capital employed in banking is more than double the rate of taxation upon capital employed in other legitimate business. Under these circumstances, to amend the banking law so as to deprive the banks of the privilege of securing their notes by the most valuable bonds issued by the Government will, it is believed, in a large part of the country, be a practical prohibition of the organization of new banks, and prevent the existing banks from enlarging their capital. The National banking system, if continued at all, will be a monopoly in the hands of those already engaged in it, who may purchase Government bonds bearing a more favorable rate of interest than the 3 per cent. bonds prior to next July.

To prevent the further organization of banks is to put in jeopardy the whole system by taking from it that feature which makes it as it now is, a banking system free upon the same terms to all who wish to engage in it. Even the existing banks will be in danger of being driven from business by the additional disadvantages to which they will be subjected by this bill. In short, I cannot but regard the fifth section of the bill as a step in the direction of the destruction of the National banking system.

Our country, after a long period of business depression, has just entered upon a career of unexampled prosperity.

The withdrawal of the currency from circulation of the National banks and the enforced winding up of the banks in consequence, would inevitably bring serious embarrassment and disaster to the business of the country. Banks of issue are essential instruments of modern commerce. If the present efficient and admirable system of banking is broken down, it will inevitably be followed by a recurrence to other and inferior methods of banking. Any measure looking to such a result will be a disturbing element in our financial system. It will destroy confidence and surely check the growing prosperity of the country.

Believing that a measure for refunding the National debt is not necessarily connected with the National banking law, and that any refunding act would defeat its own object if it imperilled the National banking system or seriously impaired its usefulness; and convinced that section 5 of the bill before me would, if it should become a law, work great harm, I herewith return the bill to the House of Representatives for that further consideration which is provided for in the Constitution.

RUTHERFORD B. HAYES.

EXECUTIVE MANSION, *March* 3, 1881.

INDEX.

	Date.
Letter of Acceptance	July 8, 1876
Inaugural Address	March 5, 1877
Letter of Instruction to the Louisiana Commission	April 2, 1877
Executive Order, Withdrawal of Troops	April 20, 1877
Report of Louisiana Commission	April 24, 1877
Proclamation convening Congress	May 5, 1877
Letter on the Conduct to be observed by Officers of the General Government in relation to Elections	May 26, 1877
Executive Order, Civil Service	June 22, 1877
Proclamation, Railroad Riot in West Virginia	July 18, 1877
Proclamation, Railroad Riot in Maryland	July 21, 1877
Proclamation, Railroad Riot in Pennsylvania	July 23, 1877
Message, First Session, Forty-fifth Congress	October 15, 1877
Proclamation, Thanksgiving Day	October 29, 1877
Executive Order, Death of Senator Morton	November 2, 1877
Message, Second Session, Forty-fifth Congress	December 3, 1877
Message returning Silver Bill	February 28, 1878
Message returning Bill authorizing a Special Term of U. S. Court to be held in Mississippi	March 6, 1878
Proclamation, Riot in New Mexico	October 7, 1878
Proclamation, Thanksgiving Day	October 30, 1878
Message, Third Session, Forty-fifth Congress	December 2, 1878
Message, Postal and Commercial Intercourse with South America	December 17, 1878
Message, New York Custom-House	January 31, 1879
Letter to General Merritt, Collector of Customs, New York City	February 4, 1879
Message returning Chinese Bill	March 1, 1879
Message, Draft of Chinese Bill	March 1, 1879
Proclamation convening Congress	March 4, 1879
Message, First Session, Forty-sixth Congress	March 19, 1879
Proclamation, Invasion of Indian Territory	April 26, 1879
Message returning Army Bill	April 29, 1879
Message returning Military-Interference Bill	May 12, 1879
Message returning Legislative, Executive, and Judicial Bill	May 29, 1879
Message returning Judicial Bill	June 23, 1879
Message returning Marshals' Bill	June 30, 1879
Message, Appropriations for Pay of Marshals	June 30, 1879
Address, Reunion, Twenty-third Ohio Veteran Volunteer Infantry, Youngstown, Ohio	September 17, 1879
Address, Michigan State Fair, Detroit	September 18, 1879

	Date.
Proclamation, Thanksgiving Day	November 3, 1879
Executive Order, Death of Senator Chandler	November 1, 1879
Message, Second Session, Forty-sixth Congress	December 1, 1879
Proclamation, Invasion Indian Territory	February 12, 1880
Message, Inter-oceanic Canal	March 8, 1880
Message, Declaration of Independence Desk	April 22, 1880
Message returning Deficiency Bill	May 4, 1880
Address, Ohio Soldiers' Reunion, Columbus	August 11, 1880
Proclamation, Thanksgiving Day	November 1, 1880
Message, Third Session, Forty-sixth Congress	December 6, 1880
Message, Ponca Indians	February 1, 1881
Message, Civil Service Commission	February 28, 1881
Proclamation convening the Senate of the United States	February 28, 1881
Message returning Refunding Bill	March 3, 1881

www.ingramcontent.com/pod-product-compliance
Lightning Source LLC
Chambersburg PA
CBHW020314240426
43673CB00039B/799